Anthropology of Contemporary Culture
Directed by James Beck

Studies in art, music, theater, film, mass media, folklore, video art, and related subjects interpreted within the context of modern life. The emphasis of this series is centered on reception by both the intelligentsia and the general public, and the monographs will have a theoretic rather than anecdotal foundation.

Tutti i diritti sono riservati. Nessuna parte del libro può essere riprodotta o diffusa con un mezzo qualsiasi, fotocopie, microfilm o altro, senza il permesso scritto dell'editore.

All rights reserved. No part of this book shall be reproduced, stored in a retrieval system, or transmitted by any means, electronic, mechanical, photocopying, recording, or otherwise, without written permission from the publisher.

Illustrations:
The author and the publisher would like to thank the following for their gracious kindnesses: Scala, Florence; Art Resources, New York; the Monte dei Paschi, Siena; ArtWatch International, New York; Columbia University, Department of Art History and Archaeology, New York; and H. M. Queen Elizabeth II.

ISBN 978-88-8398-043-5
Copyright © 2006 by European Press Academic Publishing
Florence, Italy
www.e-p-a-p.com
www.europeanpress.it
Proprietà letteraria riservata—Printed in Italy

From Duccio to Raphael.
Connoisseurship in Crisis

James H. Beck

EUROPEAN PRESS ACADEMIC PUBLISHING

Florence, Italy, 2006

Table of Contents

List of Illustrations	5
List of Colour Plates	7
Preface	9
Acknowledgements	11
Introduction	13
1 The Lost Art of Connoisseurship	23
2 The *Northumberland Madonna of the Pinks*	43
3 The *Northumberland Madonna of the Pinks*. Shortcomings	59
4 Provenance of the *Northumberland Madonna of the Pinks*	97
5 Connoisseurship Gone Astray	121
5.1 A wooden Crucifix.	121
5.2 The Piccolomini '*modello*'.	131
6 A Case Study: The *Metropolitan Duccio*	139
6.1 Addendum.	167
Coda	173
Bibliography	177
Index	187

List of Illustrations

1	Marie-Victoire Jaquotot, ceramic copy after the *Madonna of the Pinks*, Sevres, Museum.	15
2	Copy after the *Madonna of the Pinks*, Brescia, Pinacoteca Tosio-Martinengo. Infrared-reflectograph.	16
3	Copy after the *Madonna of the Pinks*, Brescia, Pinacoteca Tosio-Martinengo.	16
1.1	Cimabue and Giotto, attributed to, *Madonna with Child*, Castelfiorentino, S. Verdiana Museum.	25
1.2	Jan van Eyck, *Portrait of a Man*, London, National Gallery.	33
1.3	Antonello da Messina, *Salvator Mundi*, London, National Gallery.	34
2.1	Michelangelo, attributed to (here rejected), *Cupid*, New York, French Cultural Institute.	45
3.1	Anonymous Artist, engraving after the *Madonna of the Pinks* ("French 1").	62
3.2	Jean Couvay, engraving after the *Madonna of the Pinks* ("French 2").	63
3.3	Jean Boulanger, engraving after the *Madonna of the Pinks* ("French 3").	64
3.4	Attributed to Raphael (here rejected), *The Northumberland Madonna of the Pinks*, London, National Gallery. Infrared reflectograph.	68
3.5	Raphael, *The Theological Virtues*, Rome, Vatican Museums.	76

3.6 Copy after the *Madonna of the Pinks*. (Whereabouts unknown, formerly Tepotzotlan, Mexico). 83
3.7 Giovanni Farrugia. Engraving after the *The Madonna of the Pinks*. 85
3.8 Raphael, *Marriage of the Virgin*. Milan, Brera. Infrared reflectograph, details. 90
4.1 Raphael, attributed to. *Drawing*, London, British Museum. 111
4.2 Vincenzo Camuccini, *Drawing*, Rome, private collection. 112
5.1 Michelangelo, attributed to (here rejected). *Crucifix*, Florence, Santo Spirito. 126
6.1 Assigned to Duccio di Buonisegna (here rejected), *The Metropolitan Duccio* (detail), New York, Metropolitan Museum. 140
6.2 Duccio, *Maestà*, Siena, Museo dell'Opera del Duomo. 145
6.3 *Madonna del Veronese*, unknown collection (formerly Rome, Stroganoff Collection). 154
6.4 Giovanni Bellini, *Portrait of the Doge Leonardo Loredan*, London, National Gallery. 161
6.5 Duccio di Buoninsegna, *The Franciscan Madonna*, Siena Pinacoteca. 164
6.6 Anonymous Sienese painter, *Madonna and Child with Angels*, Montepulciano, Museo Civico. 170

List of Colour Plates

1 Attributed to Raphael (here rejected), *The Northumberland Madonna of the Pinks*, London, National Gallery.
2 Attributed to Raphael (here rejected), *The Northumberland Madonna of the Pinks* (detail), London, National Gallery.
3 Copy after the *Madonna of the Pinks*, Brescia, Pinacoteca Tosio-Martinengo (detail).
4 Collection of Maximilian Speck von Sternburg, formerly at Lütschena, since 1996 at the Museum der bildende Künste in Leipzig. Inv. no. 1666.
5 Collection of Maximilian Speck von Sternburg, formerly at Lütschena, since 1996 at the Museum der bildende Künste in Leipzig. Inv. no. 1666 (detail).
6 Attributed to Duccio di Buonisegna (here rejected), *The Stroganoff Madonna* (formerly), *The Metropolitan Duccio*, New York, Metropolitan Museum of Art.
7 Attributed to Duccio (here rejected), *The London Triptych*, London, National Gallery.
8 Unknown Artist, Copy after the *Madonna of the Pinks*, Zagreb, Strossmayer Gallery.
9 Sassoferrato manner of (attributed to), Copy after the *Madonna of the Pinks*, Detroit, Institute of Arts.
10 Raphael, *Marriage of the Virgin*, Milan, Brera.

11 Leonardo da Vinci, *Benois Madonna*, St. Petersburg, Hermitage.
12 Leonardo da Vinci, *Madonna and Child*, Munich, Alte Pinakothek.
13 Attributed to Michelangelo (here rejected), *Crucifix* (front view), Turin, private collection.
14 Attributed to Michelangelo (here rejected), *Crucifix* (back view), Turin, private collection.
15 Attributed to Raphael (here rejected, assigned to Pinturicchio), *The Journey of Aeneas Silvius Piccolomini to Basle*, preparatory drawing, Florence, Uffizi Gallery, Gabinetto dei Disegni e delle Stampe.
16 Pinturicchio, *The Journey of Aeneas Silvius Piccolomini to Basle*, Siena, Duomo, Piccolomini Library.

Preface

This is the original edition of the book, specifically prepared to appear first in Italy. Other editions will appear in the future; an Italian one is in preparation. The choice of an Italian venue for this publication is motivated by several factors, the first and foremost being that I have been a student of Italian art for over half a century and have had the great good fortune and privilege of living in Italy on and off for that span. To my personal enrichment, I have been permitted to participate in Italy's intellectual and cultural life. Besides, I have marvelous friends in Italy, at the same time that my spiritual being is defined by the unsurpassed landscape of Tuscany including Settignano and the hills of Montalbano, views of Monte Rosa in the Aosta Valley, the delicate plains on the banks of the Po. Added to them are the marvels of Rome, Florence and Venice, but also those unsurpassed jewels, smaller towns and cities in every region of the Italian Republic.

Whatever value the book may hold should be regarded as a tiny expression of my affection, respect, and debt to Renaissance Art as it unfolded in Italy in the Fifteenth and Sixteenth centuries, and the need for a moral and ethical component in its study. The book also represents a response to having been awarded the title of Commendatore della Repubblica Italiana in 1991 and with it a responsibility to treat with respect and at the same time defend the Italian artistic tradition.

Acknowledgements

A number of persons offered vital assistance with the research and the development of issues raised in this book beginning with Lisa Dangles Deeds who was a constant resource for material and enthusiasm at the early stages of the project. Others who have been extremely helpful in the preparation of this study include Alessio Assonitis, Sheila Barker, Barbara Bibb, Gabriel Blumenthal, Michael Daley, Marco Fidolini, Corrado Gratziu, Young-June Keihm, Alessandra Moscato, Kerri Pfister, Manya Piels, Pietro Scarpellini, Carolina Sloser, Alessandro Vezzosi and Frances Vieta. My friend and collaborator on other projects, the seasoned journalist, writer and editor Robert Stock looked at portions of the manuscript and made timely suggestions, while Denise Budd, with characteristic good will, read over the final version which benefited from her suggestions and corrections.

Special thanks also go to Jan Sammer, a brilliant and unflappable Raphael scholar, who has made numerous contributions of fact to this book and has generously read the proofs with his customary care and attention.

Baron Vincenzo Camuccini of Rome and Cantalupo in Sabina was more than gracious and cooperative in supplying information while Dr. Paolo Puddu of Rome kindly made available material essential to the present study and further research. It goes without saying that my Sienese friend and colleague Piergiacomo Petrioli with good nature and enthusiasm contributed to the enterprise with his usual rigor as a scholar and art historian, and served as unofficial editor of the volume. He worked alongside Chiara Francesconi and Enrico Francesconi, my publishers who are also my affectionate neighbors and friends.

The present volume will be followed by two others taking up issues which have surfaced while preparing the present book. The first, which will be written by Jan Sammer, is a complete catalogue of the 55 or more versions of the Raphaelesque composition known as the "Madonna of the Pinks" as well as at least 15 engravings of the same subject, dating back to the 17th century if not earlier. The second, which is being prepared by Alessio Assonitis, will present the documentation surrounding Vincenzo Camuccini and his brother Pietro, especially with regard to a series of inventories and other documents which deal with them as collectors and picture dealers. All together they will form a kind of trilogy, although each of these volumes will make an independent and significant contribution to the history of art, and to the history of collecting and the configuration of the art world in the years after 2000.

The credit for presenting these studies goes to Chiara Francesconi, the publisher of E-P-A-P, European Press Academic Publishing, who has courageously established a viable publishing house in Lamporecchio, an historical town already known to Boccaccio, located between Vinci and Pistoia, and between Florence, Pisa and Lucca.

James Beck
Lamporecchio, June 2006.

Introduction

Two paintings, a mini aspiring Raphael da Urbino *Madonna* and an equally tiny aspiring Duccio di Buoninsegna *Madonna* were sold for record prices in 2004. The first was bought by London's National Gallery and the second by New York's Metropolitan Museum of Art. These objects and the mode in which the attributions to their famous presumed authors were achieved, document a breakdown in modern connoisseurship. The two objects represent a total expenditure of public money exceeding 100 million dollars for pictures the size of a sheet of paper. These remarkable sales could not have transpired without the participation of art experts whose role was indispensable in offering authentications of the pictures. This book will seek to define the system of attributing works of art, examine the methodology, treat in depth case studies of recent connoisseurship including the two pictures just mentioned. It addition to what is regarded as a monumental failure on the part of the experts, the use and misuse of public funds is an issue that lies just beneath the surface.

Specifically the tiny *Madonna* painting regarded as by Raphael fetched 65 million dollars in distinction to the *Metropolitan Duccio* also representing the Madonna and Child which was sold for 50 million dollars, the highest prices per square inch ever recorded.[1] (Plates 1, 6). The National Gallery out-maneuvered

---

[1]The so-called Raphael measures 11 x 8.5 inches, [28.8 x 22.9 cm.], with

the Getty Museum of Los Angeles, who had agreed to buy the picture, in order, the rhetoric had it, to keep the picture in the United Kingdom where it belonged. Executed on fruitwood, said to be cherry, the picture is regarded by its new owners as the premier or Ur version of a composition of which there are as many as 55 other painted examples housed in European and North and Latin America public and private collections (Plates 8, 9; Fig. 1, Fig. 2). Who painted these highly valued pictures is a question of connoisseurship. It goes without saying that the Trustees of the Metropolitan and the National Gallery went along with the purchases. After all, their experts and supporters were convinced that Duccio painted the Duccio and Raphael painted the Raphael. In the case of the London picture a small number of art experts and art amateurs are not so sure. A few including this observer went farther by proposing that the National Gallery's version is a late 18th or the early 19th century copy of what appears to be a lost original.

A similar but not identical version was engraved in 1828 and described as being in the Roman collection of a leading local painter, Vincenzo Camuccini. The provenance or history of the picture which will be referred to as the *Northumberland Madonna* is non-existent until around that time, when a similar or the same picture was mentioned in a London auction sales catalogue (in 1830) as being in Rome in the same Roman collection.

The aspiring Duccio was known to have been the property of Gregorii Stroganoff and had been housed with his newly-formed collection in Rome around the turn of the 19th century. In 1904 it was exhibited publicly for the first and only time, in Siena.[2]

---

the painted surface: 27.9 x 22.4 cm. in distinction to the *Metropolitan Duccio*, whose overall dimensions with its engaged frame are 11 x $8^{1/4}$ [27.94 x 21 cm], the painted surface $9^{3/8}$ x $6^{1/2}$ [23.8 x 16.5 cm].

[2] *Mostra dell'Antica Arte Senese*, Siena, 1904, p.308, n.37 (1960); and *Il segreto della civiltà. La Mostra dell'Antica Arte senese del 1904 cento anni dopo*, Siena, 2005.

Introduction 15

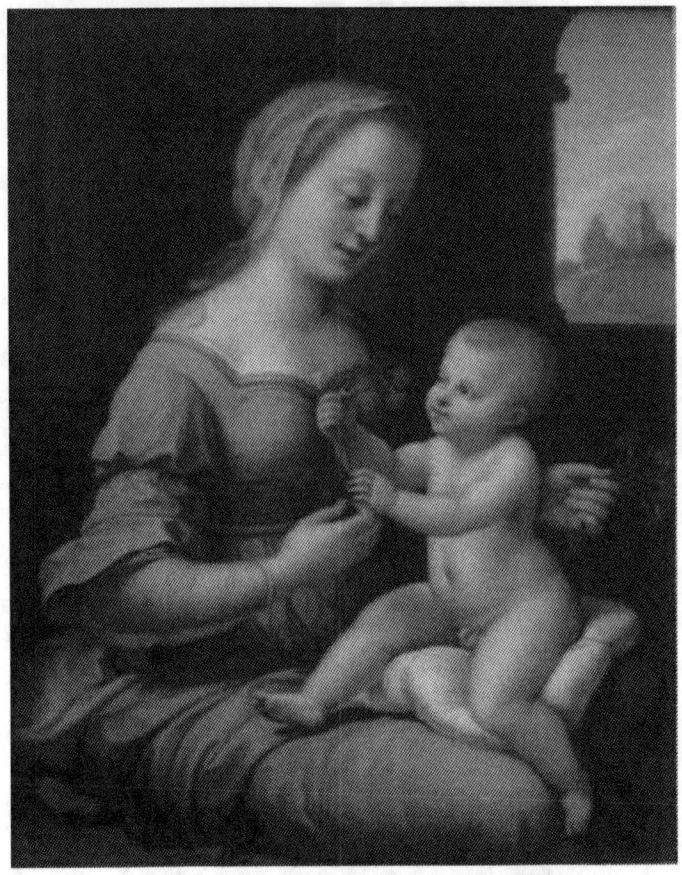

Figure 1: **Marie-Victoire Jaquotot, ceramic copy after the** *Madonna of the Pinks*, **Sevres, Museum.**

Before that point, there is no real history, except that it was purchased by Stroganoff himself from a Tuscan antique shop, according to the compiler of the collection's catalogue. It was eventually purchased from Stroganoff's heirs by Adolphe Stoclet of Brussels and was ultimately sold by his descendants directly or indirectly to the Metropolitan for about 50 millions dollars.

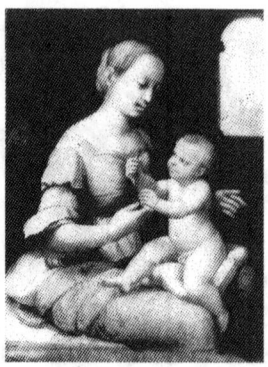

Figure 2: **Copy after the *Madonna of the Pinks*, Brescia, Pinacoteca Tosio-Martinengo. Infrared-reflectograph.**

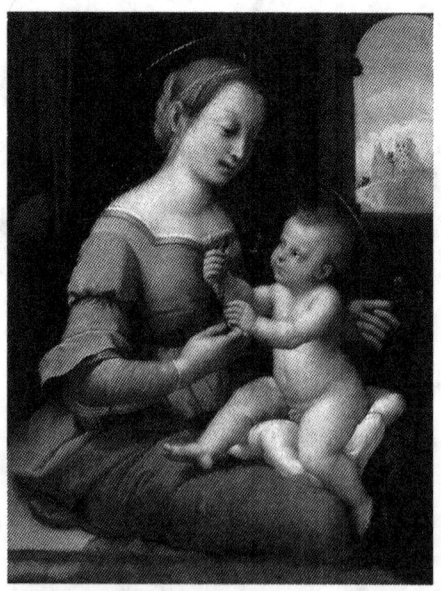

Figure 3: **Copy after the *Madonna of the Pinks*, Brescia, Pinacoteca Tosio-Martinengo.**

While the attribution to Duccio is widely held by experts, none of them had seen the picture in more than a half century; their opinions were based upon a fairly modest black and white photograph, as far as I have been able to discover. The present investigation reviews the possibilities for decoding the enigmas surrounding the two tiny paintings, together with the collateral issues.

While there are no copies or versions of the Metropolitan's Duccio, the many copies of the so-called Raphael *Madonna of the Pinks* raise issues about the identity of the composition's inventor in distinction to the authors of any particular copy. What becomes clear from the outset is that the culture out of which modern connoisseurship flourishes has permitted the grandiose attributions and their eventual sales at top prices. An appraisal of the conditions seems to be an imperative for the future health of the art market, the museums, the field of art history, and for the dignity of art in a broad context.

Behind the process of connoisseurship is the bottom-line question: are we dealing with a genuine Raphael and a genuine Duccio, as the consensus of experts vigorously assert in concert with the proud new owners of the paintings, something in between, or are they fakes as I maintain, and if so, what difference does it make anyway? After all, once admitted to the hallowed halls for eternity at 1000 Fifth Avenue or on Trafalgar Square the little Duccio or non-Duccio or the little Raphael or non-Raphael will never come up again on the art market to potentially dupe another buyer. Besides, these paintings appear enough like a genuine Duccio and a genuine Raphael to convince many experts, and are regarded as such by a wide consensus, so why make a fuss? For all practical purposes they become Duccio and Raphael by acclaim.

There had been (and still are) questionable attributions, fakes and forgeries in the collections of both institutions. Among the many Rembrandts at the Metropolitan there are actually autograph works by the master and others from his studio or workshop, replicas, works of pupils, old copies, or possible forgeries. It is common knowledge that public as well as private collections all over the world are full of problematic objects, with mistaken attributions alongside outright forgeries. Should we, then, thin out entire galleries and conduct a vast bonfire of vanities? Turning the question on its side: what is the harm of being seduced by mediocre look-a-likes including the *Northumberland Madonna* and the *Metropolitan Duccio*?

Some, even many, individuals may be inspired to lofty thoughts while contemplating them; after all, false gods are said to produce miracles.

However, such is not my view because these objects are demeaning to the dignity of art. Residing in prestigious museums where they are admired innocently by millions of viewers, their awe is reinforced by dulcet audio descriptions prepared by directors and curators singing their praise, truth, accuracy, and fairness to the memory of the artists seem to be as irrelevant as is the quality. More to the point, the life works of an artist, his *oeuvre*, should not be dependent upon the manipulation of tale spinners, academic snobs, museum fund raisers, and public relations operatives. Besides, issues of intentional or accidental fraud, interpolating spurious and by definition inferior objects into the *oeuvre* of one or another master inevitably dilutes his profile and his historical persona. The Michelangelo of the Louvre *Slaves*, the *David*, the Vatican *Pietà*, the *Medici Tombs*, is a lesser Michelangelo when a shabby fragmented *Cupid*, a modest carved wood *Crucifix*, or a ridiculous drawing representing a candelabra are added to his body of works. In most cases with such "discoveries," the artist is unfairly ground down to being more average and less magnificent than he actually was.

To have the *Northumberland Madonna* cut and pasted into the body of Raphael's autograph works makes the painter from Urbino more banal and less talented than his genuine, documented pictures allow. In simple terms, the dignity of the master is eroded and so is the history of human achievement. In the chapters of this book that follow it will be demonstrated in the context of appropriate connoisseurship that the *Northumberland Madonna* cannot be by Raphael nor by one of his contemporaries any more than the *Metropolitan Duccio* can be by Duccio or one of his contemporaries.

The process of attributing less-than-majestic paintings to leading masters is largely market driven. When the demand for high-profile works is particularly strong those few candidates with even modest claims gain in esteem beyond objective standards. Of course, the presence of anxious, deep pocketed buyers in the auction rooms and the galleries encourages generous attributions which, in turn, result in amazing sale prices. These, in turn, create an unstoppable cycle, inducing ever more "discoveries."[3]

Not without reason, when dealing with objects that are not supreme, scholars are wont to point out that even great masters from time to time have bad days, or even bad periods, when they might produce objects of lower quality than their usual standard. Consequently, according to this view, a great artist can quite possibly produce mediocre works. Pure quality, therefore, may not be the ultimate measure as one might expect, even if agreement could be reached over which works are superior. What is probably required is establishing a standard level below which an accomplished painter cannot go. For example can a prime Renaissance painter 'forget' what he had previously learned, can he ignore altogether how to model forms, render foreshortening and perspective, violate accepted anatomical patterns? In the case of Raphael, we have documented works from all periods

---

[3]New diagnostic techniques can be employed to offer indications not available in the past which can raise or lower the standing of a given object. In the case of the *Northumberland Raphael*, it was promoted from a copy status to being the original as recently as 1992.

and they should be used to establish the range of quality we can expect from the painter.

The circumstances surrounding the new Duccio at the Metropolitan Museum has parallels with the new Raphael, but significant differences as well. The consensus is also solidly supportive of the attribution, but the picture was not available for viewing for half a century if not longer, so the experts even those who wrote monographs on Duccio had to base their positive evaluations on an old photograph. Not even a decent color reproduction was available until 2003. The *Northumberland Raphael* was around for two centuries, and the type of Madonna it represents was known from engravings for much longer than that. The Duccio, instead, pops up in 1904 as a last-minute entry in an exhibition of old Sienese Painting held in Siena's Palazzo Comunale, at which time it belonged to a Russian collector in Rome. No engravings or other references whatsoever support the painting's existence before its first and only public appearance, until its purchase by the Metropolitan.

The situation surrounding the *Northumberland Madonna* was quite different because it was on public view on the walls of the National Gallery since 1993. Furthermore it has a dossier of technical and scientific tests (although circumscribed by the former owner) and was the subject of a carefully-crafted article which presented the attribution to the world along with impressive scholarly paraphernalia. For the Duccio, as far as I can gather, no technical dossier was available before the purchase by the Metropolitan Museum, at least no data of this sort has been made public. No test was made of the age of the wood in either case, which would have been helpful, and might well have been a prerequisite for a picture purchased with public funds.

The evidence points to a crisis in the area of connoisseurship. The present book seeks to isolate characteristic issues surrounding the crisis and to begin the process of establishing standards which will help to mitigate it, to protect buyers, whether public or private, and to protect the historical memory of artists whose integrity has been endangered.

Chapter 1

The Lost Art of Connoisseurship

For centuries the study of art, at least that of the West, has been centered around individual works produced by individual artists. We treasure the objects which had been produced with invention and brilliance and the creators as among the finest persons mankind has produced. In the case of painting and sculpture, the common judgment is that works of Leonardo, Raphael, Rembrandt, Rubens, Michelangelo and the rest epitomize the highest accomplishments of civilization. They represent the best of us, as it were, and hence we treasure all aspects of their contributions and of their lives. The proper identification of works of art where absolute indications of authorship are lacking is consequently central for the accurate determination of our past.

Assigning the authorship of a painting, drawing or sculpture falls under the rubric of "connoisseurship." The connoisseur must consider multiple factors including the date a work was created, the culture out of which it emerged and the degree to which it conforms to other works by the same presumed master and his contemporaries. In the case of old master works, these factors are difficult—often impossible—to establish with any objective certainty. What is required is a decision informed by skillful scholarship, by years of familiarity with the art objects themselves and, arguably, most important of all by what might be termed 'artistic intuition.' Of course, when all is said and done, the process has everything to do with the skill of seeing and being able to judge quality. The undertaking becomes especially thorny when the objects date back to a more distant past, where the data is usually elusive if not non-existent and the physical status of the objects has been compromised by time and abuse.

As for dating, even a trifling few years in the fluid condition that characterizes the Renaissance and Baroque periods (and to be sure, most others), can seriously alter the conditions under which any given work was created, as well as the *iter* of an artist, an entire movement, or "school." There are prominent artists, for that matter, whose birth dates remain only wild guesses and the presumed birth year may vary as much as 15 years from one critic's reconstruction to another's. Such is the case, for example, with Fra Angelico, Antonello da Messina, and Piero della Francesca, to cite but three examples from the Quattrocento. Any effort to sketch a pattern of their early stylistic development confronts a minefield cluttered with suppositions, assumptions, and outright guesswork. The most daring or I should say risky attributions are consistently located within the parameters of the presumed early phases of an artist's output, since these are usually the least documented and the most stylistically problematic. With the early careers almost anything is possible, it would seem.

For example, the prominent scholar Luciano Bellosi has recently put forward a nondescript *Madonna and Child* (Castelfiorentino, Museo di Santa Veridiana), a panel cut down in earlier times and over-restored in the 1930s, as a collaboration between Giotto and Cimabue[1] (Fig. 1.1).

---

[1]Bellosi, in A. Bagnoli, R. Bartalini, L. Bellosi, M. Laclotte, *Duccio. Siena fra tradizione bizantina e mondo gotico*, Milano, 2003, pp. 130-133.

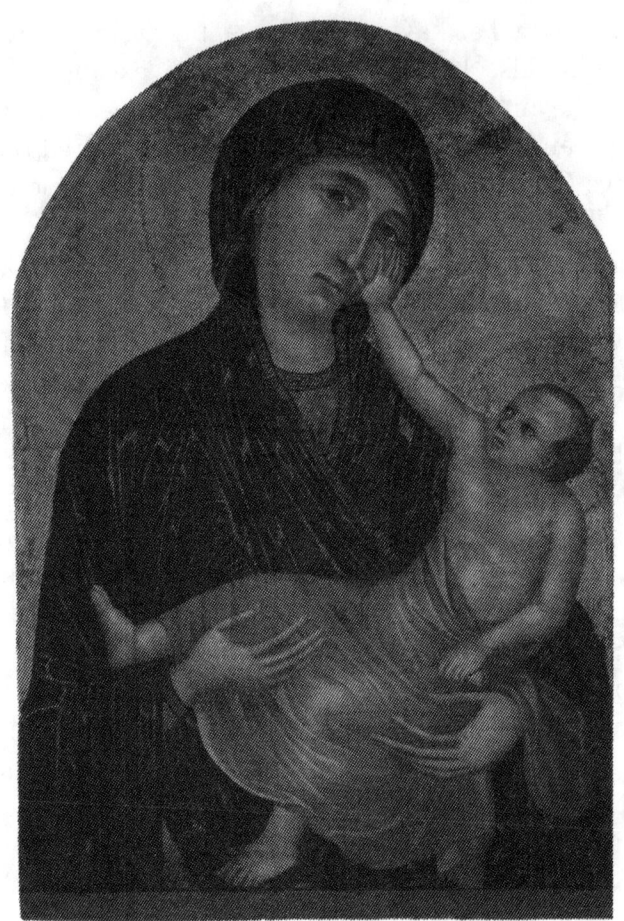

Figure 1.1: **Cimabue and Giotto, attributed to,** *Madonna with Child,* **Castelfiorentino, S. Verdiana Museum.**

Young Giotto and even early mature Giotto is impossible to pin down on the basis of confirmable objects and historical facts, starting with his birth year. There is considerable disagreement among specialists as to whether early Giotto can be spotted in the Basilica of San Francesco in Assisi at all or, for that matter, when he is regarded as having had a role, precisely which frescoes there might be his. Even the dates of their execution are very much up in the air. Hence to construct an assumed collaboration between him and Cimabue, which must have occurred before the presumptive Giotto at Assisi, is building a sand castle on a bed of shifting dunes.

In other words this type of connoisseurship seems to me a combination of wishful thinking and whistling in the dark. After all we have no indications whatsoever based upon confirmable evidence about the style of the young Giotto or even of the phases of Cimabue's career. Professor Bellosi's proposal of a Cimabue-Giotto collaboration is only possible at all because older writers beginning with Dante report that Giotto was Cimabue's pupil.

The history of the attribution surrounding this unimpressive picture demonstrates an all-too-familiar pattern of circular reasoning. Initially the painting was attributed to Duccio, then to Duccio's School, to Cimabue or Cimabue's School, then to various compromises, including a suggested collaboration between the two major masters of the time, Duccio and Cimabue. Two decades ago, and again more recently, Bellosi offered his identification of the panel as a joint venture between pupil Giotto and teacher Cimabue.

The extension of this category of reasoning upon Art History has misleading effects when applied more generally, as to teacher Ghirlandaio and pupil Michelangelo, teacher Verrocchio and pupil Leonardo, teacher Perugino and pupil Raphael.[2] Further steps along this line of reasoning become mind-boggling. Consider applying this argumentation to areas where the teachers are not known. We could have the anonymous teacher who must have collaborated with his famous pupil, as, "Young Piero della Francesca and his teacher," whoever he was. Still further

---

[2]Ironically, there is good evidence in another set of conditions to maintain that Titian completed a major painting by Giovanni Bellini, although not at the teacher-pupil stage.

along to the ridiculous, consider the possibility of being offered a construct in which anonymous masters are understood as collaborating with their anonymous pupils or, even, collaborations between two anonymous pupils of, say, Perugino.

Such flimsy constructions continue to be found in the scholarly journals and in art historical handbooks, museum catalogues and special publications for exhibitions. It is fair to assert that analogous imaginative inventions and the accompanying explicatory rhetoric have gone a long way in mystifying the connoisseurs' activity. The main beneficiary is the art market and gullible collectors whose hands shake with pride when holding their best drawing by Amico di Sandro (i.e. Friend of Sandro) or Giovanni Nessuno il Giovane (i.e. John Nobody the Younger).[3]

The likelihood that inclusive histories of Renaissance and Baroque pictures can be written is remote, and this is particularly true for panel and easel pictures in distinction to frescoes, where documents are more likely to have been uncovered. Hence the continuing need for well-tempered connoisseurship is evident and constant. In only a few instances does the evidence date back to the time of their production, when as if by chance payments or old sales records survive. Even signed and dated works are regarded with suspicion, simply because forgers, fakers and unscrupulous dealers over the centuries have tended to add dates and signatures to them in order to enhance the value of their objects. And of course, copies will also have skillfully rendered signatures when they are found on the object copied.

Older sources including Giorgio Vasari's *Lives*, are given authority simply because of the absence of better data. The governing principle seems to be that a partially informed or misinformed Vasari is better than nothing at all. Vasari himself was keenly aware of the problems of attribution. After consulting

---

[3]Bernard Berenson, "Amico di Sandro", in *Gazette des Beaux-Arts*, 1899, 1, XLI, pp. 459-471; 2, XLI, pp. 21-36, and reprinted in Bernard Berenson, *Study and Criticism of Italian Art*, London, 1901, pp. 46-69.

primary sources, he made substantial corrections and emendations between the first edition of his *Lives* (1550) and the second (1568). In one case, he attributed the vast gable marble relief of the *Assumption of Mary* on the Porta della Mandora of Florence's Duomo to the Sienese sculptor Jacopo della Quercia in the first edition, which was, stylistically speaking not really far off, but in the second edition he corrected the attribution giving it to the Florentine Nanni di Banco, on the basis of contemporary documents.[4]

The vast body of pictures which have come down to us from the *quattrocento* and *cinquecento* are not mentioned by Vasari or other early sources. Even with the expanded study of archival material in the past 200 years, the number of undocumented pictures and other unique art objects is overwhelming. Considering the circumstances, the role of the connoisseur remains crucial.

The expanded demand for authoritative attributions of Old Master paintings is closely linked with the dramatic rise of collecting in the 18th and 19th centuries, first in Italy, the United Kingdom and in France and subsequently in Germany, the United States and Russia. Admiration for Italian art was reinforced by the culture of the grand tour, coinciding with the appearance of monographs treating the *oeuvres* of individual artists. In fact, the identification of authorship became a principal activity for art specialists in the 19th and early 20th centuries until fairly recent times and was inevitably connected directly or indirectly with the booming art trade. Johann David Passavant, Giovanni Battista Cavalcaselle, Giovanni Morelli, Bernard Berenson and Roberto Longhi dominated the field and their impact as connoisseurs had a crucial effect on the art market as it did on the history of art. Their scholarly contributions and especially their influential attributions are reflected in current monographs to this day. When the confirmable *oeuvre* of an artist consists of a

---

[4]G. Vasari, *Vite...*, (1550), Luciano Bellosi and Aldo Rossi, eds., Torino, 1991, vol. 1, p. 219.

mere handful of certain works, the void must be filled in one way or another. Connoisseurship as an activity has seen a decline in authority, prestige and quality since their deaths and more recently those of Federico Zeri and John Pope-Hennessy, who both died in 1998.

Today connoisseurship is largely neglected in departments of art history and criticism as taught in the universities and as practiced in the museums. Notably in the past few decades, scholars based in these institutions have favored treating iconographic, sociological or cultural issues surrounding the art rather than identifying the authors and parsing the style of the objects they have made. Technology and implicitly science is regarded as the *porta magna* for entering the mysterious edifice of art, and have captured the thinking of the art establishment.

A recent in-depth study of the backs of Masolino's and Masaccio's panel pictures provides a case in point.[5] The way in which the various planks of a panel picture were attached, the kind of screws, the management of the batons or the pattern of the worm holes seems to take precedent over studying the pictures themselves, i.e. their fronts. The cornerstone assumption of the study, namely that Masaccio and Masolino were close collaborators who regularly worked on each other's pictures is deeply flawed. The authors write that the *Santa Maria Maggiore Altarpiece* is a work which "Masolino and Masaccio created together." And further along, "The artists would have carefully prepared their designs, collaborating and exchanging ideas before the gilder arrived on the scene." Of course, no documentary support much less historical confirmation for these confident claims has been provided. Even solid evidence for dating the diverse parts of the complex, double-sided altarpiece is lacking. The notion of joint or "good-buddy" designing is, in my view, preposterous for the period. To claim that two highly able, proven masters would collaborate in

---

[5] C. B. Strehlke and C. Frosini, eds., *The Panel Paintings of Masaccio and Masolino: The Role of Technique*, Milan 2002.

the actual conception of a single coherent work is an awesome leap in common sense.

The conditions surrounding modern museum practice are further complicated because art restorers are often called upon to evaluate and interpret the technical data, mainly because the curators are ill-equipped to do so on their own. The resulting dependence upon the restorers who also confidently offer opinions about authorship is hardly new, but nowadays they claim to base themselves on 'scientific' evidence, which lends their opinions an undeserving aura of credibility.

To reiterate: the need for connoisseurs, whose ability seems more innate and instinctive than acquired, has hardly diminished over the past couple of centuries. Works of art lacking proper credentials continue to appear on the art market, often with considerable clamor, whether an ubiquitous not to say boring Sienese Madonna with the usual gold background, an over-restored Fra Angelico look-alike or a would-be Botticelli portrait. Besides, objects new to the market turn up regularly. One source for new discoveries, is taking a heavily overpainted picture, or a sculpture whose surface has been overworked or abused, and cleaning them. More frequently than one might imagine, the "originals" are discovered under the gunk. Objects are found in junk shops and English manor houses, up-state country antique stores, and swanky galleries. The better material more often than not ends up in the commanding international auction houses. Nothing seems to delight the public more than news that a worthless art work purchased for a pittance turns out to be priceless, except when a priceless object highly touted by the experts turns out to be worthless. The exhilaration of discovery, even if only transitory in staying power, is front page news.

Back in 1989 when the undivided consensus of Raphael experts unanimously regarded the *Madonna of the Pinks* located in the Duke of Northumberland's Collection as a copy after a lost original by Raphael, it was evaluated for inheritance purposes at 6,000 pounds. In 2004 the picture was sold to the National Gallery in London for 35,000,000 pounds in cash and tax abatements, a 6000 fold increment. In an analogous case the same year the tiny so-called *Stroganoff*, also known as the *Stoclet Madonna*, was purchased as a Duccio di Buoninsegna by the Metropolitan Museum in New York for an undisclosed amount said to range between 45 and 50 million dollars to the delight the New York press (Plates 1, 6). As an indication of the absence of transparency surrounding the details of the purchase, the fact that even the exact price was not made public should raise a few eyebrows.

The attributions attending many objects housed in museums and collections often require re-evaluation as additional data and new diagnostic techniques become available and critical frameworks are redefined. Besides, from time to time new documentary discoveries can offer alternative dates and chronologies as was the case recently with Paolo Uccello's famous *Battle of San Romano* paintings in the Uffizi, the Louvre and London's National Gallery. I believe that while the need for qualified connoisseurship has persisted, the habit and the skills exhibited by later-day connoisseurs have failed to keep pace.

Indicative of current conditions is the attribution to Caravaggio of *Taking of Christ*, located in Ireland's National Gallery, which had received broad consensus approval.[6] A couple of years ago another version (which had previously been rejected by Longhi) was touted as the original when it turned up on the Roman art market. The controversy was just beginning to boil over into the media when a third version, this one in Odessa, Ukraine was called the original. The jury is still out.

The decline in authoritative connoisseurship has multiple causes. The conditions of modern life have substantially altered our

---

[6]Benedetti Sergio, *Caravaggio e la collezione Mattei*, Claudio Strinati, ed., Roma, 1995; Luigi Spezzaferro, *Caravaggio e l'Europa. Il movimento caravaggesco internazionale da Caravaggio a Mattia Preti*, Milano, 2005.

visual apparatus and visual skills. Furthermore in the past generation or so, the training of art scholars has become less effective with regard to connoisseurship. Issues of authorship become peripheral when art is studied with an emphasis on the political and cultural context. The delicacies found in a panel by a Jan van Eyck or an Antonello da Messina and how they differ have become difficult if not impossible to perceive by most viewers. (Figs. 1.2, 1.3). Study has drifted away from seeing picture *per se* as an aesthetic object.

Unavoidably and incontestably the visual environment of everyday existence frames what we see and how we see it. Current fashions in art, the main movements and the styles they represent are among the most powerful forces acting upon our mode of seeing. In broad terms the commanding art of the past hundred years has witnessed the pre-eminence of qualities markedly at odds with those that define the Renaissance and Baroque periods. One is on solid ground in maintaining that modern art in its larger compass represented a conscious rejection of the older precepts. The human figure, the core of earlier manifestations, has been relegated to a design component, while notions of modeling from light to dark, of planar construction of space, of perspective, are seen as obstacles to overcome, resulting in an abyss between the contemporary era and the past.

For the generations whose mode of seeing has been calibrated by Cézanne, Matisse and Picasso, and then Pollock, de Kooning, Alberto Burri, Franz Klein, Andy Warhol, Roy Lichtenstein and still more current manifestations including video art, the entire process of authenticating and dating, say, a pale drawing executed in silver point in 1500 is irrelevant and, for all intents and purposes, an anathema.

In other words the artistic environment defined by Twentieth Century art: Cubism, Futurism, Dadaism, Neo Dadaism, Abstract Expressionism, Post-Modern, Arte Povera, Pop, Minimalism and the other dominant movements has altered the mould.

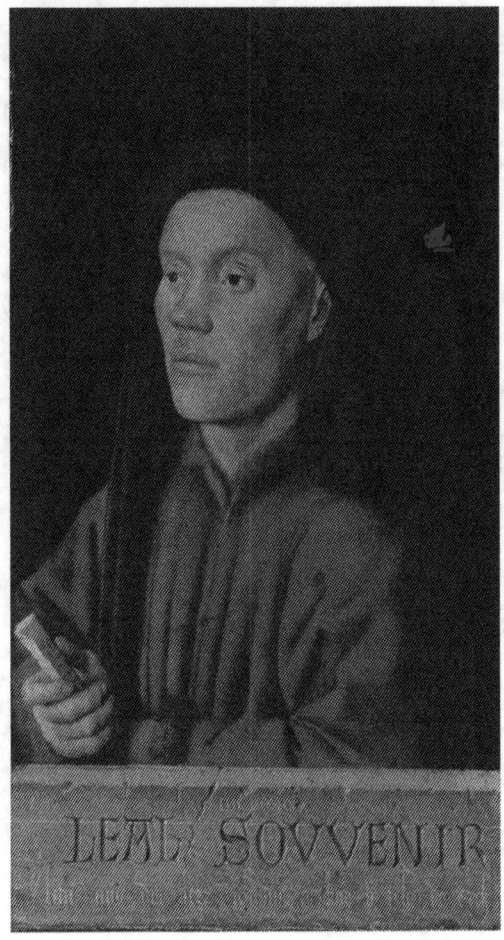

Figure 1.2: **Jan van Eyck, *Portrait of a Man*, London, National Gallery.**

The capacity to see subtle nuances has witnessed a serious decline, while the need to look at older art has been reduced.[7] Pictorial nuances found in a Rembrandt self portrait appear today to

---

[7] I am not belittling more recent art, but merely trying to underscore the changes.

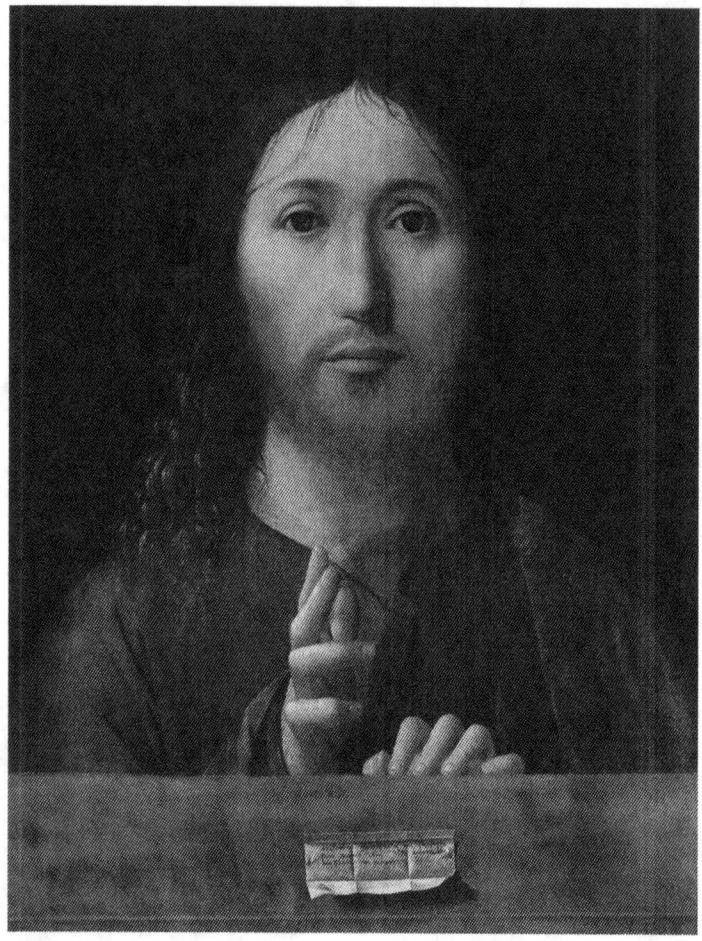

Figure 1.3: **Antonello da Messina, *Salvator Mundi*, London, National Gallery.**

be far more removed from "normal" visual experience than they were even two or three generations ago.

Also instrumental in modifying our mode of viewing pictures is an array of technological innovations, beginning with black and white photography. Before the mid 19th century, reproductions of works of art were rendered by engravers and lithographers, and hence they were in a certain sense an interpretation of the object depicted, although the skills employed in reproducing the appearance of the objects were remarkable. With the introduction of photography our habits of viewing the physical world around us, including the art of the past, changed forever and so did the way artists perceive nature. Landscape painters from Leonardo, Titian, Claude Lorrain, Turner, Corot, to C. D. Friederich transformed our way of seeing natural landscapes. Landscape is understood not only by what is out there in nature but also what is there *as filtered* by painters. With photography, which has greater claims to veracity, our vision has been modified.

The delicate variations of color, atmosphere, form, texture, and contour, of, say, a Turner seascape or the background of Giorgione's *Gypsy and the Lady* have become anachronistic. For nearly a hundred years, if not more, we have been habituated to comprehend the world as two dimensional. A further consideration when it comes to sculpture in particular is the tendency to move away from descriptive or reportorial photographs toward more dramatic or interpretive ones, presumably with the book-buying public in mind. These reproductions constitute an ingredient in the way we perceive the originals. One could easily maintain that the familiarity of a work through photographs modulates the way we see it when observing it in the flesh, while dulcet explanations by verbose curators also can predispose a particular attitude.

The invention of moving pictures first in black and white and then in color allowed for additional adjustment of the visual process. Voices and music came to impact "mere" seeing, as theatre had done in past epochs. Perhaps those degrading, canned explanations of pictures on handsets rented in museums around the world reflect today's need for an aural component to the act of looking.

Further impacting upon our ability to carefully observe older art is the viewing of images on back-lighted television and computer screens, an overwhelming part of the daily visual experience of almost everyone for at least a generation. The cellular phone is the latest image producer which will affect the act of looking, especially in terms of scale.

Another vehicle which has operated to alter the capacity to perceive subtleties are those manipulated illustrations which appear in the popular magazines printed on glossy paper. Also influential in the deterioration of viewing are billboards and signage. Our daily lives are effectively and constantly bombarded with raw, unrefined or actually charged imagery.

Beginning around 1900 the formation of art historians was structured by illustrations used in university lecture halls employing lantern slides, first with those harsh black and white monsters which were frighteningly unforgiving. They were followed by the introduction of 2 x 2 cm color slides that inevitably presented inherent problems of reliability: for decades students were initiated into the world of art whose colors were either too pink or too blue.

A central component of the instructional canon was the reliance on the comparative method (*confronti* in Italian). The pairing of slides has lingered in classrooms to this day, even though it necessarily transforms the works of vastly different dimensions, media, and periods into an identical size on the shiny white screen.

One effect resulting from the comparative method is the impression that there is no real size or real scale in art. Big, small and medium-size images appear to have the same dimension on the screen and in PowerPoint. This situation leaves a highly misleading impression about art.

Another implication of the comparative method of teaching has to do with the concept of influences and with it that of borrowing. The conclusion is that artists constantly appropriate ideas and compositions like highway robbers. What results is a simplistic view of the art of the past and of the creative process.

The newer techniques of teaching art history with PowerPoint and other computer programs are already producing changes. It is far easier to demonstrate details, and often very small ones, so that an intense study of an object seems possible, although issues of scale must still be factored in. Besides, instead of one-to-one comparisons a cluster of images can be put in front of the viewer at the same time. But most art historians practicing today learned with and perpetuate older routines. In this respect then, in terms of custom and orientation, the trained viewer cannot see an object alone, for its own unique properties, but needs some sort of confirmation by viewing other works at the same time. It goes without saying that nothing can substitute for the first-hand examination of real pictures and real sculptures.

The ability of the modern observer to relate to the objects is made more difficult by art publishers who have been adept at imparting an acceptable look to the reproductions in their books. We tend to judge how good (or bad) reproductions look, without considering how the originals really appear in the first place, or more specifically how they present themselves today in museums and private collections. Not infrequently the reproductions are more satisfactory than the object itself. Although determining in our understanding, art reproductions are, at best, third cousins to the originals, and that applies even, or perhaps mainly, to the most luxurious and elaborate art books.

Although they all have to look homogeneous in print, the works of the same artist have had different lives and come down to us in different states of preservation and with different restoration histories. Even sections from the same altarpiece may have had different treatments and consequently today appear to be significantly unalike. A generalization is in order: the better an object appears in coffee table books, the more misleading the reproductions probably are.

The process of engendering consistency in reproductions, evidently for marketing reasons, has a parallel in blockbuster exhibitions, which have been in vogue for the past generation or more. All the works, which may come from assorted countries and regions and which may have disparate histories, are usually given a uniform appearance before presentation with the aim of achieving a harmony. In other words, an acceptable average "look" is sought and often achieved, although occasionally an owner, sometimes a museum, is unwilling to go along with the offer of a free cleaning.

Contemporary viewing is also conditioned by the fact that the objects from earlier periods as well as some relatively recently created ones have undergone changes, sometimes drastic ones. Like human beings, with the passage of time, art objects, grow old and even die. In paintings, colors change, sometimes radically, varnish darkens or yellows, washes fade and disappear, wood cracks and canvas flakes. After five hundred years a work has a different appearance than when it emerged fresh from the artist's studio.

In addition to what might be called "natural" ageing, aspects of which are often prized as engendering an attractive "aura" to pictures, a host of accidents and natural disasters can affect the appearance of pictures. Floods are but one example: the notorious flood of 1966 in Florence affected the health, appearance and the very existence of thousands of art objects. Works of art are sometimes dropped, burned, or attacked by psychopaths, caught in wars, or otherwise injured by error or neglect. Thirty years after the flood, Florence's Uffizi Gallery was bombed by terrorists, killing five persons and damaging scores of Old Master paintings.

Restorations weigh heavily upon the task of the modern connoisseur by decisively altering the appearance of art objects, for better or worse. Restorations are performed according to shifting philosophies and methodologies and various national and local traditions. Among the most blatant examples is that of Leonardo da Vinci's *Last Supper*, which was restored hardly a generation after Leonardo left it, and has undergone at least six more interventions since then, the most recent aggressive one completed less than a decade ago.

In the case of more recent cleanings the dominant philosophy has been to remove all the previous restorations in the hope of getting at the original, however much is left. Apparently, a search for purity, for a return to the art work's "original glory," has become fashionable with museums and with their sponsors. In the past 25 or 30 years, almost all of the great masterpieces in public museums in Europe and America have been subjected to cleanings and restorations, some more than once.

Thus, transmutations at both ends of the viewing continuum have transpired. On the one end, our visual habits and skills, that is, how and what we see *and* on the other, the objects under observation themselves, have been modified, often oppressively. We see pictures very differently than Raphael's patrons did when he delivered them and the pictures are themselves quite different objects.

Before dealing with painting more specifically, which is the main thrust of this study, the case of an attribution of a sculpture can be helpful to better appreciate issues of connoisseurship. With a marble sculpture, modern technology cannot help much when it comes to dating, except in areas where the work has undergone repair with foreign materials like adhesives. These can be dated, but to my knowledge, no certain way has yet been developed to scientifically determine the date when a marble block was quarried or when it might have been carved.

An episode involving an under-life-size *Cupid* which stands in the center of the foyer of 972 Fifth Avenue, the former Payne Whitney mansion (completed around 1906) in New York City, today houses the Cultural Services of the French Embassy can be brought up here.[8] In 1902 the sculpture appeared in the catalogue of a London auction house, offered for sale by its Italian owner as a work by Michelangelo. Sixty six years later the Florentine art historian Alessandro Parronchi resurrected the attribution, based upon the photograph in that old catalogue, although he was unaware of the location of the sculpture.

His attribution was picked up presumably by coincidence by an American art historian, Professor Kathleen Weil-Garris Brandt of New York University, who elaborated the arguments in a scholarly article published in *The Burlington Magazine* (1996, p. 644-59) and in the international press. Her efforts provided an episode which placed connoisseurship in sharp public focus with the identification of author of the statue, called either a *Cupid* or alternatively an *Apollo*, as Michelangelo.

In treating such a work a series of steps the connoisseur may take which can have general application.

Step 1. A Visual Description of the object.

This exercise is fundamental for any critical activity and exceptionally so for attributions. The process should be conducted as clinically as possible and be restricted to describing what is seen, avoiding aesthetic and qualitative interjections as well as intuitive hunches. Also to be eschewed at this stage are art historical analogies, possible parallels with other works (i.e. *confronti*), allusions to different periods or styles, and miscellaneous analytic paraphernalia (which have a place elsewhere in the attributional process). Among the most difficult aspects of the descriptive exercise is the need to take into account the various viewing points required when dealing with sculptures in-the-round, which can be virtually infinite. Also, the point of sight

---

[8]For bibliography, see James Beck, "Connoisseurship: A Lost or a Found Art? The Example of a Michelangelo Attribution: The Fifth Avenue Cupid", in *Artibus et Historiae*, 37, 1998.

in reading the statue, that is, at eye level, from above, or from below, and the angle should be taken into account. Parenthetically, this requirement can also be relevant for viewing paintings. Elements which should be considered include:

(a) The overall appearance and presentation; (b) pose; (c) treatment of the surface; (d) state of completion; (e) figural proportions; (f) treatment of body parts, especially the torso and the head; (g) losses and additions.

Step 2. A Technical description of the object.

The measurements, type of stone, source or possible sources of the stone, its mineral characteristics which, in turn, affect the appearance of the surface, the patina, color and aging should be considered. A crucial component is a precise description of the physical state of the object, the damage it appears to have incurred over time, the condition of the surface, and areas of breakage. Ideally, laboratory tests should be undertaken and the results should be reported.

Step 3. Determination of the subject matter.

Step 4. Provenance and any documentary evidence.

The history of the object should be traced beginning with its present location and working backwards as far as possible to the originating artist.

Step 5. The historical context.

Step 6. Copies, versions adaptations and engravings of the work under review.

Step 7. Determination of the date of the object on the basis of style when no documentation is available.

Step 8. The confluence of period style and the style of individual artists.

Step 9. Comparisons, analogies and explanations.

Step 10. The formation of a consensus.

Consensus formation is a much sought-after process when it comes to an attribution. But one must recognize that a consensus view is often colored by factors outside the conditions of any given situation, such as training, teacher-pupil relationships, friendships, institutional loyalties and even self-interest. The existence of a consensus of specialists in favor or opposed to a particular attribution does not represent proof.

Step 11. Common Sense.

A determining role for common sense should be an embracing test for the validity of an attribution.

Chapter 2

The *Northumberland Madonna of the Pinks*

Due to his fame, which erupted by the time he was 25 if not before, and the consistently high marks his art has achieved ever since, Raphael is an appealing artist to study. Furthermore having died young, at age 37, while his output was ample, the number of works is not overwhelming and actually is somehow manageable. Raphael's gentle and agreeable personality, at least as it has been perceived ever since Vasari, has also contributed to making Raphael studies a favored activity, just as his pictures were copied regularly over the centuries.

A few years before the article anointing the *Fifth Avenue Cupid* as a Michelangelo appeared in *The Burlington Magazine*, the same publication carried the groundbreaking article by Nicholas Penny attributing the *Northumberland Madonna of the Pinks* to Raphael (Plate 1).[1]

The attribution, which had been gaining support, was widely solidified in 2002 by 25 art scholars and experts who attended a symposium on 8-9 November at London's National Gallery.

---

[1] N. Penny, "Raphael's *Madonna dei garofani* Rediscovered," *The Burlington Magazine*, 134, (1992), pp. 67-81.

They examined the little painting in the Science Department and, at least according to the Gallery's account, everyone appeared satisfied that the picture was indeed the original Raphael. What they may not have known was that the Gallery was entertaining the idea of buying the picture.

Since the picture, although on display at the Gallery for over ten years, was essentially on the market, a consensus among experts was highly desirable. An undocumented object that lacks the appearance of a consensus will not bring top prices and will rarely be treated seriously. In the past such an accord might have taken years to accomplish, but in today's globalized world, it can occur quickly, especially with the prodding of the public relations apparatus, amply available in world-class museums like New York's Metropolitan and London's National Gallery.

The *Fifth Avenue Cupid* appeared to be on its way to winning consensus approval, but a snag developed, and the specialists backed off *en masse* (Fig. 2.1).

Today hardly a decade after its clamorous "discovery," the *Cupid* is not taken seriously by Michelangelo scholars, and I suspect it never will be. Actually one might wish to formulate a special category for such objects that might be dubbed "Once attributed to." These objects, if nothing else, retain a sociocultural value far beyond that of the object *re* object. "Vermeers" that were produced in Holland before World War II and denounced following the war when the faker was actually imprisoned have achieved respectable prices on the auction market, presumably as curiosities.[2]

In the case of the little Raphael-style Madonna, the major event of the consensus-building was the symposium organized by the National Gallery, which had the picture on extended loan.

---

[2]P. B. Coremans, *Van Meegeren's faked Vermeers and De Hooghs: a scientific examination*, Amsterdam, 1949; John Godley, *Master Art Forger: The Story of Han Van Meegeren*, New York, 1951; Lord Kilbracken, *Van Meegeren: Master Forger*, New York, 1967.

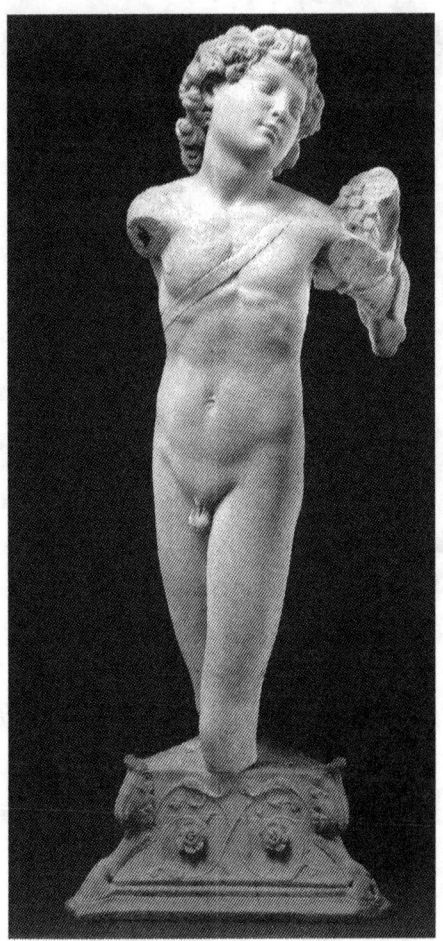

Figure 2.1: **Michelangelo, attributed to (here rejected),** *Cupid*, **New York, French Cultural Institute.**

In order to understand the mechanism in the full compass of its impact, the names of the invited participants and their institutional affiliations are instructive.

1. Beverly Brown (Independent Scholar)
2. David Alan Brown (National Gallery of Art, Washington)

3. Kim Butler (Swarthmore College)
4. Alessandro Cecchi (Uffizi Gallery)
5. Hugo Chapman Brown (British Museum)
6. Donal Cooper (Victoria & Albert Museum)
7. Charles Saumarez Smith (National Gallery, London)
8. David Ekserdjian (formerly *Apollo Magazine*, currently University of Leicester)
9. Caroline Elam (formerly editor *The Burlington Magazine*, CASVA, Washington)
10. Miguel Falomir (Prado Museum)
11. Silvia Ferino-Pagden (Kunsthistorishes Museum, Vienna)
12. Tom Henry (Oxford Brookes)
13. Michael Hirst (Courtauld Institute of Art)
14. Alexander Nagel (University of Toronto)
15. Antonio Natali (Uffizi Gallery)
16. Arnold Nesselrath (Vatican Museums)
17. Nicholas Penny (National Gallery, Washington)
18. Carol Plazzotta (National Gallery, London)
19. Lisa Pon (Harvard University)
20. Francis Russell (Christie's)
21. Patricia Rubin (Courtauld Institute)
22. John Shearman (Harvard University)
23. Bette Talvacchia (University of Connecticut and Harvard, Villa I Tatti, Florence)
24. Aiden Weston-Lewis (National Gallery of Scotland)
25. Catherine Whistler (Ashmolean Museum, Oxford)

A few writers and art historians, myself included, argued against the Raphael attribution and the controversy exploded in the British press during 2003, although curiously ignored by the U.S. media despite the Los Angeles-based Getty Museum's huge offer for the picture. In reaction to the attack on the picture's authenticity, 13 of the 25 supporters quickly signed a letter to the London *Times* reiterating their allegiance to Penny's attribution.

The letter's signers were: David Alan Brown, Hugo Chapman, Donal Cooper, David Ekserdjian, Caroline Elam, Tom Henry, Silvia Ferino-Pagden, Alexander Nagel, Arnold Nesselrath, Patricia Rubin, Bette Talvacchia, Aiden Weston-Lewis, Catherine Whistler. The art establishment was circling its wagons.

The impact of the 25 *magnifici* is not as impressive as it first appears since fewer than half of them are recognized Raphael specialists. And furthermore, among that number, a distinction may be drawn between those who are specialists on Raphael's art and those who are widely regarded as connoisseurs of his paintings. The point is that the two categories do not necessarily signify the same thing, a factor which causes confusion. For example, the late John Shearman had the reputation as far and away the leading Raphael expert of the second half of the Twentieth century, having authored influential books on Raphael and as the compiler of a massive collection of documents connected with the master. On the other hand, his track record as a connoisseur is quite another matter, and his attribution of a small portrait of a woman (said to be the sister of Eleonora Gonzaga) has silently disappeared from the body of Raphael literature, rejected even by Shearman's admirers.[3]

Among the list, those who have convincing authority are Penny and Silvia Ferino-Pagden, who has dealt with connoisseurship issues with regard to drawings with hair-splitting determina-

---

[3]The picture located in the deposits of the Uffizi Gallery in Florence is almost identical in size to the *Northumberland*, and might even be by the same author, which would be a fascinating irony. Characteristically, it seems, Shearman's presentation of the attribution was published in *The Burlington Magazine* in 1970 (see: John Shearman, "Raphael at the Court of Urbino", *The Burlington Magazine*, 112, pp. 72-78). The same portrait was published by Penny as "perhaps Raphael" in *Raphael* by Penny & Jones, London, New Haven, 1983, p. 2.

tion.[4] Other genuine Raphael experts though not strictly speaking connoisseurs include David Allan Brown and Tom Henry as well as younger scholars, museum personnel and art historians with a broad interest in Renaissance painting.

Notwithstanding the precisions I have sketched out, those who gathered at the National Gallery's symposium must be regarded as an impressive assembly, one that mirrors accurately today's art historical community. The Gallery was able to add five names of individuals who had not been at the 2002 encounter but who jumped in to support the attribution. The "new" five were Keith Christiansen and Everett Fahy (Metropolitan Museum of Art, New York),[5] Timothy Clifford (National Gallery of Scotland), who actually presented the case to keep the "Pinks" in Britain to the government, Rudolf Hiller von Gaertringen (Kustos der Kunstsammlung der Universität Leipzig) and David Scrase (Fitzwilliam Museum, Cambridge).

The 25 *magnifici* and the 5 rearguard, mop-up squad constituted an all-but-invincible force as the battle lines were drawn. The Vatican Museums had used a similar tactic by gathering committees of experts to successfully counter criticism over the restoration of Michelangelo's frescoes in the Sistine Chapel twenty years before.

The playing field was not quite level in Rome back in the 1980s nor in London with respect to the Raphael-like Madonna because, in the first place, many of the 25 participants at the Symposium had close ties with the Gallery. Several were actually staff members, including the new Director, who were anything but disinterested parties because the Gallery was seeking or at least considering to purchase the picture. In addition, they were directly involved in producing the exhibition "Raphael: From

---

[4]S. Ferino Padgen, *Disegni umbri da Perugino a Raffaello*, exh.cat., Florence, 1982, n. 57, pp. 92-96.

[5]Christiansen's presence is significant because he was the catalyst for the purchase of the Duccio *Madonna* discussed in chapter 6 of this book.

Urbino to Rome", which was held at the Gallery in November, 2004.[6] These included Henry, Chapman, Plazzotta, Penny and Nesselrath all of whom contributed to the catalogue.[7]

Simply stated, many of the attendees of the Symposium had a stake in supporting the attribution to Raphael on practical and/or cultural grounds. The entire 25 + 5 team members are trained art historians and constituted an influential cross-section of the international art community with their impeccable institutional affiliations. They functioned as a firewall against any viral invasion of dissatisfaction with the attribution. Given such a robust lobby, few potential naysayers are likely to come forward, the risks being substantial.

The institutional connections of the 25 + 5 have their own muscle to deliver in terms of fellowships, internships, jobs, research assignments and publishing opportunities. They have in hand the goodies which scholars prize, including all-expenses-paid invitations to symposia, participation in blockbuster exhibitions, writing catalogue entries and essays, service on prestigious exhibition committees and the rest. After all, museums have become an essential venue in the formulation of a *curriculum vitae* for budding scholars seeking university appointments. Actually a relatively new development in the art historical universe is the conflation of roles between museums and universities. Museum curators often teach a course or two at a nearby university while a good many university professors have close ties with the museums for research, in creating exhibitions and in placing

---

[6]H. Chapman, T. Henry and C. Plazzotta, *Raphael: from Urbino to Rome*, ext. cat., London, National Gallery, 2004.

[7]I cannot resist a comment about the recent post-Michelangelo restorations at the Vatican for which Professor Nesselrath has a role. The frescoes in the *Stanze* by Raphael, if anything, in my opinion, have been more radically restored and with greater damage to the reputation of the creating artist than the previous gravely flawed restoration of the ceiling of the Sistine Chapel. See J. Beck, *L'arte violata. Una valutazione sulla cultura del restauro*. Florence, 2002, European Press Academic Publishing.

their students there. For any art historian, especially a younger scholar, to stand up against the configuration represented by museums like the National Gallery and the Metropolitan Museum of Art is virtually unheard of.

No polling of the invitees' views concerning the putative author of the *Northumberland Madonna* was conducted at the symposium, at least as far as I have been able to determine. The National Gallery's Director reasoned that since none of the people who attended the symposium of November 2002 expressed doubts at that time about Raphael's authorship, they all favored it, interpreting silence as agreement. Given the situation in which the individuals were employees or invited perhaps with expenses included guests, one could imagine that some would have been uneasy in speaking out against their host for fear of running against the current or out of good manners.

A parallel case from the nineteenth century connected with the *Northumberland Pinks* at Alnwick can be called into play. Gustav Friedrich Waagen was surveying material for his exhaustive survey of British art collections, *Treasures of Art in Great Britain*, published in London in three volumes in 1854. A fourth supplementary volume appeared in 1857 under the title of "Galleries and Cabinets of Art in Great Britain." In this supplementary volume the author writes that "on occasion of my visit to England in 1854 I had the privilege of spending a day at Alnwick castle as his Grace's guest... The Camuccini collection, which the Duke purchased at Rome in 1856 is to be placed in this castle. On this account it appears to me more appropriate to describe the pictures as if already there." Obviously he knew the pictures from having seen them in Rome.

Surely this was a questionable procedure difficult to reconcile with Waagen's otherwise painstakingly factual approach. Equally uncharacteristic is his glowing description of the soon-to-arrive the *Madonna of the Pinks*: "It is well known that the charming composition is by Raphael and of all of the numerous specimens of the picture that I have seen, none appears to me so well entitled to be attributed to his hand as this." Three years earlier his opinion of this picture was decidedly less flattering. On page 253 of volume III, published in 1854, he dismissed it as "the small picture in the Camuccini collection at Rome which I do not consider to be the original. The tone of the flesh has something insipid and heavy. The treatment makes me suspect a Netherlandish hand." [Parenthetically I must confess my own reaction to the picture was identical.]

What could have been the reason for the radical change of attribution? One guess is that Waagen was merely being polite after having been liberally hosted at Alnwick Castle by the Duke and Duchess. In his upgraded version, however, he says, that it is "entitled to be attributed" to Raphael, not a total reversal of his earlier assessment.[8]

The explication and demonstration of the authenticity of the picture at the meeting was carried out largely by the Gallery's scientists and technical experts, a procedure which at least implied that the attribution had a scientific foundation. Once again the Gallery opted for a tactic that the Vatican Museums tested to good effect in seeking support for the restoration of the Sistine Ceiling. Since today's art scholars are usually in awe of science, they are disposed to go along.

Although an overwhelming majority of the participants were persuaded, and hence a credible consensus was achieved, the claim of unanimity is unwarranted. I learned that at least three of the original 25 do not agree that the picture is an autograph

---

[8]Waagen refers to the Camuccini picture a decade earlier in a letter written on 11 November 1843 in *Kunstwerke und Künstler in Baiern, Schwaben, Basel, dem Alsass und dem Rheinpfalz*, Leipzig, 1845, p. 301, "Maria mit dem Kinde, die liebliche Composition, welche in der Sammlung Camuccini und auch anderweitig, aber immer klein, als Raphael vorkommt, befindet sich hier in Lebensgrösse. Der Kunsthändler Wocher, welcher dieses Bild früher besass, hielt es auch für Raphael. Es ist indess meines Erachtens ein besonders schönes and anziehendes Bild des Sassoferrato."

painting by Raphael. Indeed, one participant told me with indignation that he had spoken out against the attribution at the Symposium itself.[9]

For the connoisseur the lesson of the *Northumberland Madonna* must be: beware of the consensus. Factors outside the specific issue can be determining factors, including personal friendships, national and institutional loyalties, and the distinction and power of the museums represented. Arguably in the case of the *Northumberland Madonna* the entire Anglo-American Art Establishment was co-opted, including Christie's auction house by the presence of one of its staff, while Sotheby's was directly involved and did take credit for the sale to the National Gallery, according to their own advertisements.

What makes this consensus attribution so intriguing is that until 1991 an equally solid consensus among Raphael scholars held that the picture was nothing more than a good copy.[10] The only name I can find in the earlier period who considered it an original was a certain Francesco Longhena, a translator and dealer in the early 19th century, if indeed he was referring to this particular copy.

From the point of view of connoisseurship the picture has massive problems. The malformed feet of the Child, the flatness of the planes, the odd color, the shiny surface, and the un-

---

[9] It is indicative of the climate of such encounters that this dissenter insisted that I not identify him.

[10] The observation was made to me by Michael Daley. In dealing with the *Fifth Avenue Cupid*, I have taken up the question of consensus as well as general considerations in " Connoisseurship: A Lost or a Found Art?"*op. cit.* One should also recall that a solid consensus of leading experts favored the authenticity of three sculptures as by Amedeo Modigliani which were found in a canal in Livorno over a decade ago, until the faker, actually two different fakers, came forward and admitted their authorship. Until then, the consensus among experts had been compact in supporting the fakes, with few exceptions. The same solid consensus initially supported the attribution of the Van Meegeren Vermeers, published coincidentally in *The Burlington Magazine*.

characteristic landscape are deficiencies actually recognized by the proponents of the attribution to Raphael. Individually and globally they raise a classic dilemma: "Can a great artist make bad pictures or bad drawings?" In other words, is it not possible that Raphael himself, and other great masters simply turned out some flawed works? Alternatively must we assume that all his paintings were celestial and drum out any objects that fail to live up to the highest standard?

Unquestionably, like everybody else, an artist can have bad days, weeks, months and even years. Problems with patrons, projects, materials, with the subject or in his private life may affect his creative abilities. Indeed, variation in quality within the authentic output of many artists is common. The crucial question is, how great a variation would a master like Raphael reveal from one of his paintings to another? How many and what kind of weaknesses, omissions, mistakes, and unsatisfactory features could he sustain? In connoisseurship terms, how bad can Raphael get and still be Raphael?

Part of the connoisseur's task is to determine when a work under study was created, a dating that conforms to the artist's known and confirmable chronology. In the case of the *Northumberland Madonna* a genuine difficulty in fitting the little picture into a specific historic moment arises. To be sure, Raphael shows a fairly clear development, more so than most artists of the Renaissance, yet the National Gallery's picture does not readily fit into any definable moment. Instead it falls between the stylistic cracks.

One explanation is to see it as very early within Raphael's career because of the overall tightness of the treatment and the stiffness of the Child, say, between 1502 and 1504, before his extended stay in Florence. However, the painting contains no echo of his master Perugino, and we know that as late as 1504 and perhaps into 1505, Raphael was still working close to Perugino's style. In considering this moment in Raphael's career, the signed and dated *Marriage of the Virgin* in the Brera is the best control (Plate 10).

Another feature of the *Northumberland* is the full, somewhat monumental conception of the figures, which is regarded as exemplary of Raphael's Florentine style. At that time (1504-1508) his art reflected an admiration for Leonardo's paintings including *Madonna and Child and St Anne*, the *Mona Lisa*, and *Battle of Anghiari* cartoon, all works that were executed after Leonardo's return to Florence from Milan. They should be understood in distinction to his pre-Milan period. Leonardo's contemporaries including Raphael surely knew the difference.

The compositional concept, in distinction to the figure style, revealed in the *Northumberland Madonna* type appears to owe a good deal to Leonardo's early that is pre-Milanese Madonnas (Plates 11, 12). The little picture in London reflects elements from both Leonardo's early and mature styles and, to my eyes, combines features from Raphael's early or first phase with those of his second, all in an incongruous mix. The stylistic inconsistencies inherent in the painting are accentuated by totally uncharacteristic color for Raphael at either phase.

A necessary step in building the case for Raphael's authorship is the formulation of the provenance or history of the object. Ideally, a letter or a payment referring to a picture at the time it was painted could turn up or the picture could be traced in inventories, which would reveal its location over the centuries. With most paintings of the Renaissance indications of this sort are not preserved. In contrast, for frescoes and to some extent larger-scale altarpieces, the chances are greater of finding contemporary data upon which to build, including contracts and payments.

With the goal of formulating an approach in an ongoing quest for an appropriate methodology, the range of possibilities for the *Northumberland* version of the *Madonna of the Pinks* composition may be itemized schematically as follows:

1. The picture is entirely by Raphael, the pictorial surface as well as the preparatory drawing beneath it and everything in between.

2. The surface layers are by Raphael based upon preparation and underdrawing by a workshop assistant, that is, what is visible is by Raphael himself.

3. The surface layer is by a workshop assistant based upon Raphael's original preparations, including the underdrawing and layers immediately over them.

4. Raphael prepared a fully developed cartoon from which an assistant or collaborator executed the painting from start to finish.

5. Raphael made one or more compositional sketches which he passed on to someone in his workshop. From the sketches a *modello* or cartoon was prepared and then transferred to the wood panel.

6. The entire painting, the surface and everything beneath it is a copy of uncertain authorship and uncertain date, produced at an undetermined period between the 16th and the early 19th century, when the picture was documented in the collection of the Camuccini brothers in Rome.[11]

---

[11] Perhaps a refinement of point 6 could be entertained by creating a distinction between old studio [i.e. *bottega*] and contemporary 16th c. editions, and considerably later ones, including those of the early 19th century. Using a 17th century (?) Raphaelesque picture in Wilton House, Wiltshire, which has a patently fake inscription referring to Raphael and interpreted to show the year 1508, as even an oblique evidence to support the *Northumberland* picture's hegemony, as Penny does (1992, p. 68 and n. 7), represents an inadmissible leap. (Penny, 1992, fig. 5). J. Shearman incredibly treats this picture as a document, in the monumental but idiosyncratic *Raphael in Early Modern Sources*, 1483-1602, New Haven and London, 2003, p. 122. P. Joannides [cf. *The Burlington Magazine*, no. 1220, vol. Cxlvi, pp. 749-752]

With an eye towards approaching the task of identifying the author of the *Northumberland Madonna*, a number of avenues are recommended:

(a) A credible reconstruction of the picture's provenance.

(b) A precise determination of the wood support upon which it is painted, is it cherry, or another type of fruitwood, and if so what kind? Examples of the use of the particular type of wood, once ascertained, and their relation to Raphael's procedures during his Florentine phase.

(c) The age of the wood upon which the picture is painted should be tested.

(d) An analysis of the precise structure of the preparatory ground found on the panel and a possible rapport with grounds found on other paintings of the period by Raphael and by his contemporaries.

(e) The determination of the medium employed in the picture and in the preparatory layers, using visual evidence as well as physical samples.

---

uses the Wilton House Madonna, which he compares to the *Nortumberland*, in building other attributions. Seemingly he is paving the way for another "discovery." The article in part functions as a timely defense of the National Gallery's attribution which he takes as fact, although he describes the *Northumberland* as exhibiting "a certain stiffness in design." The author lists a number of versions and adaptations of this composition and even a copy of a lost Raphael drawing. None of these are from the 16th century, in my opinion, except for an engraving by Marco Dente which he says is based upon Raphael as well. This engraving, in turn, is placed in context with a terra cotta work, attributed to Pietro Torrigiani. One can expect that one or more optimistic owners will come forward with their newly rediscovered Raphaels hoping to repeat the outcome of the *Northumberland* and as things stand they may well succeed.

(f) A comparative analysis of at least a selection of the better versions of the composition whose total number now exceeds 55.

(g) A discussion of the color in the picture and its relation to color used in other versions of the composition and in confirmed pictures by Raphael.

(h) Scientific testing of at least a selection of other versions/copies of the compostion.[12]

(i) A formal and stylistic analysis of the function of light in the picture, the anatomy revealed in the figures, the system of modelling, the treatment of landscape and still life elements including the column and the buildings in the landscape.

(j) An evaluation of the quality exhibited in the picture.[13]

---

[12] As far as I have been able to determine the impressive and unequaled dossiers of Raphael paintings compiled by Maurizio Seracini, Editech, Florence, have yet to be consulted by proponents of the attribution. Very recently the administration of the Pinacoteca Comunale Tosio Martinengo have placed their fine copy, which was studied by Seracini in the past, under scrutiny with encouraging results (Figs. 1, 2).

[13] In terms of sources which would could give the *Northumberland* picture authority, a rapport with a drawing by Fra Bartolomeo in the Uffizi has been proposed by Penny (1992, p. 68 and fig. 9) and repeated by the London experts. But the implications for this reference are, of course, true for all the copies, so to raise a big name of an artist Raphael is known to have studied (and vice versa), is used misleadingly to add to the *Northumberland's*, pedigree. In the UK's governmental report we find the language "there is more than a hint of Fra Bartolommeo's influence..." *Department for Culture, Media and Sport; Export of Works of Art 2002-2003, Case 18.* Actually the Fra Bartolommeo is a reflection of Leonardo, which in turn is based upon a relief by Desiderio da Settignano, both in London, the former in the British Museum and the latter in the Victoria and Albert Museum. See now A. Parronchi, *Proposte per Leonardo Scultore*, Milano, 2005, esp. ills. 8-15.

A gathering of all the versions of the composition which have any claim to quality should be undertaken. After all, to sustain the attribution, the *Northumberland Madonna* must be demonstrably superior in design *and* in execution to all the others as a starting point.[14]

According to the proponents the most persuasive indication that the *Northumberland* is in fact a Raphael is the "evidence" supplied by the 'underdrawing' which can be visualized or rather reconstructed by means of Infrared Reflectography. Penny and the Gallery claim that the underdrawing is by Raphael and that therefore, as night follows day, the surface painting must be by him.

Of course the assessment of the underdrawing is itself only an attribution. The result is that the proponents of the primacy of the *Northumberland Madonna* are in an untenable situation. The attribution of the painting is based upon the attribution of "underdrawing." The reasoning is circular. But worse, any connoisseur worth his salt would be very reluctant to base judgement on a photograph of a work of art, whether a painting or a drawing. He would want to see the real thing. In this case with the IR, *there is no real thing*, only a shadow of the real thing, constructed by a mosaic of small photograms patched together and coalesced with computer technology.

In my view, the underdrawing, to the extent it can be at all read, reveals a Neo-Classic flavor, indicating it as the work of an artist of the late 18th or early 19th century, not that of an early 16th century one. My connoisseurship leads me to reject both the underdrawing and the painted picture as Raphael's as will be amply demonstrated in the following two chapters.

---

[14]It is quite likely that some copies were made from other copies and not from the original and the same may be hypothesized for the engravings of the same composition. The reader is reminded that shortly a complete catalogue of the known versions will be presented by Jan Sammer, in a volume to be published in the same series as the present volume.

Chapter 3

The *Northumberland Madonna of the Pinks*. Shortcomings

In order to properly approach the *Northumberland* painting with an eye to determining its proper place in Raphael's catalogue a more thorough examination of its shortcomings must be undertaken. The connoisseur would do well to determine the *Northumberland Madonna*'s proper niche among the known versions (and any others which might turn up) not to mention its relationship to the approximately fifteen renderings of the composition engraved over the centuries. Had the London picture not been proposed as the original or prime version in 1992 by a prestigious scholar, in a prestigious journal, and then exhibited as a Raphael in a prestigious museum for over a decade, the need would have been negligible. Surely it would have remained in that limbo where it had rested for nearly two centuries.

At the start of any discussion, a fundamental distinction should be drawn with a heavy stroke between the original concept or idea on the one hand and the identified versions on the other. The proponents of the *Northumberland*'s authenticity claim it as the original painting, and have effectively won over many specialists and art experts to their opinion, as we have seen. But, as will be demonstrated, their judgement is based upon assumptions that cannot survive close scrutiny. Below I have selected problematics raised specifically by the London picture (and shared with those versions possibly derived from or intimately connected to it), but not inherent in the original (Ur) composition. The weaknesses or aberrations associated uniquely with the *Northumberland*, some of which have already been highlighted in previous pages, will now be reviewed. I am not including here the substantial ambiguities, not to say the fantasies, surrounding the picture's provenance which will be treated separately in the following chapter.

The *Northumberland* exhibits a series of qualities uncharacteristic of Raphael making his authorship impossible. A corollary issue, not connected with any specific attribution, can be raised: if the *Northumberland* could not have been painted by Raphael, is he nevertheless the inventor of the idea behind it and all the other versions, as the general opinion holds? In other words, is the Ur picture (or pictures) by Raphael himself or, on the contrary, by a follower or imitator? Merely raising the question, which to my knowledge has never been done, although Crowe and Cavalcaselle came close, provides a rewarding exercise, at least for the sake of tidiness. But it needs to be borne in mind that the eventual resolution of this question does not in the slightest affect the status of the *Northumberland* picture, once it is removed from consideration as an original work by the master.

The National Gallery experts continue to insist that the *Northumberland* is the original version executed by Raphael with pictorial solutions that are predicated upon Leonardo da Vinci's inventions before he left for Milan, in a style practiced in Verrocchio's workshop. Of course, compositional "sources" located here are pertinent to all the versions, not exclusively to the London copy. On the other hand, the execution of the *Northumberland* picture exhibits a heavy dosage of Raphael's early or first manner, that is, his pre-Florence style, which reached its fulfilment, so to speak, in the *Marriage of the Virgin* (Milan, Brera) (Fig. 3.8). At the same time, however, elements from Raphael's Florentine period, from 1504 to 1508, may be isolated as well. Hence, as will be demonstrated, due to these ambiguities, the dating of the London picture has caused problems for nearly 200 years.

Although ignored in 16th century sources, the *Pinks* composition, *nota bene* not the *Northumberland* version, demonstrably was appreciated in France in the 17th century, when engraved at least four times. Whether Raphael actually invented the idea or not, at that time and ever since, it has been regarded as Raphael's.

Under any circumstances, we are on safe ground in maintaining that an original or at least an authoritative old version, and quite possibly two, must have been in France early in the century, if not before. The *Madonna of the Pinks* gained renewed popularity with the rise of Neoclassicism in the later 18th century and the ascendancy of Raphael's reputation, when it continued to be copied and engraved.

The French prints, whose precise dating will be taken up in a future publication, reproduced and disseminated the composition far and wide. Among the first which has come to light, referred to here as *French 1* (Fig. 3.1) is among the earliest visual documents of the idea behind the composition of the *Madonna of the Pinks*, although one or more of the others may have preceded it (Figs. 3.2, 3.3).

The complex account of the engravings and their relationship to the original concept has yet to be unravelled, although under any circumstances it does not affect the connoisseurship issue at hand, a clarification of the attribution of the *Northumberland* painting to Raphael. While the alleged dependence of these en-

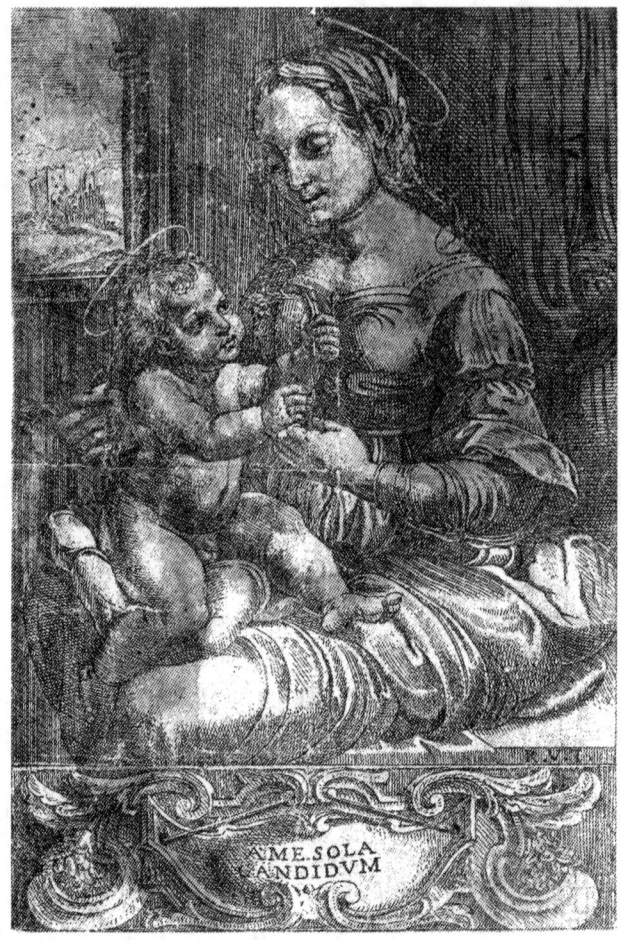

Figure 3.1: **Anonymous Artist, engraving after the *Madonna of the Pinks* ("French 1").**

gravings on the *Northumberland* is at the core of the National Gallery's case, it will be demonstrated that the picture could not have given rise to any of them due to differences in details, modelling, and expression.

I consider it desirable to offer what should be regarded as

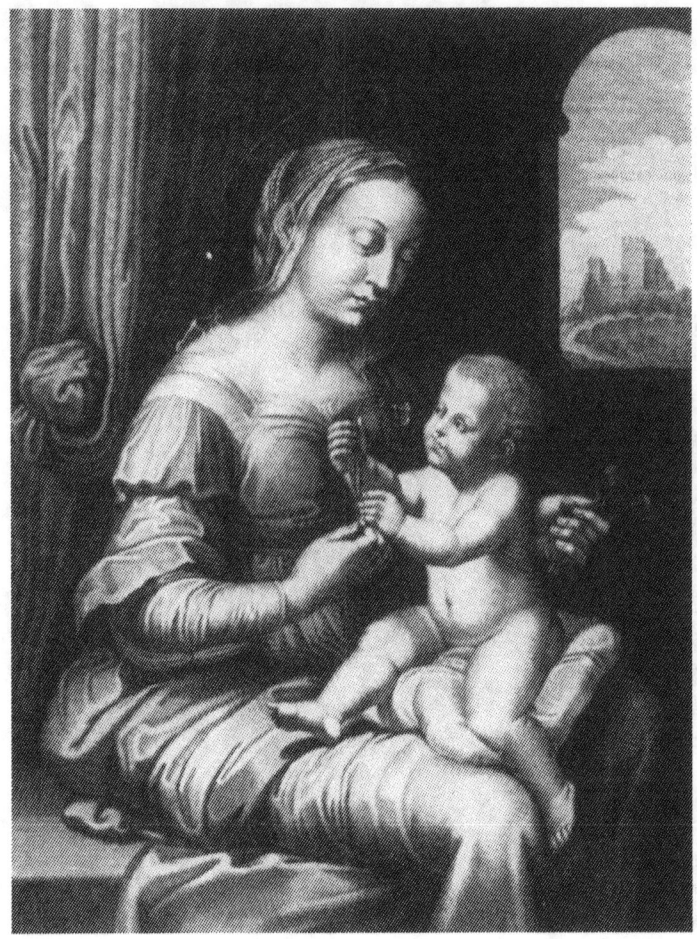

Figure 3.2: **Jean Couvay, engraving after the *Madonna of the Pinks* ("French 2")**

shortcomings or problematics inherent in the argumentation supporting the primacy of the *Northumberland* picture. They constitute an insurmountable barrier to claims of authenticity. Some are basic, while others are superficial. But what becomes apparent is that the number of unusual, uncharacteristic or unique

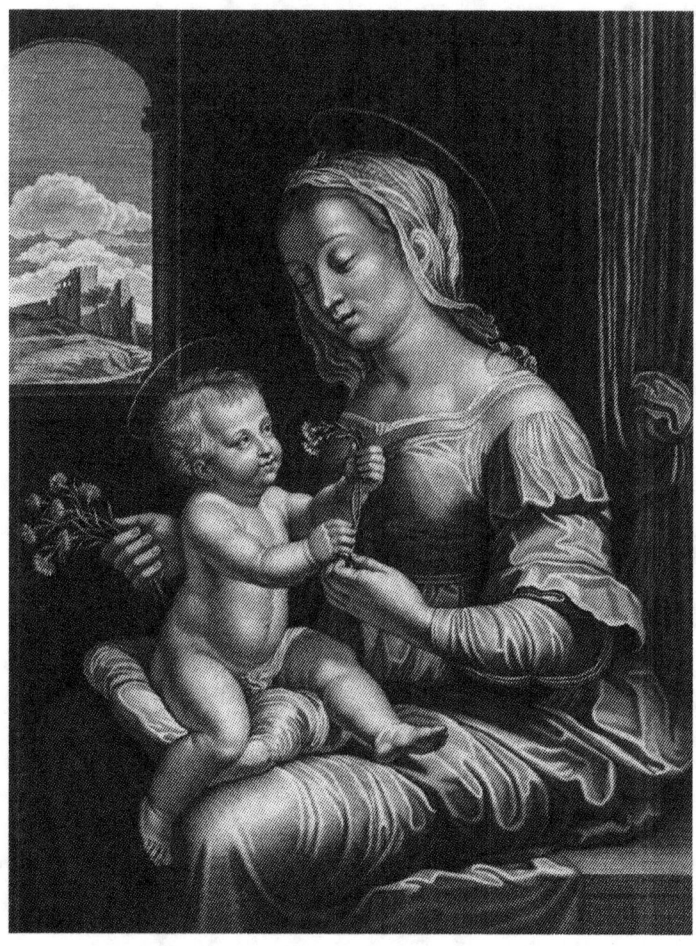

Figure 3.3: **Jean Boulanger, engraving after the *Madonna of the Pinks* ("French 3").**

elements found in the picture is overwhelming. Each of these issues surrounding the *Northumberland* painting is enumerated below and is followed by a commentary.

1. **The proportions revealed in the condensed picture and especially the lack of space available on all four sides provide for a crowded field in which a third flower held in Mary's left hand is cut off.**

Two connected issues raised here are: (1) the actual physical size, namely the real dimensions, and (2) the amount of space implied within the composition, regardless of the actual size. In the case of the *Northumberland* and related examples, the sacred figures are squeezed into a restricted, cramped area. The window arch is truncated, the head of the Virgin is close to the top edge of the picture, and so on. Furthermore, the implied depth is shallow.

Evidence confirms the existence of at least two different sizes of the composition. Among the earliest printed references to a picture representing the *Pinks* theme is a London auction catalogue of 1830, which will be discussed in the following chapter. It specifically refers to a version of the composition in Rome owned by the local painter Vincenzo Camuccini, calling it smaller than and inferior to the one in the sale.[1] Hence, we can group the extant copies into at least two distinct sizes: (1) the smaller one, which includes the *Northumberand* and in fact the majority of the fifty-five versions, and (2) a substantially larger prototype. All that we can say for now is that some of the known painted

---

[1] In the 1839 edition J.D. Passavant *Rafael von Urbino und sein Vater Giovanni Santi*, (volume I under item no. 55) gives the following unflattering report on the picture: Es gibt mehrere alte Copien dieses hübschen Madonnenbildes, ohne dass ich bis jetzt noch das Original endeckt hätte. Die mir bekannten sind alle von einem sehr kleinen Format, und stimmen darin überein, dass sowohl der Charakter des Madonnen Kopfs, als auch des Faltenwurfes die spätere Florentinische Epoche Rafael's bezeichnet, von 1506 bis 1508. Ich will hier die vorzüglichen mir bekannten Exemplare angeben: a) In der Sammlung des Cavaliere Vinc. Camuccini in Rom. Sie sitzt links und ist rechts gewendet. Die Behandlung hat etwas zartes; die Färbung ist kalt. Es kommt sicher aus der Schule Rafael's. Leider hat es durch Retouchen mit Ölfarben ein etwas fleckiges Ansehn erhalten.

versions and engravings are as much as twice as large as most of the others.

A central question grows out of the conditions surrounding the *Northumberland* version, one which is devastating for claims of its primacy: ***Can more detailed and spacious versions with un-crowded pictorial fields be regarded as having derived from a cramped and airless prototype?*** Or putting it in reverse: ***Can a crowded and cramped version give rise to airy and spatially harmonious pictures?***

If the National Gallery's expensive new property is the genuine, original Raphael, the more spacious versions which are also more informative and more visually satisfying must be regarded as expansions of it produced by copyists who sought to improve the concept. If not, the attribution to Raphael of the *Northumberland* is not viable right from the start.

Furthermore, to accept the *Northumberland* as the original Raphael it must be not only superior in quality but superior in invention to all the other versions. Can a situation be imagined in which anonymous copyists have effectively improved upon Raphael and have produced paintings superior to their model? The rubric I have labelled "common sense" should be called upon. The question alone provides a potent warning about the validity of the *Northumberland* attribution to Raphael.

The French engravings offer insights for unravelling at least part of the puzzle. *French 1*, located in the Istituto Nazionale per la Grafica in Rome, belongs to the smaller category. Published in the Institute's already cited catalogue *Raphael Invenit*, it was mentioned but not illustrated by Penny, who failed to notice the date of 1648 incised in the central left side of the print and he mistakenly dated it to the late 16th century describing it as Italian (Fig. 3.2). *French 1* contains the letters "R V I", which should be taken as a reference to Raphael of Urbino as the inventor and as such represents not only an early reference to the existence of the composition but an early reference to Raphael as its author. In terms of the pictorial field, at the bottom it shows even less than the *Northumberland*, with most of the bench upon which Mary sits blocked out. I suggest that the engraver needed to make room for the elaborate Baroque cartouche.

According to the explanation offered by Penny, the engraving, *per force*, must be based upon the *Northumberland* version. His reasoning begins with the assumption that the picture is the original. All the versions, painted or engraved, necessarily must be derived from it (directly or possibly indirectly). Although *French 1* shares a smaller format with *Northumberland*, the evident differences rule out a dependence. These include an alternative treatment of the landscape, the head and hair of the Child, Mary's expression, and the handling of drapery, which in the engraving shows greater complexity, especially on the Virgin's extended leg. Also we find a convincing three-dimensional modelling in rendering the Child and greater authority in drawing the hands and feet than in the *Northumberland*.

In *French 1*, as well as in some painted versions, the back leg is visible while in the London painting it is not. Ironically, the 'missing' leg is present in the underdrawing of the *Northumberland*, as revealed by infrared reflectography (Fig. 3.4).

If we were to accept Penny's account, we would have to assume that the author of the engraving saw the underdrawing, an impossible eventuality.

French 2 and *French 3* can also be called into play. *French 2*, by Jean Couvay (1605-1675) (Fig. 3.2), is dated to circa 1670 by Penny, but could have been produced considerably earlier.[2] Noting the differences with the *Northumberland*, including the

---

[2] As mentioned already, the chronology of the engravings will be taken up in a subsequent publication. In the latest official statement by the Gallery, Couvay is regarded as one of the interpreters who reproduced their picture, for which see *Raphael From Urbino to Rome, op. cit.*, p.190. Of course, Couvay depicts the type, but not, under any circumstances, the actual *Northumberland* picture. This sleight-of-hand constantly burdens the National Gallery's analysis of the picture.

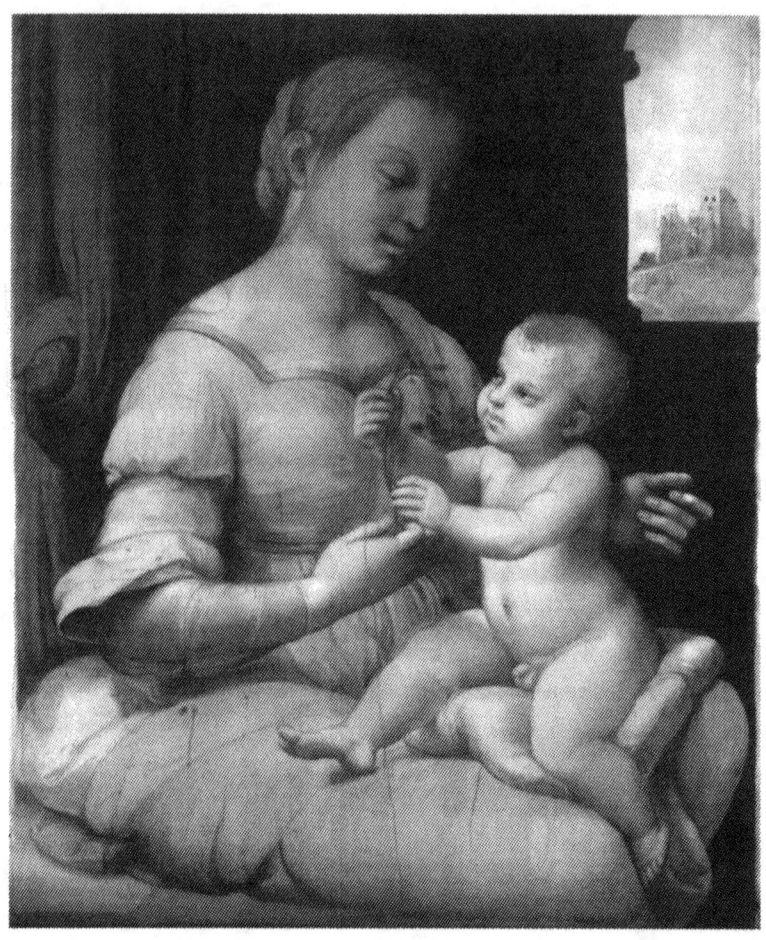

Figure 3.4: **Attributed to Raphael (here rejected),** *The Northumberland Madonna of the Pinks*, **London, National Gallery. Infrared reflectograph.**

larger pictorial space, Penny postulates that there may have been other copies of the painting available to the engraver.[3] Of course

---
[3]Penny, p. 80.

these must, following this rationale, have depended upon the *Northumberland* picture somewhere along the line. *French 2* is substantially different than the *Northumberland*: nearly the entire arch of the window embrasure at the top right is rendered, a tell-tale element which will be addressed later. Furthermore Mary's extended front leg has a highlight on the knee, while the lower leg is resolutely indicated by vertically oriented drapery folds. The bench upon which Mary sits is given greater elaboration, increasing the logic of the pose which is so unsettling in the *Northumberland* copy.[4]

None of the French engravings can be regarded as based upon the *Northumberland*. And the reader/connoisseur should continue to keep on the front burner of his mind the question: which could come first, a cramped, restricted image or one with greater logic, air, space and cohesion? Specifically, can the original version be one which is smaller, characterized by less figuration and the near elimination of the bench upon which Mary sits, as well as a reduced number of flowers and an amputated window embrasure? At this point, I find it appropriate to claim, given the situation as has already been sketched, there is no chance whatsoever that the *Northumberland* painting is an original Raphael. Actually, the connoisseurship story on the picture could very well end here, but for the sake of of completeness, other problematics are treated in the following pages.

---

[4]There are two other French engravings of the period by Boulanger (cf. *Raphael Invenit*, Madonne, III, 2, measuring 391 x 299 and 450 x 308 mm), both of which are significantly larger in physical size than the Northumberland painting. Penny's proposal that they are based upon the Couvay engraving (French 2), which measures 337 x 257 mm, is unlikely, and the opposite explanation is equally tenable.

2. The highly irregular width of the borders or edges formed by the space between the painted surface and the actual edge of the panel are untypical, if not unique, among Raphael's certain works.

Seeing the picture outside its frame demonstrates that the panel was not cut down (Plate 1). In other words the tiny, crowded picture is today what it was when it was painted, and nothing has been shaved off the edges.

The irregular border that separates the painted surface, i.e. the actual painting, and the edges, must be the result of the creating artist's awareness that it would be framed after its completion. If he were to have painted to the extreme edge of the panel, a portion of his work would be buried by the lip of an eventual frame so he would not have placed there any meaningful elements. Penny punctiliously reports: "A border varying from 6 mm. (at left of the lower, and right of the upper, edge) to 1 mm. (at the sides towards the top) has been left unpainted but is covered with the gesso ground. Such a border is unusual in Raphael's small panel paintings only in its irregularity."[5] Whatever explanations one might invent for such a deviation from his usual practice, its presence has to be regarded as injurious to the case advocating Raphael's authorship of the *Northumberland*.

Evidently the painter of the *Northumberland* lost his way while copying, which is especially evident in the landscape, where his pictorial rendering spills over into the area which will necessarily not be visible. I believe that the irregularity of the strip confirms the fact that we cannot be dealing with an original, created *ex novo*, but a copy.

The underdrawing raises the issue of the number of flowers held by Mary in the various copies. In *French 2*, which is reversed, Mary holds seven flowers in her left hand, while in the *Northumberland* she holds only two, with a hint of a third in the border of the panel or the bud of a flower, as the National Gallery

---

[5] Penny, *op. cit.*, p. 67 and note 2.

experts suggest. If the carnations have a relevant function for the overall meaning of the picture, as the National Gallery's learned iconographers maintain, how can one explain the restricted number? In terms of Christian iconography, three flowers, a number which appears in numerous versions, is surely preferable to two. Furthermore, if the *Northumberland* was the original, the others must be understood as expansions, an impossible scenario. In other words, the number of flowers visible makes the attribution to Raphael impossible.

3. The cherry wood (or fruitwood) support is unknown for Raphael during the first decade of the Sixteenth century.

According to the National Gallery's Director, the wood support of the *Northumberland* picture is cherry, although it has also been referred to as "fruitwood, probably cherry."[6] Since cherry was not used for other Madonnas by Raphael or in fact for pictures painted in Florence during the period, the kind of wood is only one more unique feature of the picture. Recognizing the rarity of cherry for Renaissance paintings, the Gallery in its defence has pointed to Raphael's *Transfiguration* (Vatican Museums), which was painted on boards of cherry wood. Of course, this imposing altarpiece was executed a decade after the presumed date of the *Northumberland*, in a diverse cultural milieu. Its existence does not change the fact that the choice of cherry for a small Madonna painting is unheard of in the period.

As for the *Transfiguration*, it has been speculated that cherry was chosen because originally the altarpiece was designed to be shipped to France.[7] In the Gallery's argumentation to explain

---

[6]It does seem odd to me that a world-class museum is prepared to purchase for millions of pounds a picture whose support is a question mark. Of course, cherry is quite distinctive in color, and while the back was painted over (see below, point 4), the edges and the sides should help tell the tale.

[7]On this point see F. Mancinelli, "La Trasfigurazione e la Pala di Mon-

away the unusual type of wood, they also point out that Raphael's *Doni* portraits are on limewood indicating that Raphael used "unusual" supports when in Florence, so that cherry could have been a legitimate possibility, the common feature being uncommonness.[8]

But a curiosity with regard to the *Transfiguration* requires attention: the individual in charge of the restoration in the early 19th century was none other than Vincenzo Camuccini, the presumptive owner of the *Northumberland*.

4. The back of the panel has been polished and covered with a dark substance, obfuscating the wood surface and whatever, if anything, might have been on it.

Just as the disregard of the pictorial edge of the painting and the unusual support are damaging to the case for Raphael's authorship, so is the polishing of the back of the panel. Whatever the case here, any reference to a pre-19th century history of the painting or other evidence in the form of labels or inscriptions, if there were any, has been obscured. Collectors and museums alike relish clues concerning the history of a work and usually retain and even treasure them. Obfuscating the back is inevitably suspicious to people familiar with the art trade, who tend to wonder: "Is there something to hide?"

As the picture now appears, according to the National Gallery, the back has only 19th century seals, one of Pietro Camuccini, one of Vincenzo and one of the city of Rome, presumably for export purposes; alternatively it is possible that one is the

---

teluce: Considerazioni sulla loro tecnica esecutiva alla luce dei recenti restauri," in *Princeton Raphael Symposium. Science in the Service of Art History*, J. Shearman and M. B. Hall, eds., pp.149-50, note 2.

[8]In addition to wood, almost always poplar, Raphael also used canvas from time to time, as with the early *Marriage of the Virgin* (which was attached to a wood surface, however), or the later *Sistine Madonna*, the *Donna Velata*, and the *Castiglione* portrait. This practice was common in the Perugino shop (as per Ashok Roy, etc., *Technical Bulletin*, 2004, p. 5).

seal of Giovanni Battista Camuccini, son of Vincenzo, and the effective owner at the time of the sale in 1855. There is no single indication or hint of a vaunted Perugian, much less a French, provenance. The presence of Pietro's seal can be taken as confirmation that this is the version owned by him at his death in 1833, which passed on to Vincenzo and later to his son. This bit of evidence seems to belie the official line to the effect that Vincenzo bought it in Paris. In an unpublished account book Pietro reports that he bought it for a substantial sum, but does not indicate where.[9]

Related to the same point was the inability of the National Gallery to thoroughly test the panel before the purchase due to restrictions imposed by the owner. After the object became the property of the Gallery, in February 2004, such restrictions became moot, but as I write they seem unwilling to conduct testing of the wood which could reveal the age and the type.[10]

Although wood dating is not absolutely precise, it could help, even if fakers often used old wood in their operations.[11]

---

[9] I would like to thank Professor Paolo Puddu of Rome for making the manuscript available to me, and generally for his enormous help. This entry reads: *"[No.] 241 Madonna e Bambino Originale di Raffaello d'Urbino di tavola alto palmo 1.o[ncie] 3 L 1 palmo"*. On another page, he specifies that he paid 500 Luigi and that the selling price was 750, but it was really worth 1500 Luigi. The high inventory number, i. e. 241, might indicate that the picture was not purchased very early in Pietro's activity as a dealer. The evaluation in the inventory taken at the death of Pietro in 1833 reads: *"No. 11 Madonna e Bambino con garofoli* [sic] *in mano, alto pal.* 1½ *Maniera di Raffaello s*[cudi] *[100]."*

[10] According to the National Gallery, the explanation for not examining their other tiny Raphael, the *Vision of the Knight*, is "due to its small scale and excellent condition" (from *Technical Bulletin*, 2004, p. 5) which, to be sure, also raises questions in my mind, especially since that picture has unresolved problems of its own.

[11] Due to the sensitivity of the matter, if and when the Gallery were to test the wood for age, it would be desirable to have it done by an independent expert, with a disinterested observer present to verify the results.

5. Locating the picture within Raphael's stylistic development and offering a convincing date has been a long-standing challenge.

As has been signalled already, the style exhibited in the *Northumberland* picture is inherently difficult to pin down. Since its appearance in the early 19th century, specialists have vacillated mainly between placing it in Raphael's first or second style. The dating offered by the National Gallery's experts of ca. 1507-08 which has shifted a little to 1506-07,[12] that is, smack in the middle of the artist's Florentine period, fails to take into account the stiffness of the poses, especially that of the Child, as well as the tight, miniature-like treatment, the reduced modelling and the ineffective interaction between Mother and Child. In fact, the flexibility in terms of the dating indicates the intrinsic problem of determining its period style within Raphael's well-defined artistic itinerary.

Since coming to light, the painting has been dated to Raphael's pre-Florentine period (i.e. before late 1504), *during* his Florentine years (1505-08), or *after* Florence (1508+), that is, the early Roman period (for example, K. Oberhuber as 1510). Berenson would have dated it still later, at least in 1897, when he attributed it to Giulio Romano, although he subsequently changed his mind. Common sense tells us that such disagreements are symptomatic of an inherent problem of period style which, in turn, speaks against an attribution to Raphael.

As a means of testing the National Gallery's dating, the confidently dated *Deposition* (1507) presents a touchstone for comparison in terms of Raphael's chronology for the assumed

---

[12]See H. Chapman, T. Henry and C. Plazzotta, *Raphael From Urbino to Rome, op. cit.*, p.190, as "about 1506-7," which has a double equivocation, the "about" and the bracketed years, documenting the insecurity of the officials. The "about" and the bracketed years leave open the possibility, I suppose, that it is 1505 or even 1504 at one end of the range, and 1508 or perhaps 1509 on the other. Dr. Henry told me personally that he would date it specifically to the winter of 1506-07.

date of the *Northumberland*. It fails to fit in as it should. The monochrome *Virtues* which formed the predella of the *Deposition* should reveal common features if they really are contemporary. The treatment of the children and the concept of their design are totally different from the Child in the *Northumberland* and clearly superior (Fig. 3.5).

As referred to earlier, a few specialists believe that a painting known as the *Wilton House Madonna*, which shares features with the *Madonna of the Pinks* composition, especially the extended hand of Mary holding flowers (reversed) helps to confirm a dating of ca. 1508, since the mixed-up date on it could be interpreted as such. The Wilton House picture has a scrambled inscription, which includes "RAPHAELLO VRBINAS", and has a faulty date, which "corrected" would read "MDVIII". Still, Penny, who sees the anomalies in this modest work, uses it to help with the dating of the *Northumberland*, in an inexcusable leap of faith.[13]

6. The color and surface treatment are uncharacteristic among Raphael's securely attributed works.

Even the proponents of the attribution, including Penny and Saumarez Smith, recognize that the surface appearance and color in the *Northumberland* are uncharacteristic for Raphael. An examination of the surface with the naked eye reveals cracking unlike that found in any other of his works. Furthermore, no other painting by the master for the presumptive period or any period, for that matter, reflects the same cold tonalities. The smooth, slick surface is atypical of Raphael and more generally for Central Italy in the first decade of the Cinquecento. Efforts

---

[13] He is followed by Shearman, *Raphael in Early Modern Sources*, op. cit., I, p. 122, who calls the Wilton House picture a "variant" or a copy of Raphael's *Madonna of the Pinks* (i.e. for him the *Northumberland*) and goes on to use it as a fixed document in his collection, surely an improper use of the evidence.

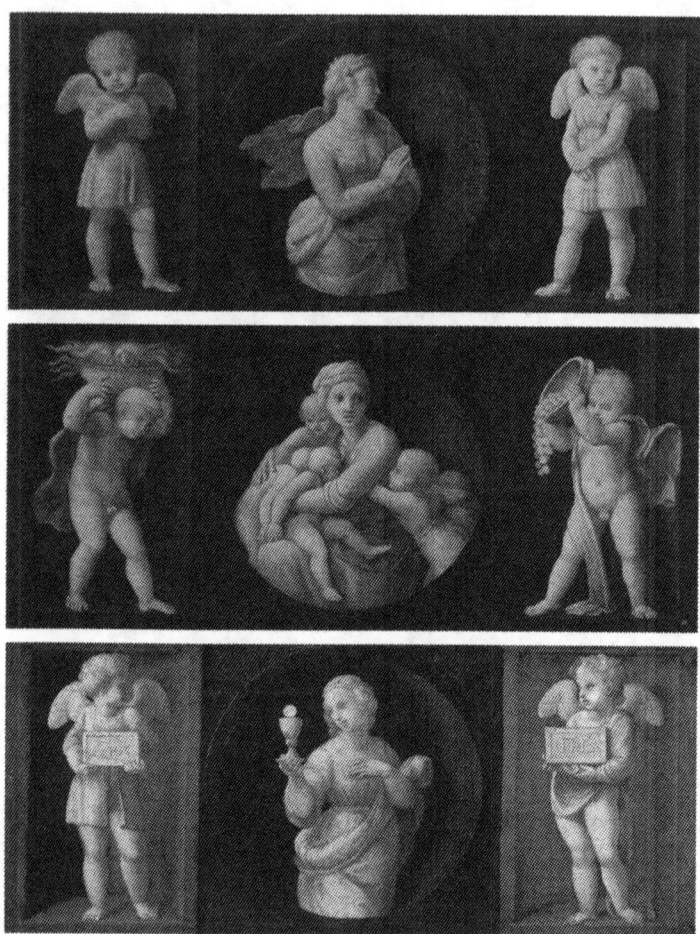

Figure 3.5: **Raphael, *The Theological Virtues*, Rome, Vatican Museums.**

have been made to ascribe this treatment to Raphael's interest in Flemish painting or to his imitation of Leonardo's usage. However, these suggestions fail to explain away the porcelain effect which has more in common with Neoclassical habits than early 16th century ones, Italian or otherwise.

If there were any doubts, the 2004 exhibition devoted to early Raphael at the National Gallery demonstrated that the color in the *Northumberland* is incongruous with all the other examples in the show and, I would add, all the genuine paintings by the master.

7. The overall appearance of the picture reveals an uncharacteristic miniature-like quality, especially noticeable in the head of the Child.

The tight, mechanistically rendered details, particularly in the treatment of the head, hair and facial features of the Child and Mary, but also in the landscape and flowers, are distant from Raphael's known style. Hardly illuminating are comparisons with other "small" pictures, like the *Dream of a Knight* or the two *St. George* panels, because the scale of the figures vis-à-vis the whole is dissimilar. The fact that Raphael worked on a small scale from time to time cannot be used to support the authority of this picture. Where the scale is analogous, no such pedantic detailing can be found, as in the *Large Cowper Madonna* or the *Bridgewater Madonna*.[14]

While the highly detailed rendering of the London painting is on the whole dissimilar to Raphael's known style, the chip on the window sill in the *Northumberland* version, a minute, fool-the-eye detail, has been cited as evidence of Raphael's authorship. Yet, there is not enough evidence to determine whether this element was present in the Ur version. Most copies do not have this element. Nonetheless, it does appear in a few, including the one in Zagreb (Plate 8), a work painted on a metal sheet and certainly datable to the end of the 18th or the early 19th century.

8. Suppressed three-dimensional modelling of the figures has resulted in a series of disorderly, shifting planes.

Convincing modelling, which is referred to as "relief" in con-

---

[14]These two pictures are not well documented either.

temporary Renaissance texts, produces a much sought-after sculptural quality, a feature fundamental to Raphael's language but fatally understated in the *Northumberland* picture. Nevertheless robust modelling, signifying an appreciation of convincing space-occupying form, is evident in the early engravings.

A side effect of the underdeveloped modelling, as manifest in the nude Child and the flesh of Mary, is a general flattening out or compression of the planes. Instead of establishing the scene within a structured system on a stage, the unstable planes appear to shift and slide, unable to hold their place. The side of Mary's face, her neck and her right shoulder all lie, impossibly, on the same plane.

9. Mary's awkward pose, especially the position and the extension of her right thigh and the obfuscation of her left leg, is uncharacteristic of Raphael.

Using the early engravings as a benchmark, Mary's pose, the position and extension of her overly long right thigh, as well as the missing left leg become troublesome qualities of the National Gallery's picture. In them and in some painted versions, the existence of the lower portion of the leg is implied by a highlight at the knee and by vertical folds, producing a more solid base to the entire composition. The downward thrust breaks the oppressive horizontal stress found at the base of the *Northumberland* picture.

The extra space at the base of the composition is evident, especially in *French 2* and but also in *French 3* where the side of the bench upon which Mary sits offers the necessary balance and stability. Read together with the bench, the extended thigh functions more agreeably within the composition when more space is available below and, all things considered, we must assume that such space must have been present in the Ur *Madonna of the Pinks*.

We might ask, how could an engraving supposedly derived

from a picture be more convincing and more satisfying than the presumptive original?

10. Mary's face, neck, and hair are ineffectually and uncharacteristically depicted.

The contour of Mary's shoulder and neck forms a harsh edge which continues upward in the direction of the ear, resulting in the formation of an incongruous single plane in the *Northumberland*. In fact, the ear which lies flat on the plane rather than being foreshortened, appears to be too high on the head. *French 1* mitigates this sensation of harshness by interrupting the edge. The material of the veil or scarf on Mary's head which flows down the side of her face is more substantial in all of the French engravings than in the *Northumberland*, thereby avoiding an incongruous emphasis.

In addition, the conception of Mary's hair is more orderly in *French 1* than in the *Northumberland*, while the braids toward the back of her head are also less confused (see also *French 2* and *French 3*). In comparison, the treatment of Mary's hair is weak and unresolved in the *Northumberland*. Other painted versions manage to avoid this pitfall, which undercuts the National Gallery's claim for the primacy of their picture. Actually the underdrawing seen with IR shows a stronger control of the hair than the painting on the layers above, a condition which in my opinion further underscores the reality that we are dealing with a copy here (Fig. 3.4). In the first stages, when the painter was closer to his model, whether an old painting or possibly an engraving, he seems to have been more exacting in his copying, but when he was more exclusively on his own during the painting stage, he went ahead and either forgot or dropped the refinements in Mary's hair.

In the *Northumberland*, Mary's mouth is open, a condition which conforms to "Raphael's preoccupation in 1507-08 with parted lips," as Penny has it.[15] What he fails to mention is that the element is not found in the old engravings. Instead of reflecting the Ur version, the teeth baring "incident" may have been the invention of a creative copyist somewhere along the way, and is reflected in other copies belonging, as it were, to the same family of objects connected with Camuccini's Rome. Martin Kemp has observed, "In reality, for any Renaissance woman to be portrayed showing her teeth, American-style, is unthinkable".[16] A source for the exposed upper teeth may have been the angel in Raphael's early *Coronation of the Virgin* located in the Vatican Museums, which was available to the owner of the *Northumberland*, Vincenzo Camuccini, who was for many years in charge of the collection.

11. In the *Northumberland*, the treatment of Mary's hands differ between themselves, indicative of an odd if not awkward condition.

For centuries art students have recognized that hands are among the most challenging portions of the human anatomy to draw. The study of the treatment of hands is one of the standard controls used by connoisseurs in the 19th century to help determine authorship. Even copying them, especially if the model is not especially precise in the first place, can create difficulties. In the case of Mary's hands, two observations should be offered. First, they are so un-alike as to appear belonging to two different people. Second, the relationships between the thumb and the other fingers are faulty.[17]

Mary's fleshy right hand, with a swollen, rubbery forefinger, unconvincingly holds the stems of the flowers which the Child grasps uneasily as well. Her left hand, which holds the stems of

---

[15]Penny, *op. cit.*, p. 72.

[16]M. Kemp, *Leonardo*, Oxford-New York, 2005, p. 242.

[17]I would like to thank Bruno Andreis for his insights about the weaknesses of the *Northumberland* picture, especially the Virgin's hands.

two carnations, has a more refined appearance but the thumb is decidedly out of proportion with regard to the other fingers. The disparity between this hand and the conception of Mary's left hand with its spiky fingers is hardly noticeable in the old engravings. Apparently, however, the origin of the problem stems from the Ur picture, but is aggravated in the *Northumberland*.

12. The static pose of the Infant is uncharacteristic of Raphael.

The Child fails to participate as an organic form in the composition; instead he appears like a collage cut-out which has been pasted in place. He balances himself only with difficulty on Mary's invisible raised left leg.

13. The shape of the head of the Infant and especially the treatment of the hair and scalp raise doubts about Raphael's authorship, while his hands and feet are among the weakest features in the entire painting.

As has been widely observed even by the advocates of Raphael's authorship, the hands and the feet of the Child represent problems, particularly the right foot which appears broken in the middle. The origin of the problem stems from the foreshortening of the foot in which confusion occurs between the shadows under the foot and the contour of the foot at the bottom. The Child's other foot is not immune from anatomical lapses, including a failure to distinguish the foot itself from the ankle, and the ankle from the lower leg.

If the feet of the Child cause uneasiness about the authenticity of the *Northumberland*, the treatment of his hands is hardly reassuring. They fail to convince the viewer that they are capable of holding anything.

Christ's head, with an exaggerated extension at the top, high forehead, and low placement of the ear, raises other doubts. Its deformities include the bulging contour of the side of the face and unconvincing hair with the exaggerated receding hairline of the Child on the left side of his head.[18]

Another devastating element for the authentication of the *Northumberland* picture, which is unique to it, is the representation of the Child as walleyed. His right eye looks sharply to his right and upward while the left eye looks slightly to the right, and straight on. Not registered in the early engravings, a walleyed Christ Child is unknown in other works by or attributed to Raphael, and is probably merely the result of a dab of misplaced paint.

14. The truncated window embrasure with its severed arch makes for an uncharacteristic and unpleasant element in the painting.

As observed by Penny, who nonetheless failed to recognize the implications, the painter of the *Northumberland* has for all practical purposes eliminated the arch of the window. The absence of the arch or even an indicative fragment produces an uneasy if not an intolerable passage. Versions including *French 2*, which portray nearly the full arch of the window, make it quite clear how unpleasant the sharply severed window arch is in the *Northumberland*. A number of painted copies also give the full arch or a much larger portion, including the one in Mexico (Fig. 3.6) and the one in Brescia (Figs. 2, 3).

15. The landscape elements and especially the clouds are uncharacteristic for the early 16th century; instead they are consistent with the late 18th or early 19th century academic painting.

Although highly admired by Penny, the landscape seen through the window in the *Northumberland* is far from satisfying in terms

---

[18]To be sure, there is an odd confluence between the treatment of the head here and in the *Metropolitan Duccio*, for which see Chapter 6, although it would be overly zealous to see any genuine connection.

The Northumberland Madonna of the Pinks. Shortcomings   83

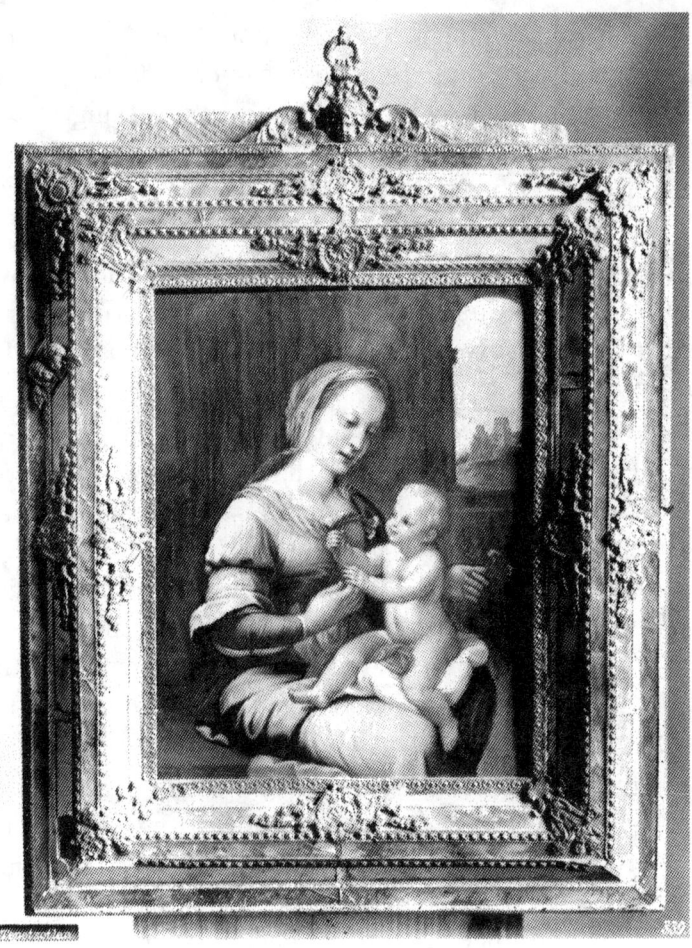

Figure 3.6: **Copy after the *Madonna of the Pinks*. (Whereabouts unknown, formerly Tepotzotlan, Mexico).**

of Raphael. The reading of the element, perhaps a path or rock formations in the foreground, is frustrating. In the distance between the two fragmentary castles a distracting spiky tree which forms a dark silhouette calls attention to that point well out of the central pictorial image. Furthermore, the brilliant clouds and the bright light compete with the sacred scene within the interior room. The landscape in the London painting is at odds with and inferior to that found in the three old French engravings, as well as in other painted copies.

16. The brothers Pietro and Vincenzo Camuccini owned at least two versions of the composition, one showing the Child completely nude and another with the Child's genitals covered.

Along with Penny and the National Gallery experts, at the start of my study I had assumed that the Camuccini brothers owned a single version of the *Madonna of the Pinks* type, the one sold to the Duke of Northumberland in the mid 1850s and purchased in 2004 by the National Gallery. Presumably it surfaced publicly in the 1820s, when it was engraved in Milan by Farrugia and was said to be the property of Vincenzo Camuccini (Fig. 3.7). But a serious problem arises because the engraving is by no means identical with the *Northumberland* painting.

The main but not the only divergence is that the Child's genitals are covered in the engraving but not in the picture. Could this be merely an addition placed by the engraver for the sake of modesty? That is unlikely, since it turns out that the tradition of covered and uncovered types occurred already in the 17th century, making such an explanation inappropriate for Farrugia's engraving. Besides, in the Farrugia version there is greater space at the top, and also in distinction to the *Northumberland*, the Child has a full head of curly hair while Mary sports a benign, even vaguely Leonardesque, smile. While *French 1* does show the Child naked, he is covered with a loincloth in *French 2* and *French 3*, whose design is not consistent with Farrugia's engraving. The Camuccini must have had two versions, one with the genitals exposed, the *Northumberland*, and a second with the genitals covered, which was depicted by Farrugia.

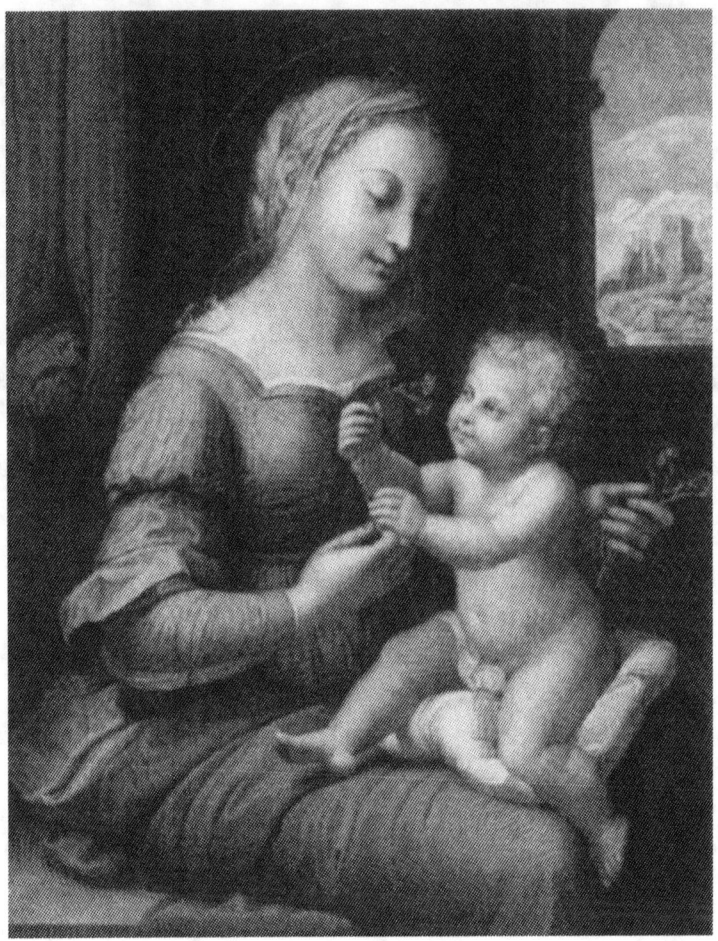

Figure 3.7: **Giovanni Farrugia. Engraving after the *The Madonna of the Pinks*.**

Under any scenario one might seek to invent the conditions surrounding the composition and the Camuccini are hardly as neat as Penny and the National Gallery experts would have it.[19]

---

[19]The possibility that the Camuccini had at least a third and even a fourth version will be taken up in a subsequent publication.

17. **The underpainting/underdrawing revealed by infrared reflectography (IR) of the *Northumberland* picture is unique for Raphael (Fig. 3.4). Instead, it can be more comfortably datable on the basis of style to the late 18th or early 19th century.**

Relatively new technologies using infrared reflectography have allowed a virtual viewing of the drawing or underpainting beneath the surface of pictures. Despite appearances, the determination of the authorship of underpainting/drawing which has been retrieved in this manner, however, has little to do with "science." Instead the process is pure connoisseurship, as will be explained. Before entering into particulars, the limitations of the technology behind IR require attention.

In no instance among Raphael's certain paintings of the pre-Roman (i.e. before 1508) is the drawing applied without any guidelines or signs indicative of transfer from a *modello* or cartoon. As for freehand or *alla prima* underdrawing, one example has been cited by the National Gallery, *La Fornarina* in the Barberini Gallery in Rome. This painting falls much later in Raphael's career than the presumptive date of the *Northumberland* and actually is not a certain work by the master anyway, although the consensus is supportive.[20] In other words, the freehand application would be yet another unique feature for Raphael.[21] This condition has been interpreted by the proponents of the attribution as evidence of its originality. In an inventive twist of logic, they would have it both ways. First, they claim with justification that when Raphael's normal practice of transferral is found, it can represent a confirmation of his authorship. Yet, when an abnormal application is found on the *Northumber-*

---

[20] *Technical Bulletin*, 2004, p. 5. I personally have reservations about the autograph status of the painting, but it has been so severely over-cleaned recently that making an attribution is more difficult than ever.

[21] The National Galley's position was effectively countered by the painter George Leonard in his article "Raphael Saved," *Jackdaw*, 39, June 2004.

land, such a condition seems just as good, for they rhetorically ask, who else could have been so clever as to have done it without any aids? What results is a win-win play, but common sense has it otherwise.

In assessing the technique of infrared reflectography, its inventor, J. R. J. Van Asperen de Boer cautioned that "interpretation is sometimes complicated because of interference from overlying paint layers."[22] This is the unstated but precise situation surrounding the IR of the *Northumberland*, since what is shown is not exclusively underpainting, but a conflation of underdrawing *and* portions of later applications of paint, even some from the surface itself (Fig. 3.4).

The value of technology and science in connoisseurship practice is often overrated. The point was raised effectively by Simon Schama with regard to Rembrandt, "...the effectiveness of using x-rays to distinguish Rembrandt and his imitators seems to depend upon prior subjective assumptions about exactly which kind of brushwork exemplified the true techniques of the master."[23] Schama even more pointedly speaks about "techno-toys" to bring "...irrefutable verdicts." He continues, "No self respecting Rembrandt exhibition catalogue these days is complete without x radiographs, infrared spectrographs [*sic*], auto radiographs, canvas warp and woof counts, dendrochronology (tree ring) analysis of panels, and microscopically differentiated strata of grounds, glazes, and pigments. But the techno-kenners had hardly donned their lab coats before it became apparent that scientific investigation was a lot stronger on promise than on delivery."[24] Parenthetically, calling upon such esoteric data to

---

[22] J. R. J. Van Asperen de Boer, "Current Techniques in the Scientific Examination of Paintings," in J. Shearman, M. Hall. *Op. cit.*, p. 5.

[23] Cited in R. D. Spencer, ed., *The Expert versus the Object. Judging Fakes and False Attributions in the Visual Arts*, Oxford-New York, 2004, p. 203.

[24] Spencer, *op. cit.*, pp. 203-4.

support the attribution of any picture is an effective strategy because art historians and their humanist cousins generally are in awe of science and technology, being unaccustomed to critically evaluate such data.

The style of the underdrawing as revealed creates a major obstacle for the defenders of the painting's authenticity as a Raphael. Regardless of the tools employed and their effectiveness, a connoisseur's judgement is required right at the start. The experts assert with biblical authority that the underdrawing *is* by Raphael. They base their assumption on the painting, which is connected to Raphael in the first place. Then the attribution of the drawing, which is not strictly speaking a drawing anyway, is attached to the painting. The reasoning goes that since the underpainting is by Raphael, the painted surface above it must be by him too. We have gone the full circle.

For the record, my connoisseurship tells me that the underdrawing especially as visible in the heads has nothing to do with Raphael at all; rather what can be made out reveals a late 18th- or early 19th- century academic hand. Of course, if the underlayers are datable on the basis of style to the late 18th or early 19th century, the painted surface cannot, under any circumstances, be by Raphael.

Without an acknowledgement of the inherent limitations of the evidence, the IR underdrawing has been regarded as the strongest visual support favoring Raphael's authorship of the painting by the National Gallery. The wall display there (in February 2004) alongside the painting reads: "...the attribution of the painting to Raphael was supported by the technical examination at the Gallery. Infrared reflectography revealed a spontaneous underdrawing entirely characteristic of Raphael's work." In effect, they have based the attribution of the painting on the attribution of a drawing which is only partially visible and which is the result of a reconstruction by means of computer technology.

Due to a host of variables, interpreting the reliability of the IR photograms, whether used in isolation or in comparisons, can be hazardous. Differences in supports and their density, the quality and composition of the ground, and the thickness of the painted surface above, as well as varying methods applied to the readings all effect an evaluation. Regarding comparisons using IR imaging, Penny has recognized the necessity for making allowances.[25] The process is anything but pure science. In terms of the procedure used by Penny and the National Gallery in making the attribution of the *Northumberland Madonna*, a fatal omission of method should be cited. Not a single comparison using infrared reflectography (or X-rays) has been offered between the *Northumberland* picture and any of the other versions, numbering more than fifty-five, on a variety of supports including canvas, wood, and metal.

Furthermore, a reading of images visible in reflectograms is a far cry from visually examining original drawings. Reflectograms, which are patched together "mosaics," are dependent upon photographic and computer generated technology. Worst of all, we never see with the naked eye these under-layers, but only reflections or shadows of them. For a connoisseur, seeing the original mark—the stroke, the look, the aura—is regarded as a paramount requirement, a process which is excluded with IR.[26] In the case of the *Northumberland* IR, what is revealed of the underdrawing is quite unlike Raphael's known practice. A particularly fruitful example which should serve as a guide is the *Marriage of the Virgin* in the Brera, under which a well-developed linear drawing is found, along with pentimenti, or the *La Muta* in Urbino (Fig. 3.8).

---

[25] Penny, 1972, p.7.

[26] Actually, examples are occasionally found where underdrawing can be seen with the naked eye due to the transparency of the painted layers. Such is true for portions of Leonardo's unfinished *Adoration of the Magi* in the Uffizi.

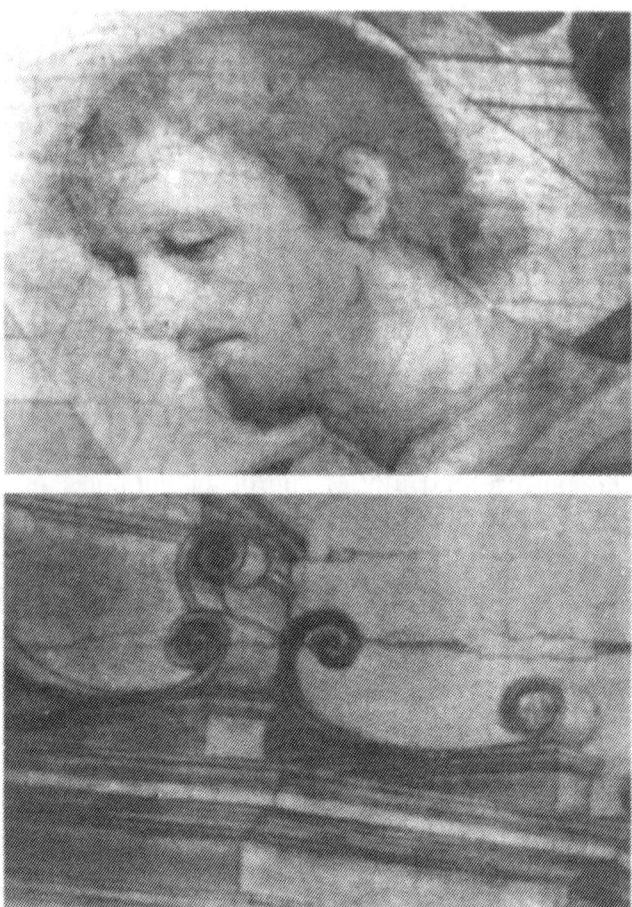

Figure 3.8: **Raphael, *Marriage of the Virgin*.** Milan, Brera. Infrared reflectograph, details.

Also damaging for claims of authenticity for the *Northumberland* picture is a comparison with the under-layer of the presumably contemporary *Garvagh Madonna* in the National Gallery, which contains a fully developed drawing and which is totally unlike the *Northumberland* one.[27] There is hardly any wonder that the National Gallery experts fail to offer it as a comparison.

18. Incomplete and insufficient scientific analyses were applied to the *Northumberland Madonna* before as well as after the purchase.

The application of science for discovering the authorship of a painting or sculpture, a much desired event, is, I believe, a long way off. Peter C. Sutton seems to hold the same opinion in his description of conditions surrounding Rembrandt attributions. He observes that "Although scientific and technical studies... have advanced scholarship and can expose the material inconsistencies of latter-day forgeries, they have played a relatively small role in changing opinions about individual paintings' authorship and authenticity."[28]

---

[27] For which, see J. Dunkerton and N. Penny, "The infra-red examination of Raphael's 'Garvagh Madonna'," *National Gallery Technical Bulletin*, 14, 1993 (cf. esp. figures Figs. 3.2 and 3.1). To appreciate how approximate an infrared reflectogram can be, the technique, according to Washington National Gallery's K. Christensen (*Studies in the History of Art*, Washington National Gallery, 17, 1986, p. 47), utilizes a camera fitted with an infrared tube, which produces an image on a television monitor. The image is photographed, and the photographic print is called a reflectogram. However, the technology seems to be evolving with infra-red reflectogram mosaics (for which see J. Dunkerton and N. Penny, *op. cit., passim*, but esp. note 7. This is the kind of evidence that has been used to support the originality of the *Northumberland* picture. Hence in actual fact, we really never see the drawing. I have taken up the larger issue of the need for seeing the original in a paper "Restoration II: Debunking the 'have you seen it?' myth," *Source. Notes in the History of Art* 19/2: pp. 2-5. Recently, I discussed issues surrounding infrared reflectographs with Dr. Maurizio Seracini, who introduced the technique in Italy. Cf. Maurizio Seracini, "Il disegno sottostante nella pittura di Raffaello: esempi dei periodi fiorentino e romano," in: *Raffaello e l'idea della bellezza*, a cura di Alessandro Vezzosi, Firenze, Relitalia Studi Editoriali, 2001. Many pictures by Raphael are documented in the well-stocked archive of his firm, Editech, in Florence.

[28] P. C. Sutton, "Rembrandt and a Brief History of Connoisseurship," in

More effectively, science can be used to prove a work is not original.

While the scientific claims surrounding the painting are complex, one salient point should be raised in the context of connoisseurship. In confirming their attribution and for the sake of the purchase, neither the Getty Museum nor the National Gallery undertook tests involving physical samples of the wood panel to determine its age, the exact composition of the ground, the medium, or the pigments. To be sure, a restriction against such testing was imposed by the owners prior to the sale, and apparently neither institution was prepared to confront the seller on the matter, notwithstanding the amount of money involved.

A superficial reading of the defense of the purchase which appears on the National Gallery's website may leave the impression that scientific evidence supports their contention that the *Northumberland* painting was executed early in the 16th century. According to the Gallery, the best evidence for them was that they found traces of the pigment lead-tin yellow. Using the standard of common sense, which has been advocated throughout this book, one is forced to ask: how can a pigment which was highly popular until the early 17th century and surely was known for another century thereafter, be proof that a painting was painted in the early 16th century?[29] The fact of the matter is that it cannot. Of course, pigment analysis in certain cases can help to evaluate the age of a particular painting. But this method is valid only if the painting contains pigments which were not used in the epoch presumed for the picture. The classic case is Prussian Blue, although other blues were not abandoned after its introduction in the early 18th century.[30] After around

---

R. D. Spencer, *op. cit.*, pp. 29-30.

[29]The issue of the usage of lead-tin yellow is complex and continues to be studied. In a subsequent publication, I plan to take it up in greater detail.

[30]G. Matthaes, *Manuale illustrato del collezionista d'Arte: saper distinguere tra autentico e falso*, Vol. I; Garzanti Vega Ed., Milano 1997, p. 32.

1730 lead-tin yellow seems to have been gradually replaced with lead-antimony yellow, which was eventually substituted for lead-tin yellow completely sometime after 1800, although the reader should keep in mind that these dates are very approximate and are changing as our knowledge expands. There are indications, however, that it was available later, for stained glass and mosaics.[31] Did Vincenzo Camuccini and his older brother Pietro, along with other painters operating in the last quarter of the 18th century and after, use that particular yellow? For now, there is no evidence one way or another, largely because of the lack of data surrounding the pictures they authored. Furthermore, being restorers, they may well have used it in their work anyway.

That the Camuccini brothers knew about the particular yellow is a near certainty, especially due to the fact that it is mentioned by Cennino Cennini, and after all Vincenzo was a restorer who for decades was actually in charge of major treatments in Rome. His older brother and mentor, Pietro, was also a trained painter, although he made his living as an art dealer. As such he was involved in treating the pictures he sold (mainly to English collectors).

One oddity should be noted regarding the technical study of the *Northumberland* painting. I would have thought that the National Gallery would have conducted tests to determine the age of the wood of their panel. If the tests showed that the wood was contemporary with Raphael, it would have gone a long way in buttressing their attribution. In the past taking the samples necessary for such tests was prohibited by the owners. However, the London National Gallery now owns the *Northumberland* and no longer requires approval except their own.[32] It is my guess

---

[31] F. Frezzato, ed., in *Il libro dell'arte di Cennino Cennini*, Vicenza, p.252.

[32] Of course, were the wood to date to the first decade of the 16th century, the attribution would have a substantial lift, although we do know that fakers used old wood, so it would not be a final and absolute proof in any case. We are not even absolutely sure that the wood is cherry.

that an independent examination including the participation of disinterested observers would confirm once and for all that the *Northumberland* picture is very far from Raphael in date of manufacture. Molecular spectroscopy IR has been used for some time to date various types of wood, including cherry, within a range of +/- 15 years. The testing does not pose the slightest danger to the object, because for the analysis only a very small particle of the wood is required as a sample, which can be taken from the back or the edge of the panel, so as not to interfere with the painting at all. Furthermore up-to-date C14 analysis could also be performed on the *Northumberland*.

20. Who painted the *Northumberland Madonna of the Pinks*?

While naming or even suggesting the author of the painting does not alter the case against Raphael's authorship, the connoisseur might wish to seek to suggest some plausible identification. To approach the larger issue, presumably one might need to examine many of the other copies and versions, a project which goes beyond the intentions of the present study. It is sufficient to say that the historical facts together with connoisseurship at the present time lead me to tentatively conclude that the *Northumberland* version was executed in the studio of Vincenzo Camuccini, possibly in collaboration with his brother Pietro.

After all they owned at least two versions of the *Madonna of the Pinks*. Furthermore they had the skill and the experience, as well as knowledge of the techniques of the old masters, whose works they copied abundantly and whose works they also restored and frequently sold. On the basis of connoisseurship, I believe that a case can be made for Vincenzo Camuccini as the author of the underdrawing of the *Northumberland* (Fig. 3.4).

Vincenzo had an authoritative role in influential restorations in Rome, as he had been appointed *Ispettore alla conservazione delle Pubbliche Pitture* in 1814.[33] In this guise, he saw to the restoration of a *Madonna and Child with a donor* in the Church of Sant'Onofrio said to have been painted by Leonardo and Raphael's famous *Prophet Isaiah*, a fresco in the church of Sant'Agostino. Besides, he oversaw work on the Caravaggios in Santa Maria del Popolo, and later on he restored Raphael's *Transfiguration* in the Vatican Museum.

A final decision on the identity of the author requires further research and analysis of the evidence, including data from other copies. However, it should be quite clear to the reader that settling on the identity of its maker does not change the fact that the *Northumberland* is not a 16th century painting nor is it by Raphael.

21. Who invented the composition known as the *Madonna of Pinks* and when did it first appear?

If the Neoclassical Italian painter Vincenzo Camuccini, together with his older brother Pietro, had a hand in producing the *Northumberland* painting, as I propose, who was the inventor of the composition? The type goes back to at least the 17th century, at which time it was already regarded as Raphael's invention. Of course, the painting or paintings upon which the engravers based their work would have to be earlier, but was the prototype early enough to support an attribution to Raphael?[34]

All the indications uncovered thus far point to the presence of two, rather than one, original or Ur versions, one in which the Child is covered and one in which the Child is nude. The reader

---

[33] See A. M. Corbo, "Il restauro delle pitture a Roma dal 1814 al 1823," in *Commentari*, XX, 1969, p. 236.

[34] Many of the versions which have emerged will be presented in a catalogue being prepared by Jan Sammer. The one I find most engaging, a version documented in Mexico in the previous century, is known to me only from a black and white photograph. To draw any conclusions from it would be a violation of all the rules of good connoisseurship, but at least an oblique reference to it seems appropriate. See fig. 3.6.

should again be reminded that this suggestion has nothing to do with the status of the *Northumberland* picture.

Since what were probably 16th century originals have not been identified as yet, to insist upon identifying the specific creator of a non-existent picture is not easily justifiable. With that caveat, on the basis of style it appears most likely that the original dates to the early decades of the 16th century. The originator of the composition may have been Raphael, perhaps when he was living in Florence, since the inventor was acquainted with Leonardo's early Madonnas and was dependent upon the older master for the idea.

An alternative scenario concerning the Ur composition can also be postulated. Instead of Raphael, the invention might be attributed to an as yet unidentified but competent painter active during the late 1510s and 1520s, probably operating in Florence or Umbria, a painter who was well acquainted with the art of both early Leonardo and early Raphael. In this reconstruction, an artist like Ridolfo Ghirlandaio could have produced a small *Madonna with the Pinks* or possibly two, of different sizes, similar to a composition already twice explored by the young Leonardo. One of the reasons that such a possibility has merit is that Raphael, once in Florence (1504), was deeply engaged with Leonardo's more recent work done after 1500, such as the *Madonna and Child and Saint Anne* and the *Mona Lisa*, and not the much earlier *Benois* and *Munich Madonnas* which constitute a much less revolutionary phase. So the throw-back to early Leonardo revealed in the composition is a clue to the eventuality that the inventor was, indeed, not Raphael at all. At the very least, the stylistic process exhibited in the painting does not easily fit into Raphael's pattern for his Florentine years.

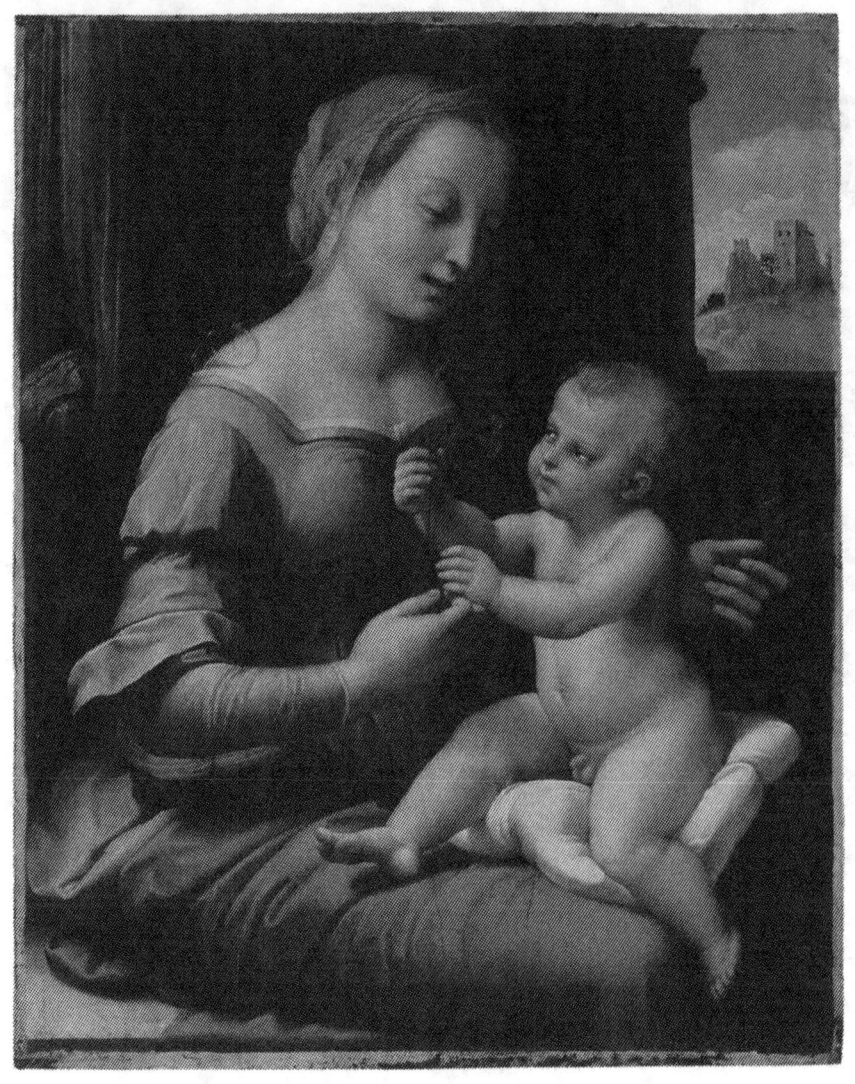

Plate 1: **Attributed to Raphael (here rejected)**, *The Northumberland Madonna of the Pinks*, London, National Gallery.

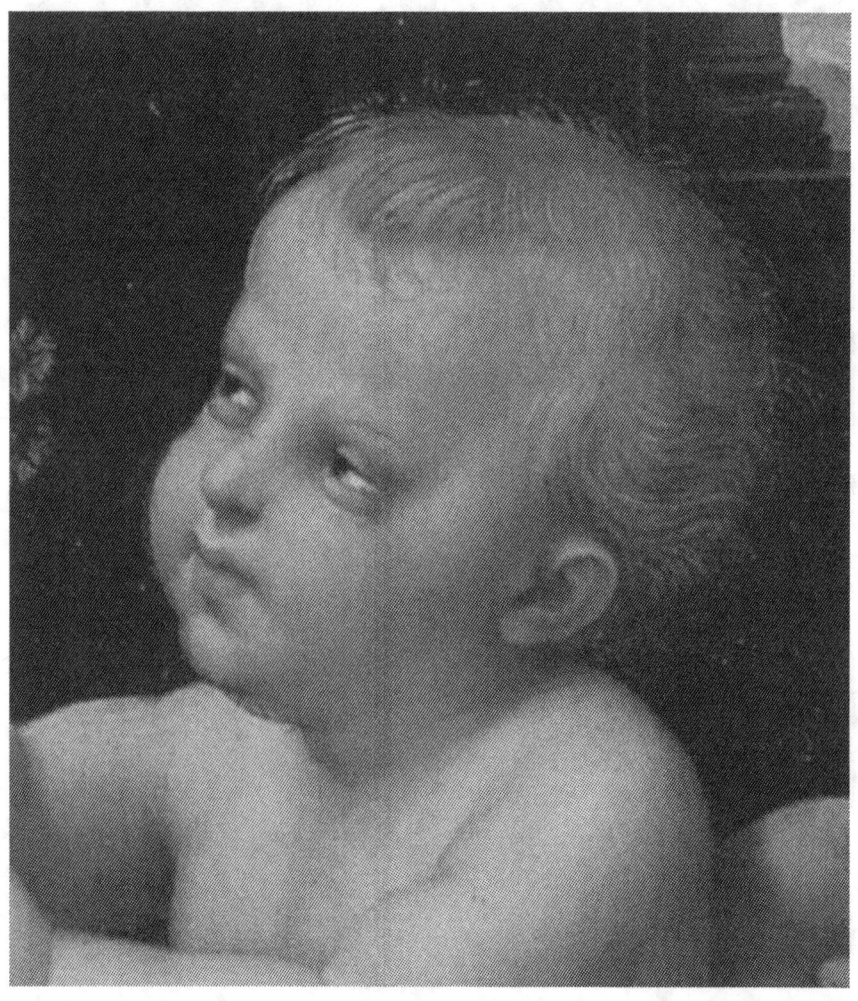

Plate 2: **Attributed to Raphael (here rejected)**, *The Northumberland Madonna of the Pinks* (detail), London, National Gallery.

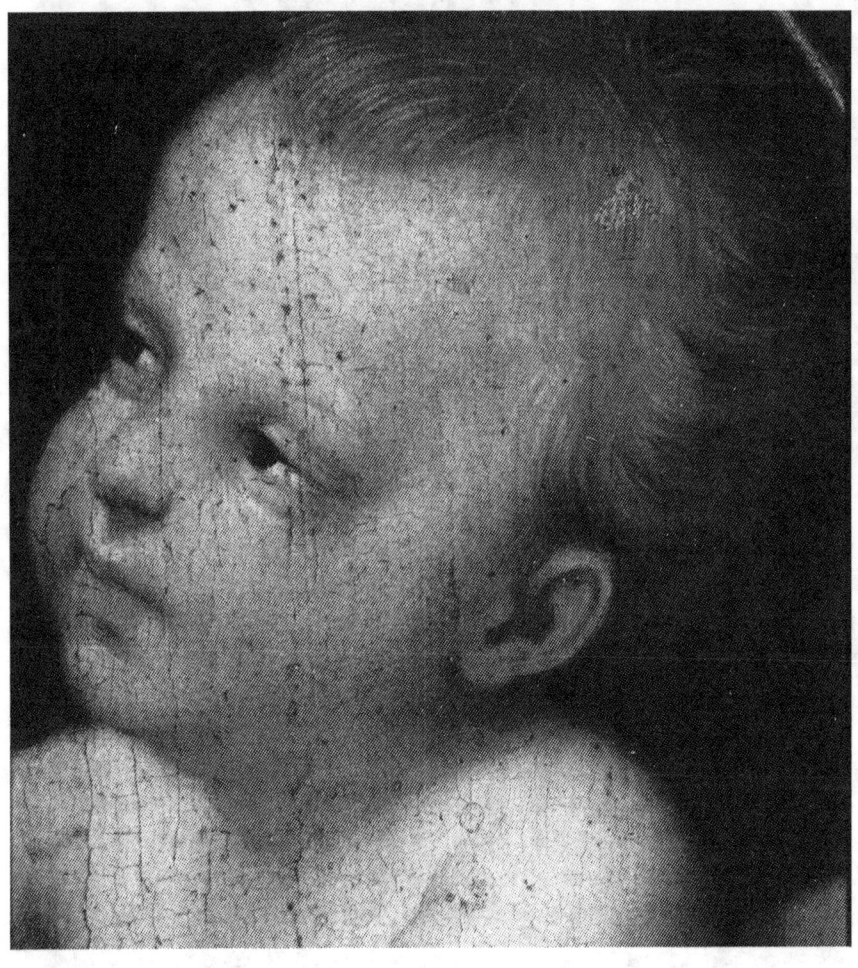

Plate 3: Copy after the *Madonna of the Pinks*, Brescia, Pinacoteca Tosio-Martinengo (detail).

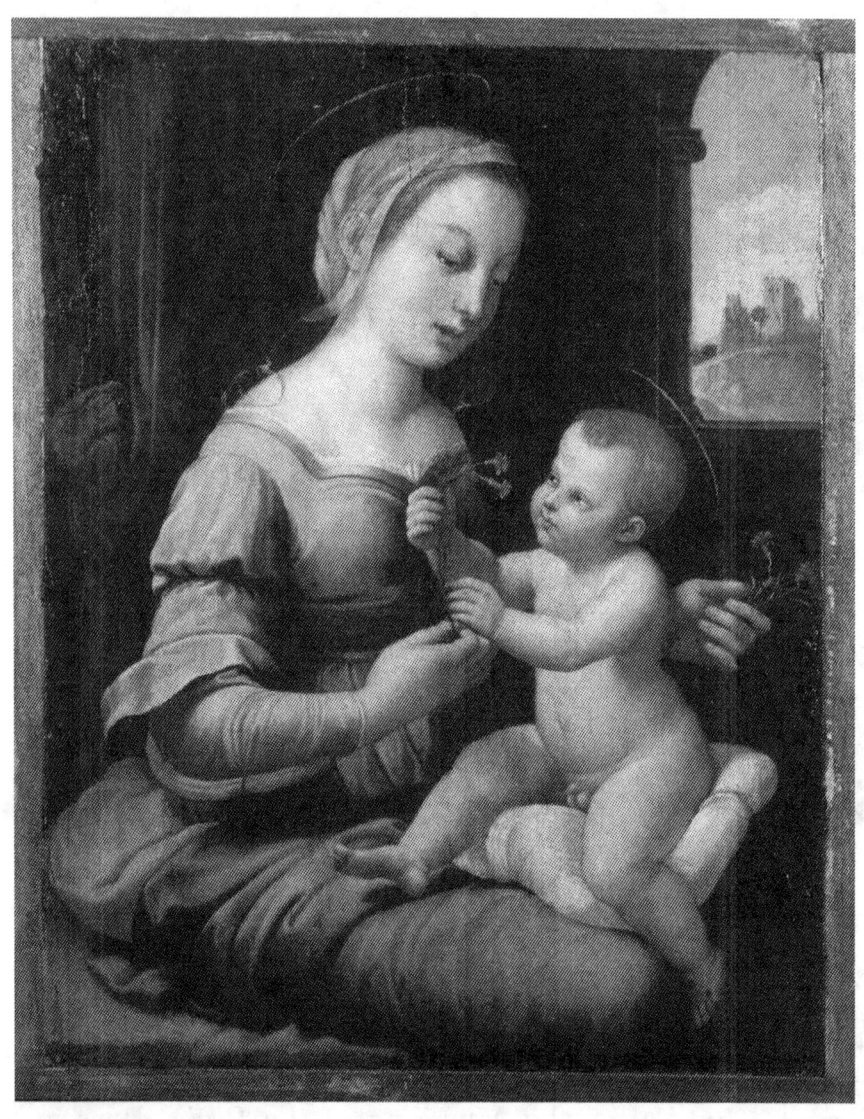

Plate 4: Collection of Maximilian Speck von Sternburg, formerly at Lütschena, since 1996 at the Museum der bildende Künste in Leipzig. Inv. no. 1666.

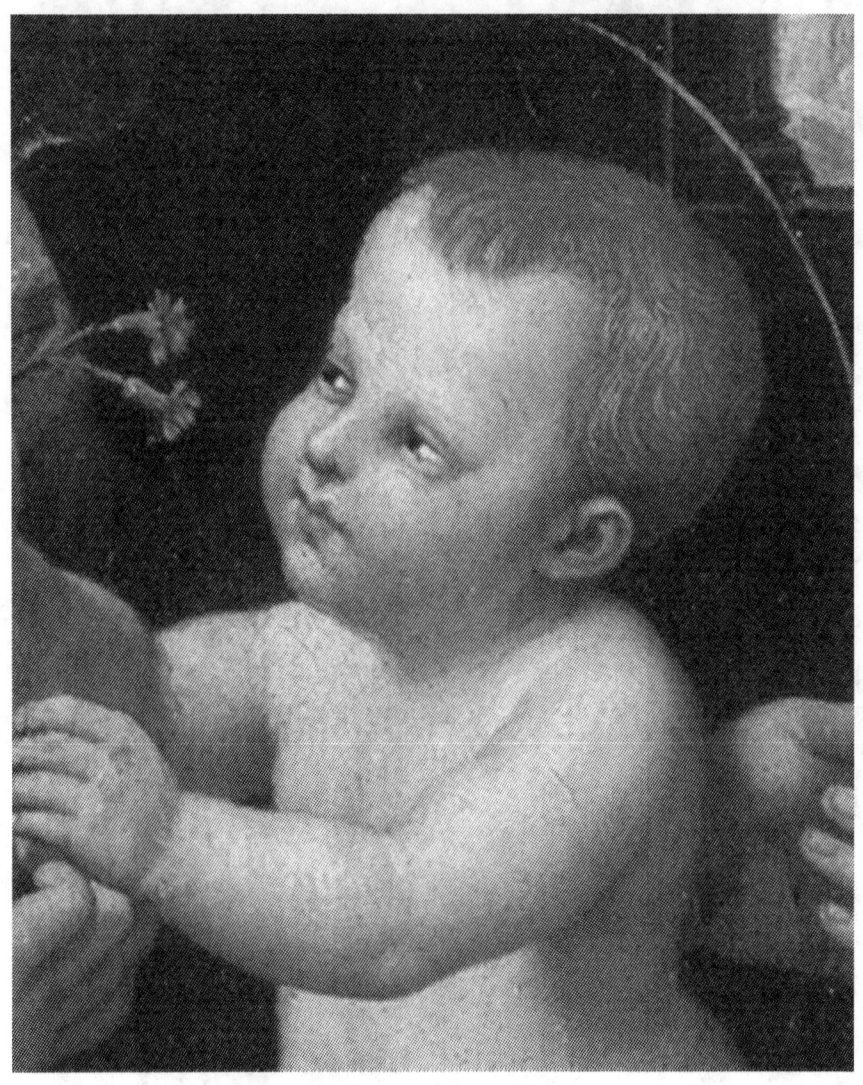

Plate 5: Collection of Maximilian Speck von Sternburg, formerly at Lütschena, since 1996 at the Museum der bildende Künste in Leipzig. Inv. no. 1666 (detail).

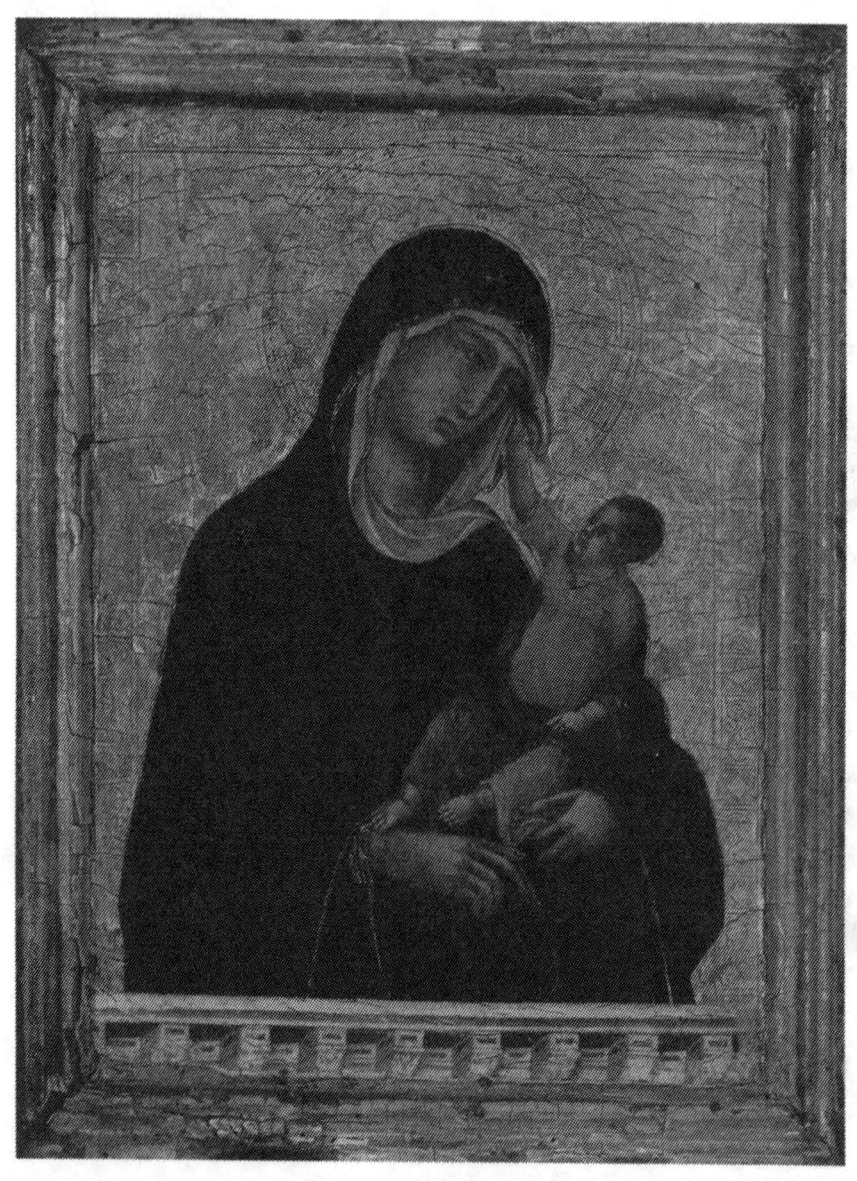

Plate 6: **Attributed to Duccio di Buonisegna** (here rejected), *The Stroganoff Madonna* (formerly), *The Metropolitan Duccio*, New York, Metropolitan Museum of Art.

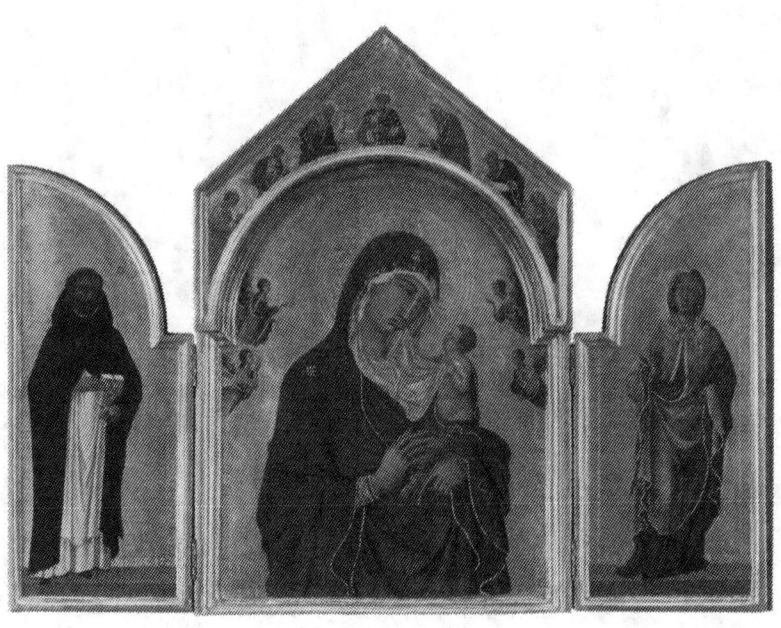

Plate 7: **Attributed to Duccio (here rejected),** *The London Triptych*, London, National Gallery.

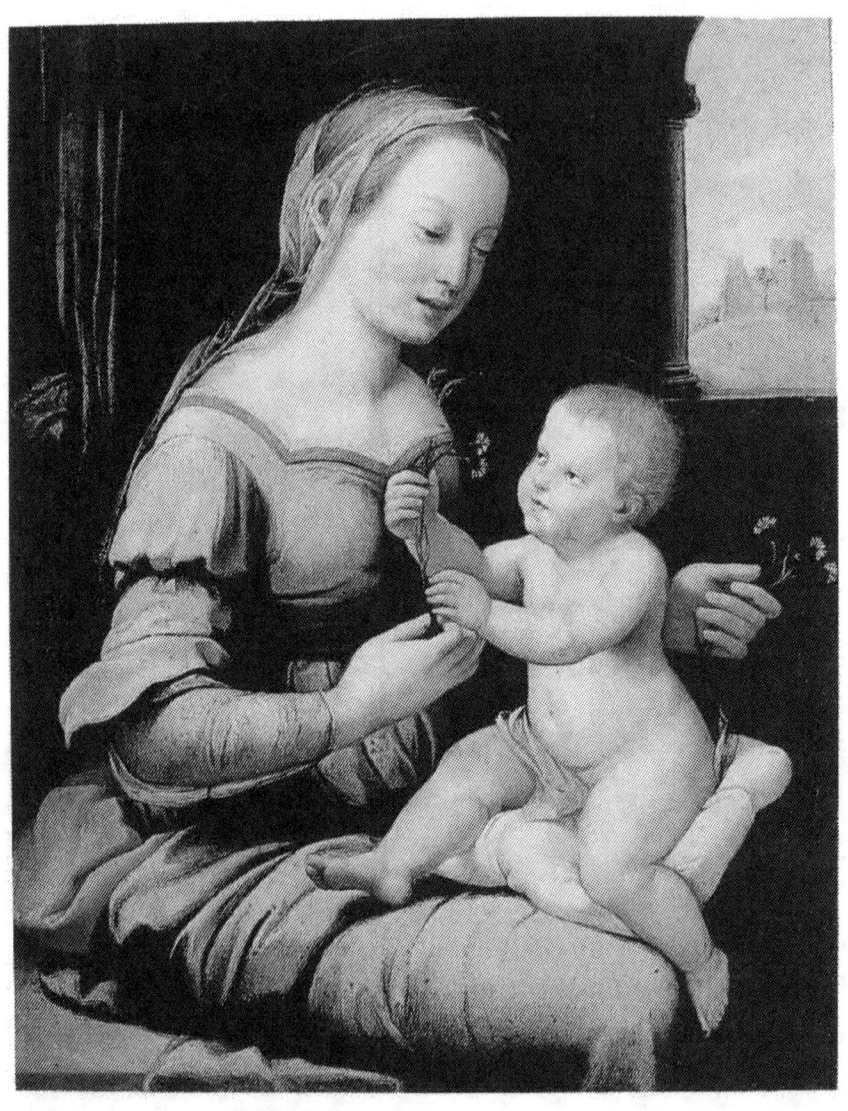

Plate 8: Unknown Artist, Copy after the *Madonna of the Pinks*, Zagreb, Strossmayer Gallery.

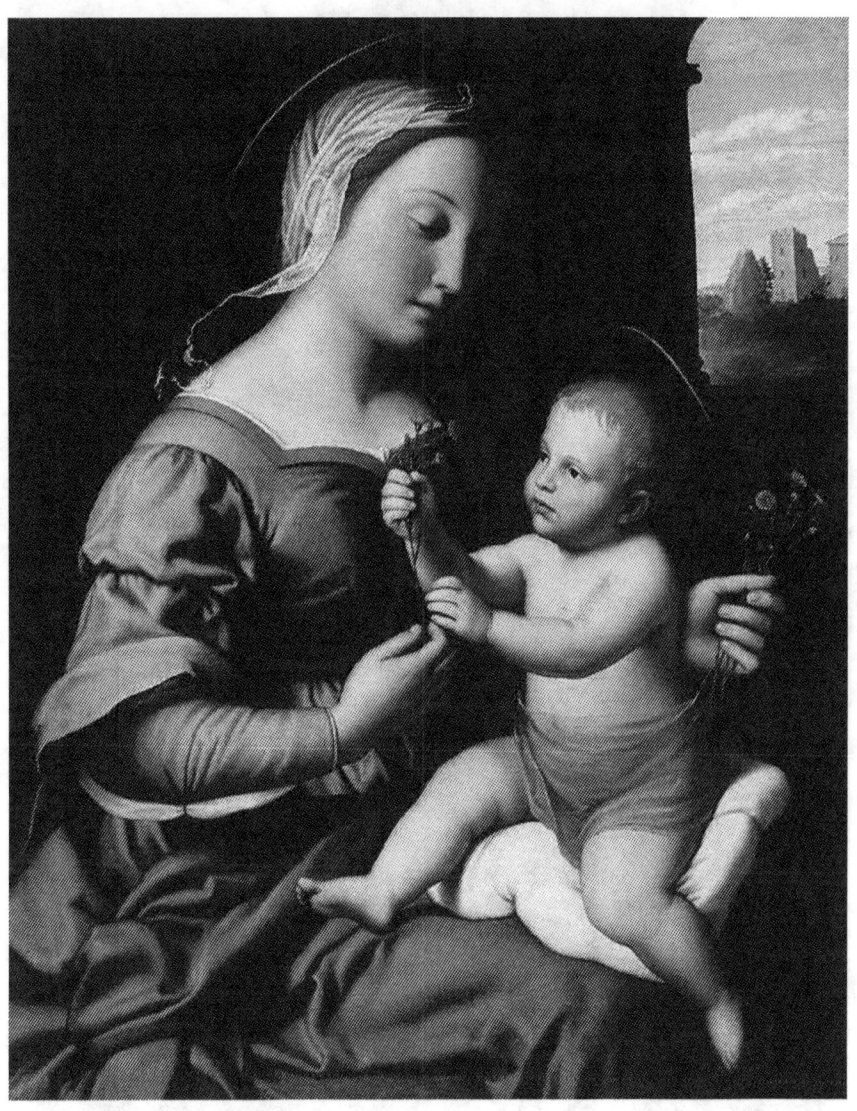

Plate 9: **Sassoferrato manner of (attributed to), Copy after the *Madonna of the Pinks*, Detroit, Institute of Arts.

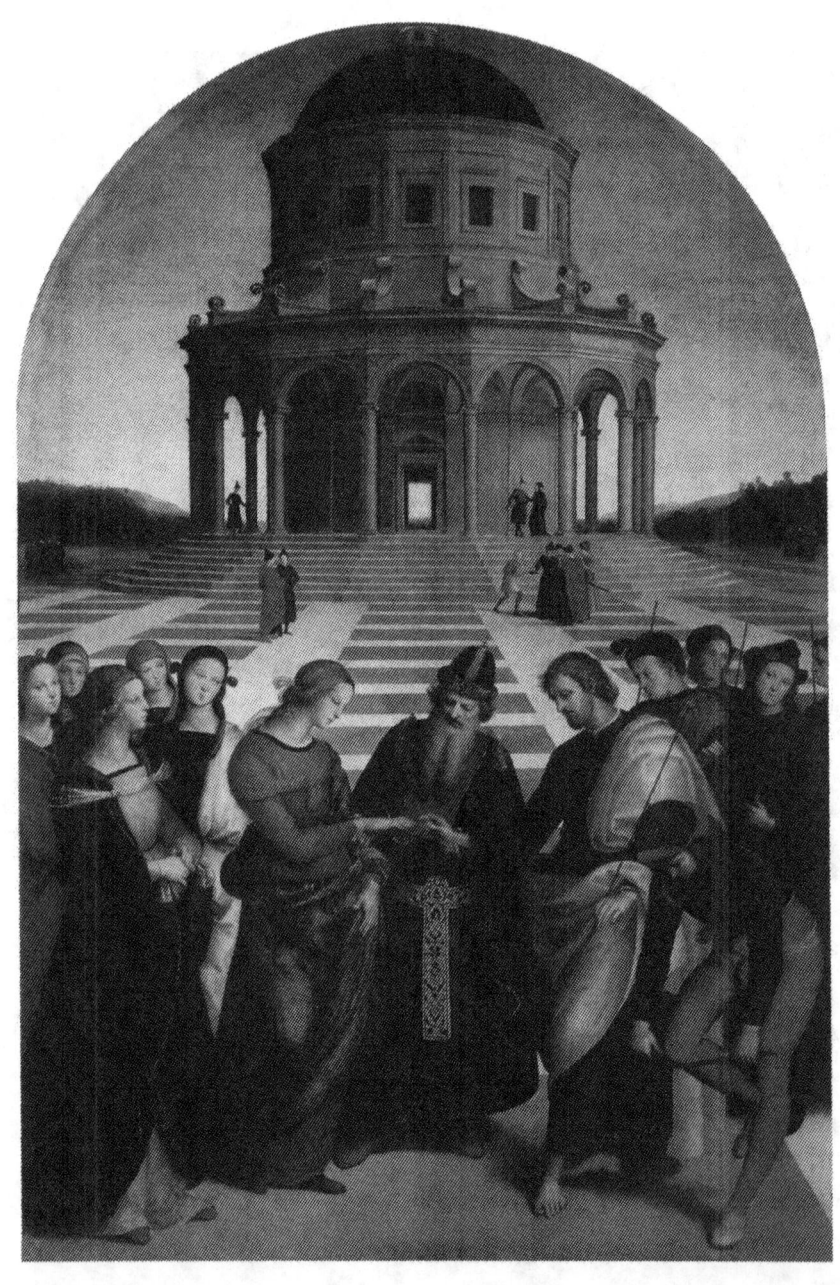

Plate 10: **Raphael**, *Marriage of the Virgin*, Milan, Brera.

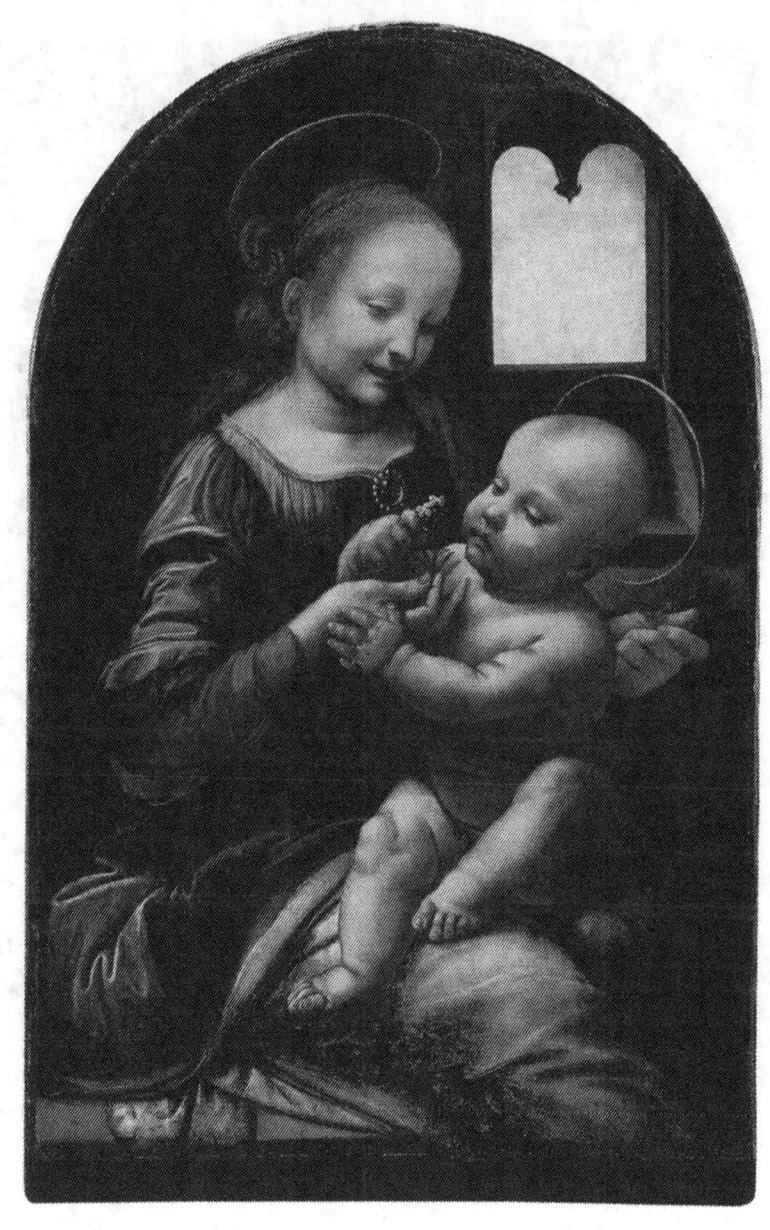

Plate 11: Leonardo da Vinci, *Benois Madonna*, St. Petersburg, Hermitage.

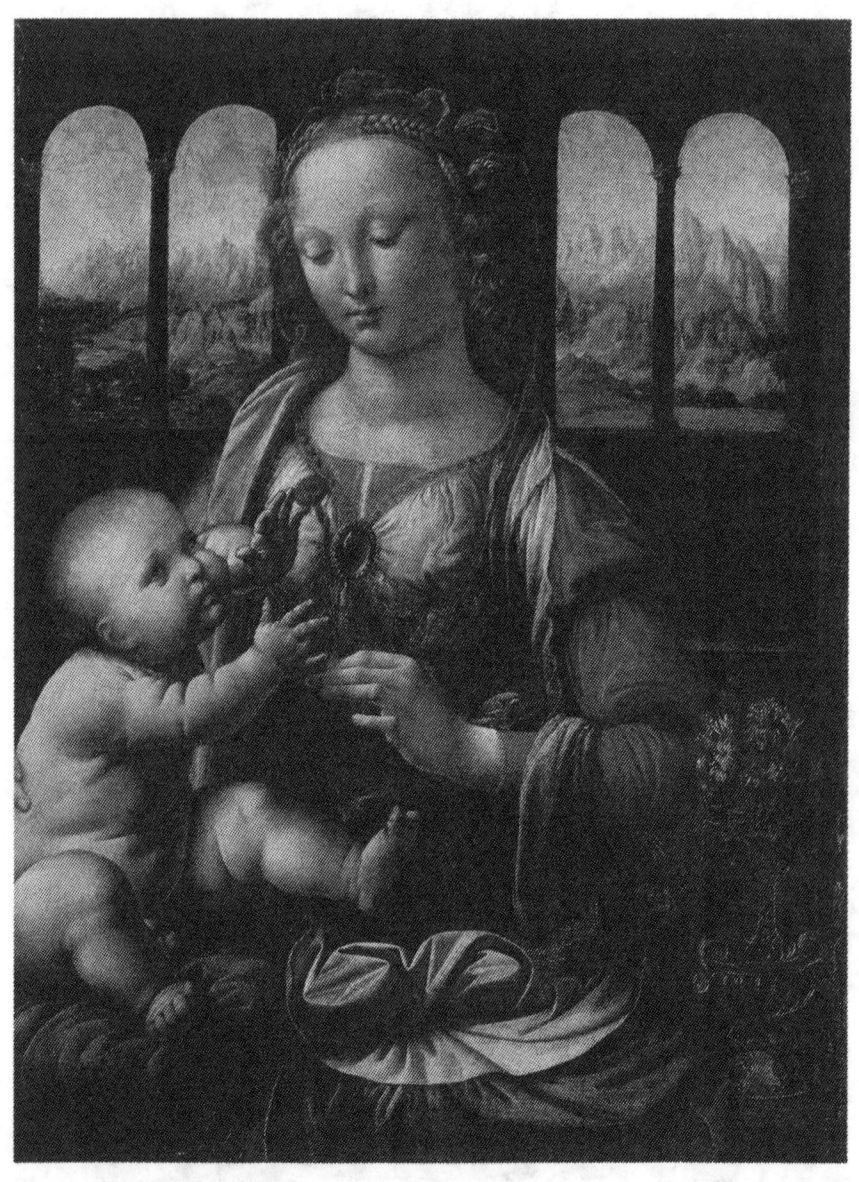

Plate 12: **Leonardo da Vinci**, *Madonna and Child*, Munich, Alte Pinakothek.

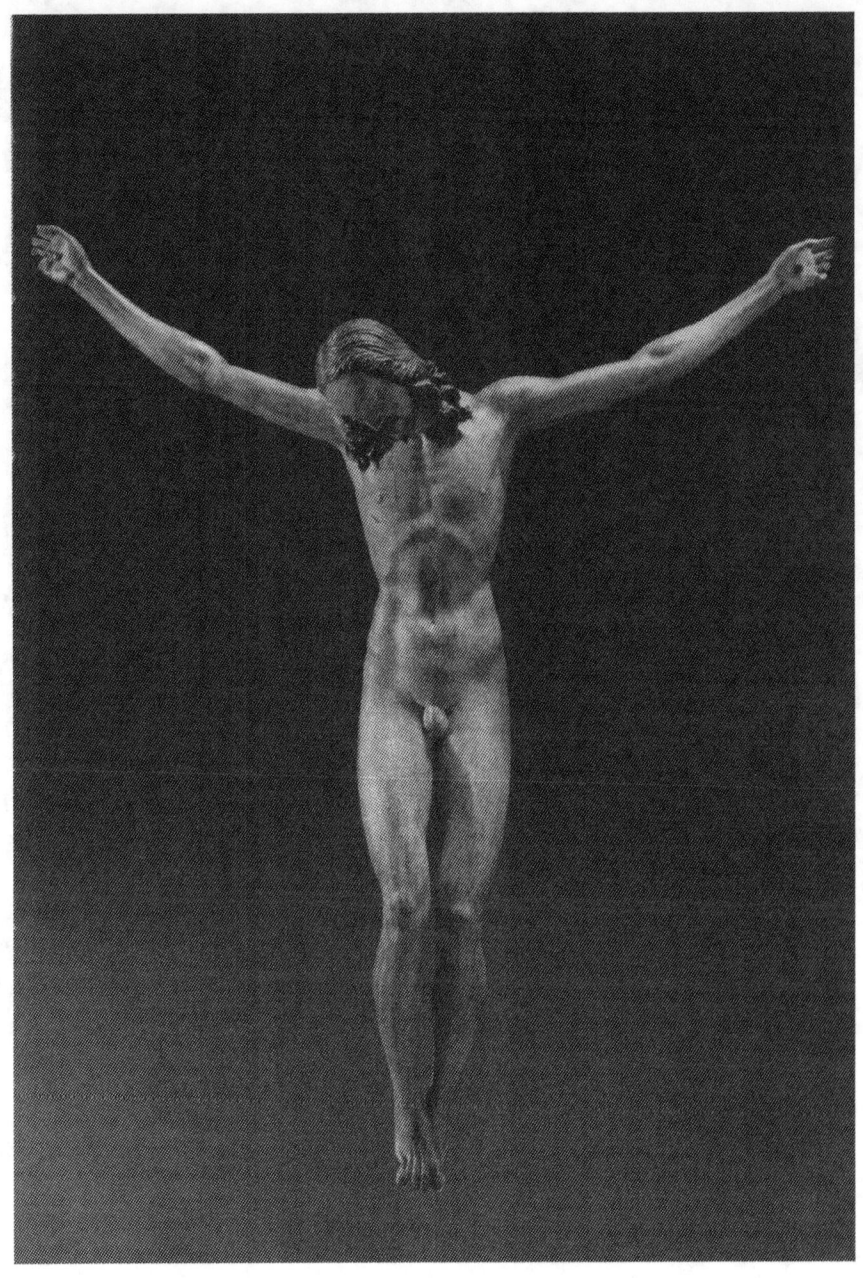

Plate 13: **Attributed to Michelangelo (here rejected)**, *Crucifix* (front view), Turin, private collection.

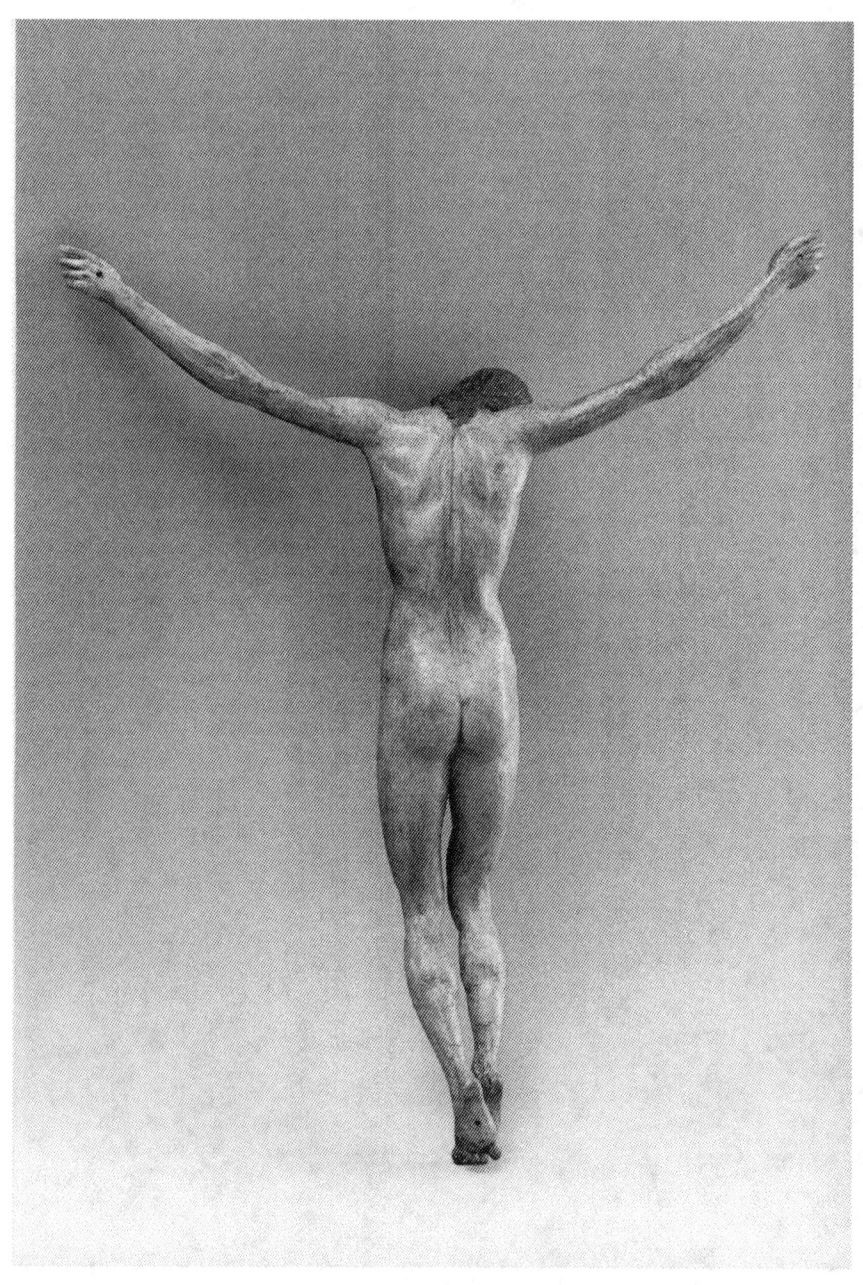

Plate 14: **Attributed to Michelangelo (here rejected)**, *Crucifix* (back view), Turin, private collection.

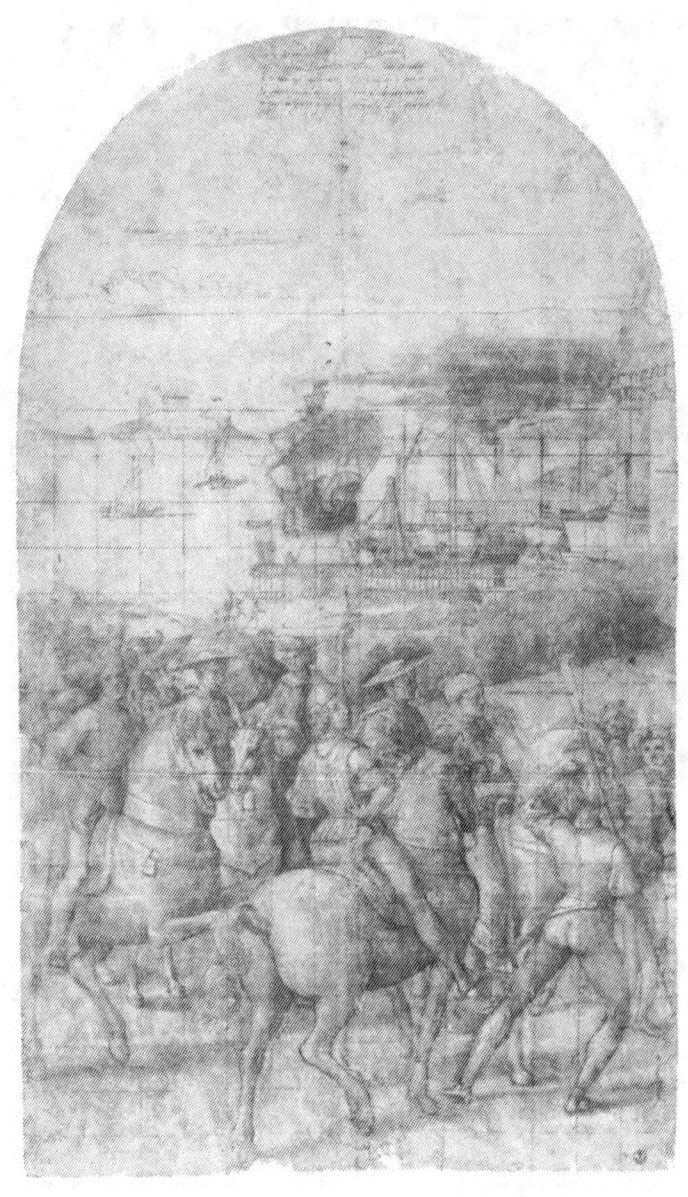

Plate 15: **Attributed to Raphael (here rejected, assigned to Pinturicchio)**, *The Journey of Aeneas Silvius Piccolomini to Basle*, preparatory drawing, Florence, Uffizi Gallery, Gabinetto dei Disegni e delle Stampe.

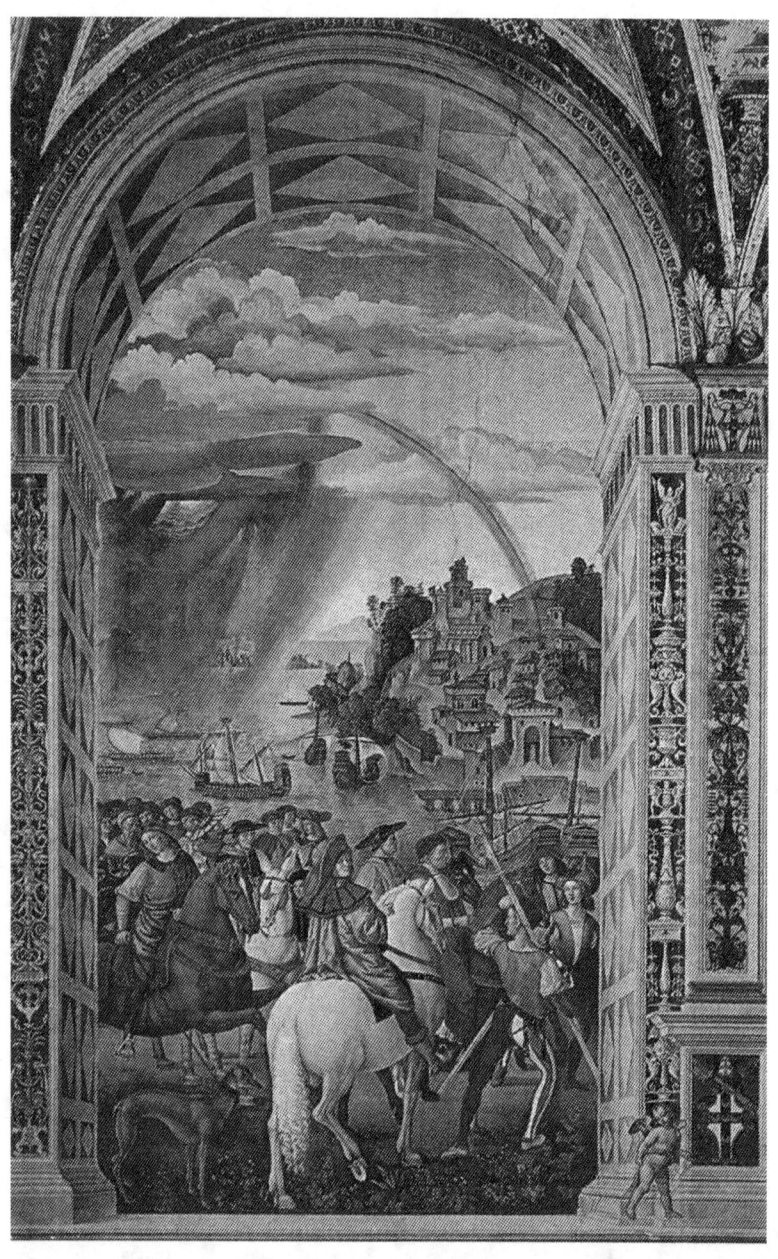

Plate 16: **Pinturicchio**, *The Journey of Aeneas Silvius Piccolomini to Basle*, Siena, Duomo, Piccolomini Library.

Chapter 4

Provenance of the *Northumberland Madonna of the Pinks*

In the litany of problematics regarding the attribution of the *Northumberland* painting to Raphael, a prominent one has been left aside. Provenance should be considered the port of embarcation for the connoisseur's journey in confronting an attribution of a painting or sculpture, once, that is, quality is determined. In this chapter, the history of the tiny picture will be rehearsed.

The first hard-and-fast confirmation of the *Northumberland* painting's existence, in distinction to the other the fifty-five versions, is regarded by its new owners as a print engraved by Giovanni Farrugia, dated 1828, Fig. 3.7.[1] Unquestionably a picture

---

[1]Penny, 1992, no. 24, and p. 78. Very little is known about Farrugia's artistic career. The Maltese artist is discussed in the bimonthly Maltese publication, *L'arte*, anno I, (1863), pp. 3-6 (Information generously supplied to me by Jan Sammer). It is curious to observe its author dates the engraving of the *Madonna dei Garofani* to the period of Farrugia's stay in Rome, which can be fixed as 1826, while the engraving shows the date of 1828. As a a lad, he was taken in by a local prelate. Trained locally in printmaking and in art, he went to Rome. After his Roman stay, he went

of the type was sold to the Duke of Northumberland by the Camuccini estate in the mid-1850s, and in fact the inscription in the engraving locates the image in Vincenzo Camuccini's collection.[2] First impressions and opinions of the National Gallery experts aside, Farrugia's engraving is definitely not based upon the London picture. As already observed, in addition to slight differences in size, the Child in the *Northumberland* is completely nude, while in the engraving he is shown with a loincloth. Besides, marked differences between the two include the treatment of the Child's head and the conception of his hair. Mary's expression is likewise significantly at variance in the two versions; in the engraving she is about to smile, while she actually bares her teeth in the painting.

Since Farrugia's engraving definitely does not depict the National Gallery's picture, and since the inscription on the engraving states that the picture illustrated is in Rome in the collection of Vincenzo Camuccini, one is required to recognize as has already been stated that the Camuccini brothers had (at least) two versions of the *Madonna of the Pinks*: one with the Child covered, the other showing the Child nude. The latter painting is known to have been owned by Vincenzo's older brother and mentor, Pietro Camuccini. This version of the subject is listed in an inventory of 1833 taken after his death and must be the one purchased by the Duke of Northumberland and subsequently by the National Gallery. The revelation that the Camuccini had (at

---

on to Milan, where he worked under Giuseppe Longhi and devoted himself to engraving famous works. Following twenty years in Italy, he returned to Malta where he died at the age of 63 in 1861. His relationship with Camuccini is not known. It does seem quite possible that he saw and presumably drew the Camuccini painting in 1826, but only executed the engraving two years later. If this explanation holds up, the version he engraved, which belonged to Vincenzo, was already visible in Rome by 1826.

[2]The text in the bottom margin reads in part: "L'originale della stessa grandezza esiste in Roma nella galleria del celeberrimo pittore Sig.^{re} Cav.^{re} Camuccini."

least) two versions of the same subject, a fact unknown to Penny and the operatives at the National Gallery, has formidable consequences for the entire discussion of the *Northumberland Madonna*.

For the sake of clarity, the painting with a loincloth which served as the basis of the engraving will be referred to as the *Farrugia-Camuccini* and the second, which shows the Child nude, as the *Northumberland-Camuccini*. The *Farrugia-Camuccini* has not yet been identified, but one can expect it will be, when a systematic study of all the versions is completed, presuming that it has survived.[3]

As part of the search for a provenance of the *Northumberland* painting, much earlier indications of the composition are found in other engravings treated previously (Figs. 3.1, 3.2, 3.3). They provide evidence that the composition known as the *Madonna of the Pinks* was in existence by the middle of the 17th century at the latest. The determination of which picture (or pictures) served as the model for the various engravings is elusive. One thing is certain: the *Northumberland* was not and could not be the foundation example, as Penny and the National Gallery experts claim. *French 1*, as has been demonstrated, although showing the Child nude, could not have used the *Northumberland* painting as its model (Fig. 3.1). As for the *Northumberland* picture itself, its existence cannot be confirmed for many years before 1833, although the fact in itself only provides an *ante quem*. At the same time, the provenance and the specific appearance of the Ur example remains a mystery. The official statement of the National Gallery: "The precise date given for the picture's move to France is confirmed by several French engravings made *after* [my italics] it in the second half of the 17th century" is patently incorrect.

An enamel copy by Marie-Victoire Jaquotot (Musée national

---

[3] As already promised, a complete catalogue is being prepared by Jan Sammer of all the versions for publication shortly.

de céramique, Sèvres) confirms the existence of a painted version in France (Fig. 1). While her copy could have been based upon a print, the color appears to me to be such that a painted prototype must have been available to her. This enamel is of capital interest for the larger attributional issue because it is securely dated to 1817 by documents. Yet Penny's claim, as he must to sustain the *Northumberland* attribution, that it was copied from the *Northumberland* is quite impossible because of size differentials alone. The enamel is nearly one third again as large as the *Northumberland*, hardly the "same size" as Penny would have it.[4]

Furthermore, although a contemporary account points to the reliability of Madame Jaquotot, whose work is described as having "une incroyable fidélité", the differences between the enamel and the *Northumberland* picture go far beyond sizes. Variations include "the 'correction' of the anatomy of the Virgin's left hand and of the Christ's foot" as Penny has it.[5] Following such a statement, for the official opinion to be accepted, we would have to believe the impossible: that a 19th century enameller, dissatisfied with what she saw in an original, "corrected" Raphael. The treatment of the drapery in which the folds are more generalized and less fussy—one might even say more Raphaelesque—reflects another major difference between the National Gallery's painting and the enamel. Also pertinent, the tell-tale window arch is more ample in the enamel. As it turns out, in the search for reconstructing a proper provenance for the *Northumberland* example, the enamel is irrelevant. Furthermore, at least according to the National Gallery, their painting left France in 1810, seven years

---

[4]The *Northumberland* is 27.9 x 22.4 cm = 624.96 square cms., while the Jaquotot enamel is 31.4 x 26.6 cm = 835.24 square cms. Hence the difference is 210.28 square cms. This may appear to be a petty point, but based on the relationship between the dimensions of the work and the price, the difference runs into the millions of dollars.

[5]Penny, 1992, p. 79.

before the enamel "copy" of it was made, so even their chronology, in distinction to Penny's, seems askew. In simple terms, the Jaquotot enamel has nothing to do with the provenance of the *Northumberland* painting.

Neither the *Farrugia-Camuccini* nor the *Northumberland-Camuccini* seem to have been present in Camuccini's atelier as of 14 June 1828, when Stendhal visited it.[6] At least the French writer does not mention the existence of such a painting there, and considering its presumptive fame as a popular Raphael still in a private collection, we must assume (1) that it wasn't there, or (2) that Vincenzo was loathe to show it to him, or (3) that it was there but not regarded as worth mentioning. Stendhal actually describes Camuccini as "un homme fort adroit" who made vast pictures and goes on, "M. le chevalier Camuccini a le talent assez commun de faire d'excellentes copies... Je louerai avec plaisir les dessins de M. Camuccini, d'après des figures isolées de Raphaël; ils annoncent réellement beaucoup de talent."[7]

The year 1829 marks a second printed mention of a composition of the *Pinks* located in the Camuccini collection. In his Italian edition of the life of Raphael by Quatremère de Quincy, Francesco Longhena refers to it as an "...opera similmente de' primi anni di Raffaello, sparsa d'infinita soavità...".[8] While it is not certain to which of the two Camuccini versions he refers, no

---

[6]Stendhal, *Promenades dans Rome* (1828), V. Del Litto, ed., Grenoble, 1993, pp. 237-38.

[7]*Loc. cit.*

[8]Antoine Quatremère De Quincy, *Histoire de la vie et des ouvrages de Raphaël*, Paris, 1824, p. x. Francesco Longhena, *Istoria della vita e delle opere di Raffaello Sanzio da Urbino*, (1829), Rosario Assunto, ed., Urbino, 1977, p. 12. The picture is regarded by Longhena as of the first manner, i.e. *primi anni*, not the second manner, which is an indication of an inherent stylistic and chronological problem in the picture's critical history. I took up this issue in the previous chapter. Longhena is alone in praising the picture. He praises a number of other dubious Raphaels in private Italian collections in no less extravagant terms (cf. 101, n. 23).

mention at all of a *Madonna of the Pinks* is found in the original French edition published in 1824 or in the second or third French editions of 1833 and 1835, so the reference to the picture was clearly by the Italian translator not the French writer.

The still-to-be identified *Farrugia-Camuccini Madonna of the Pinks* is probably the picture referred to in the Phillips auction sales catalogue of 1830 in an entry for a sale of yet another version of the same subject: "*Signor Camuccini, the painter, at Rome, has a smaller picture in the earliest manner of Raphael, but which was admitted to be cold and hard...*".[9] In concordance with Longhena's reference from the previous year, the entry specifically refers to Raphael's earliest manner, meaning his pre-Florentine years. The cataloguer of the London auction house seems to go out of his way to belittle the quality of the picture. The language is categorical, and must reflect a current of opinion regarding the painting in Camuccini's collection.

The ambiguity over style, which I have referred to from time to time, appears to hold for the *Northumberland* version, specifically mentioned in the inventory taken in 1833 of Pietro Camuccini's collection. Since Vincenzo was present when the inventory was prepared, apparently he agreed to the characterizations and perhaps even supplied information.[10] The painting was consid-

---

[9] I am grateful to Jan Sammer for this citation: "Catalogue of a Cabinet of Pictures, the property of a Gentleman, to be sold by Mr. Phillips, 73 New Bond Street, in the month of May, 1830.
No. 27. *Raphael* Madonna and Infant Christ.
Few of the works of Raphael have been more frequently copied than this. These copies are generally, however, below criticism. Signor Camuccini, the painter, at Rome, has a smaller picture in the earliest manner of Raphael, but which was admitted to be cold and hard, when placed beside this. This picture appears to be a repetition, executed at a more mature age, and in a greatly improved style of art."

[10] Pietro mentioned this painting, its cost and its value, certainly sometime before in his private account register, but it is difficult to determine precisely when. See *supra*, p. 67, n. 9.

ered as "in the manner of Raphael" rather than by Raphael.[11] Vincenzo incidentally claimed that half of the collection was already his, possibly for tax reasons.

To recapitulate, we have the following references: the *Farrugia-Camuccini* engraving of 1828, Longhena's Italian edition of Quatremère de Quincy's monograph of 1829, the Phillips sale of 1830 and the inventory of Pietro Camuccini's estate of November 1833. The first three must be the *Farrugia-Camuccini* picture. The last, on the other hand, must be the *Northumberland-Camuccini*, which ended up in the National Gallery, with, as we have already seen, Pietro's seal on the reverse.

Most early 19th century sources characterize the Camuccini version they saw as falling into Raphael's first manner. Presumably, after 1833 the two versions belonged to Vincenzo, so any distinction between them becomes increasingly difficult to isolate. Nothing of the ambiguity between first or second style is found in Raphael's masterpiece of this period, the *Deposition/Entombment* altarpiece (Rome, Borghese Gallery), which was executed at approximately the same time claimed for the *Northumberland*.[12] The painting is recognized for what it is, a product of Raphael's second or Florentine phase, although he probably painted it in Perugia.

Actually, reading between the lines, doubts must have circulated in Rome concerning the attribution to Raphael of the

---

[11]L. Finocchi Ghersi, "'Il moccolo che va avanti, fa lume per due' Pio IX, il marchese Campana e la vendita della collezione Camuccini," *Rivista dell' Istituto Nazionale d'Archeologia e Storia dell'Arte*, 57, (III serie, XXV), 2002, p. 371. The author points out "La presenza attestata di Vincenzo durante la stesura dell'inventario successivo alla morte di Pietro, del resto, è un elemento di rilievo che spinge a dare fiducia ai pareri riportati riguardo alle attribuzioni..." The author also goes out of his way to give credit to the authority of the attributions ("la generale attendibilità delle attribuzioni").

[12]Ironically, a brilliant copy of it by Vincenzo is in Cantalupo. The original in the Galleria Borghese was recently restored to its distinct disadvantage, as has been recognized even by the Roman press.

Camuccini versions. In a remark by Stendhal (ca. 1835), after a subsequent visit, when referring to the painting of the *Pinks* in the "Galerie Camuccini," he described it as pertaining to Raphael's "second manner." It is not clear to me which of the two versions Stendhal was describing. He admired the purity of expression and the beauty of the Virgin and then dropped the following fascinating tidbit: "...il ne peut exister aucun doute sur son originalité...,"[13] which of course indicates that he was responding to doubts which had been circulating.

The inventory of Pietro's collection undertaken in 1833 has a role in confirming the provenance which was written for the first time in the early 1850s for the *Northumberland*. The elder Camuccini who was without an heir had prepared the way for the sale of his collection specifically in order to assure the well-being and prosperity of his family.[14] Nothing whatsoever is said about keeping the pictures in his collection for the benefit of Italy or for Rome, which has become a topos of the official National Gallery account.[15] Quite to the contrary, he *wanted* them to sell it.

The revelant entry on the picture in question reads:

"*No. 11 Madonna e Bambino con garofoli [sic] in mano, alto pal. $1^{1/2}$ Maniera di Raffaello [scudi] 100.*"

Presumably the purpose of the inventory was to establish valuations for tax purposes. Dated 16 November 1833, it was prepared by the appraiser ("perito") Giovanni Antonio Pasinati, a Roman painter.

The language is unequivocal: the expert did not consider the

---

[13] A. Constantin, *Idées Italiennes su quelques tableaux...[Oeuvres de Stendhal]*, v. 35, p. 133. This would indicate however that Stendhal at this time supported the attribution to Raphael.

[14] L. Finocchi Ghersi, *op. cit.*, p. 357. I am grateful to Baron Vincenzo Camuccini of Rome and Cantalupo for calling my attention to this extremely helpful article and for his general kindness is allowing me to visit the collection.

[15] There is no mention either to the effect that the picture had been purchased in Paris.

picture to be an autograph original by Raphael, but instead in his manner.

In terms of connoisseurship and market value, the distance in signification between "*di Raffaello*" and "*Maniera di Raffaello*" is immense. The terminology the appraiser used in describing other paintings in the collection is worth reviewing to establish his intention in the case of the Raphael and in general his reliability in terms of his characterization of the *Northumberland*. When dealing with authorship, besides "*manner of,*" he uses "*by,*" "*style of,*" "*school of,*" "*copy after or from,*" "*by unknown author,*" "*ordinary copy,*" "*ugly copy* [copiaccia]" and "*modern copy.*"[16] He is sophisticated and well informed in his categorizations. The term "*maniera di*" was used in only one other case in the entire inventory, when referring to a *Susana* by Annibale Carracci, which was evaluated for forty scudi, clearly not an original autograph work either.

Pietro's parting wish, that his heirs sell the collection, is in direct conflict with Penny's claim along with that of the Gallery's, to the effect that the collection was not intended to be sold: "There is no reason to doubt that the two brothers had hoped to preserve it [the collection]...".[17]

In September 1833, a couple of months before Pietro's passing, Raphael Sanzio's body was exhumed so that his remains could be venerated and studied. On the occasion a book was prepared describing the ceremonies and the persons involved. Among the prime movers was Vincenzo Camuccini who actually recorded the event with drawings, "con quella virtù dell'arte che

---

[16] There were even objects of no value at all, according to the punctilious expert. To be sure, the evaluation in price of the little painting, though high, 100 scudi, is hardly top dollar in terms of the place Raphael held in the art world at the time and certainly not in terms of the price paid in 2004 in London. In fact, it corresponds nicely to the amount of eighty scudi paid for the *Count Spada* (Lucca) copy, which was recorded on the back of the picture.

[17] Penny, 1992, 77.

lo fa salutare primario dipintore dell'età nostra," according to Carlo Falconieri.[18] In his short life of Raphael in the appendix to the publication, while treating many of Raphael's paintings, including Madonnas, Falconieri fails to mention a *Madonna of the Pinks* in Rome, in the collection of Camuccini, a man he esteemed. If it had been what it was supposed to have been, i.e. an original Raphael of a popular theme, one might have expected a reference. Certainly Raphael afficionandos would have known of its existence, were it regarded as an original. Evidently, it was not.

The next mention of the *Northumberland* painting comes two decades later, from about 1855. Tito Barberi, a mosaic maker said to be a member of the Camuccini circle, prepared an annotated catalogue which remains unpublished to this day.[19] By this time Vincenzo was already dead (1844) and the collection of both Camuccini brothers, which became the property of Vincenzo's son Giovanni Battista (1819-1904), was on display in Rome's Palazzo Cesi. The palace, now the *Procura Generale Militare presso la Corte di Cassazione*, was purchased by Giovanni Battista apparently only in 1851, for the purpose of exhibiting the pictures which had formerly been shown in the Camuccini habitation on Piazza Borghese.[20]

Following the recommendations in Pietro's will, the bulk of the collection was sold to the Duke of Northumberland. With the benefit of hindsight, I would suggest that the prestigious display space together with Barberi's catalogue were part of a plan to sell the collection, designed not for casual visitors but

---

[18] *Memoria intorno il rinvenimento della Ossa di Raffaello Sanzio con breve appendice sulla di lui vita*, Rome, 1833, p. 11.

[19] He prepared a pamphlet about another collection which was published in 1869, *Della Collezione dei Quadri e di altri oggetti d'arte posseduti da Monsignor Federico de Falloux*, Rome.

[20] F. Ceccopieri Maruffi, "La galleria Camuccini nel racconto di un prezioso manoscritto," *Strenna dei Romanisti*, vol. 35, 1974, p. 133. Palazzo Cesi was sold at the same time as the collection.

for potential buyers.[21] In the catalogue, any doubts about the authenticity of pictures in the collection, including the Raphael, which had been so carefully differentiated in the rigorous inventory of 1833, were obliterated. All the works became "by" the various masters, no ifs, ands or "manners of." Hence a sweeping upgrade was performed. This kind of sleight-of-hand hardly speaks well for Barberi's integrity, much less that of the catalogue, and leads to the inevitable conclusion that its purpose goes beyond the category of simple informational listings to that of brilliant merchandizing.

The *Madonna of the Pinks* had become an impeccable Raphael and to embellish the designation Barberi provided an elaborate provenance which, *mirabile dictu*, has been appropriated by the National Gallery experts, hook, line, and sinker:

"*Innanzi l'anno 1636 un francese acquistò esso dipinto dagli eredi Oddi e lo portò seco in Francia, ove fu finché Vincenzo Camuccini recomperatolo in Parigi, la restituì alla Italia ed a Roma, collocandolo fra i migliori quadri della propria galleria.*" ["Before the year 1636 a Frenchman purchased this painting from the Oddi heirs and brought it with him to France where it was until Vincenzo Camuccini repurchased it in Paris, returning it to Italy and to Rome, and locating it among the best pictures of his gallery."][22]

The words should be pondered carefully by the connoisseur/

---

[21] Tito Barberi, "Catalogo ragionato della Galleria Camuccini in Roma descritto da Tito Barberi," ms located in Cantalupo, Sabina. A copy exists at Alnwick Castle.

[22] From F. Ceccopieri Maruffi, *op. cit.*, p. 135. The author continues, that "Quatremère de Quincy nella storia di Raffaello, volta in Italiano da Francesco Longhena che dice: lo stesso Camuccini possiede altro cimelio del divino Sanzio, cioè una piccola tavola rappresentante la Beata Vergine col Bambino in grembo che prende un fiore dalla Madre, opera similmente di Raffaello, sparsa di infinita soavità. Questo quadretto bisognò che fosse tanto nell'amore delle persone d'arte che fu più volte da Benventuo Garofalo, dal Sassoferrato e da altri antichi maestri ricopiato."

researcher because the National Gallery puts a heavy weight on them. At the beginning of the passage we are faced with a semi-fact: the picture having been purchased "before the year 1636...". Ostensively the year of the purchase appears specific, but really is not. Was it actually 1635, that is one year *inanzi* (before) or 1626, ten years before? The combination of specificity and vagueness should raise a scholarly eyebrow or two about the reliability of the information. Another word seems odd: Vincenzo Camuccini "re-purchased" [*recomperatolo*] not "purchased" the picture in Paris. Was this merely a loose application of the word, or does this signify that Camuccini had sold the picture at some point earlier and then repurchased it in Paris at an unspecified date? As will be demonstrated shortly, this parsing of the word is not a purely academic exercise.

Barberi's indefinite "before" 1636 for a Frenchman's purchase, becomes the fixed date of 1636 for the National Gallery experts, and so does Camuccini's purchase, not repurchase. If such an important picture by the unanimous favorite of all time was really purchased in Paris (or elsewhere), one can expect that the news would have spread like wildfire in Paris, in the Camuccini family ambiente and in all of Rome. But such was not the case.

From the evidence we have the *Northumberland* was not obtained by Vincenzo but was purchased by his brother Pietro. Here too the authenticity of Barberi's story comes into question.[23] In fact, the evidence also points to Penny's assumption that the *Northumberland* picture was not in the Camuccini collection in 1825 when a list of their best pictures had been formulated, since the *Madonna of the Pinks* was not on it, and

---

[23] The National Gallery remains convinced of the reliability of the manuscript, though perhaps they have to, in order to maintain their impossible position. See H. Chapman, T. Henry and C. Plazzotta, *Raphael from Urbino to Rome, op. cit.*, p. 190. These authors are part of the team, and were joined by D. Cooper ("New documents for Raphael and his patrons in Perugia," *The Burlington Magazine*, no. 1220, vol. cxlvi, p. 742), who are disposed to regard the text of the catalogue as authoritative.

according to Penny it would have been, of course. To have left it off the list seems unlikely were it actually there, as the National Gallery persists in asserting. On the other hand, if doubts about its authenticity circulated in Rome and as far as London, a few years later, then it would have been sensible to keep the picture under wraps.

On the other hand, if Barberi's account is accepted at face value, namely that Vincenzo repurchased it in Paris, he must have done so in 1810, the year of his only trip to that city.[24] In fact, the National Gallery authorities now advocate that year, revealing a break from Penny's reconstruction of the situation: *"The Madonna of the Pinks is first recorded at the time of its purchase in Paris by Vincenzo Camuccini around 1810."* [25] That presupposition is indefensible as Penny realized because it has to mean that the "famous" picture was in Rome and nobody knew about it for eighteen years. Besides, it was 'copied' in France in 1817, as we have already seen.

Still taking Barberi at face value for the moment, one might speculate that Vincenzo sold the picture to a French collector or dealer at some undisclosed period, possibly in 1810, and then bought it back at an unknown date before 1826-1828. The notion of buying back pictures would not have been unique for Vincenzo since he bought back others, the most striking of which was his copy of Raphael's *Entombment,* produced in 1789 for Lord Bristol, and now in Cantalupo. He repurchased it from the sale of Lord Bristol's effects in Rome in 1805.[26] According to his

---

[24] Although he could have made other trips which are not documented, having been such a famous personality and one who kept records of his activities, this eventuality should be regarded as quite unlikely. Hence if the account is to be believed, he should have purchased or repurchased the work in 1810.

[25] Why they do not say 1810 instead of "around 1810" is puzzling to me.

[26] Cf. Ulrich Hiesinger, "The Paintings of Vincenzo Camuccini, 1771-1844," *Art Bulletin,* v.60, (June 1978), p. 301 footnote 23. I cannot fail to observe what an outstanding article this is, with a mass of unpublished

contemporary biographer Visconti, Vincenzo Camuccini was actually inclined to repurchase his works, "because he was anxious to have his work back" (perché fu vago di riavere la sua opera).[27] Did the *Northumberland Madonna* have a similar history? Was it made by Camuccini when still very young, at a time when he by his own admission was making copies of Old Masters for English gentlemen, and when the occasion arose he bought it back? It seems quite possible that the *Northumberland* picture dates to the same period as the copy of the *Deposition*, that is the 1780s and or early 1790s.[28]

Barberi also supplied the patriotic motivation for the supposed purchase, which the Gallery has latched onto: Vincenzo wanted to bring the work back to Italy and to his beloved Rome. True, he along with his brother was unquestionably a devoted admirer of Raphael, and thus the idea planted by the cataloguer has appeal. Nonetheless, it must be a total invention. As we have seen, Pietro, the real owner, provided in his will that the pictures in his collection, including the *Madonna of the Pinks*, should be sold to provide the family with sufficient means to rise in social rank. That is, in fact, precisely what happened. There was no mention of saving Raphael for Italy and for Rome. Other evidence makes a patriotic claim especially hollow: despite Vincenzo's reverence for Raphael, he sold at least two drawings regarded as by Raphael to collectors, one of which is today in the British Museum (Fig. 4.1), as well as a pair of small paintings which until recently had been in the Contini Bonacossi collection.[29] In other words, Vincenzo was prepared to part company

---

material on Camuccini.

[27] *Op. cit.*, p. 7. Many artists particularly treasure their early works and often keep them around.

[28] One way to reduce the doubts about the *Northumberland* would be to make a technical and pigment analysis of his copy of the *Deposition*, and compare the findings.

[29] See J. Meyer zur Capellen, *Raphael. The Paintings*, I, Landshut, 2001, pp. 186-187. Earlier on, Pietro Camuccini sold two Raphael paintings in

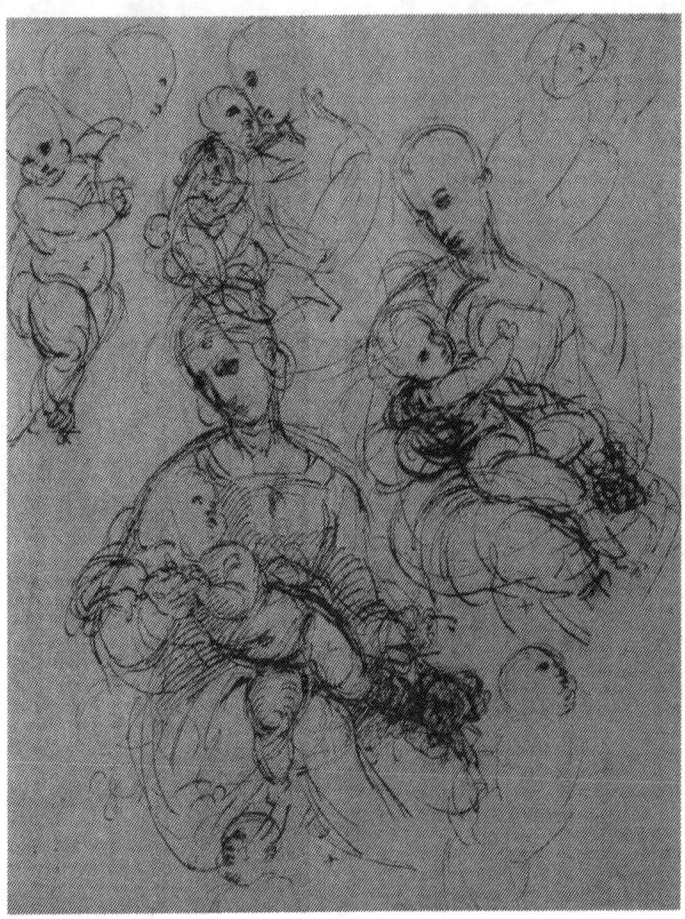

Figure 4.1: **Raphael, attributed to.** *Drawing*, **London, British Museum.**

for himself, for Rome and for Italy, with works by his beloved idol.

Barberi's provenance of the *Northumberland* painting becomes ever more fantastical, as does its defense on the part of the

---

London.

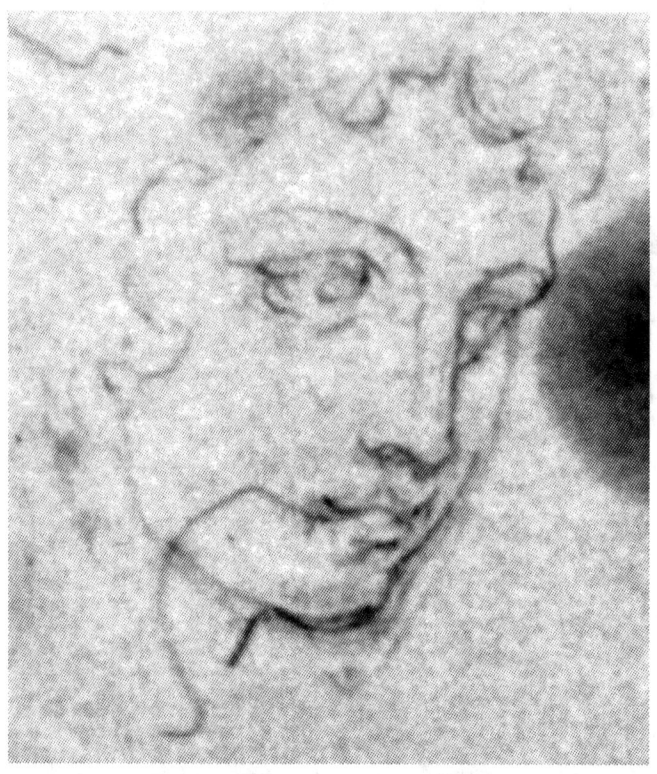

Figure 4.2: **Vincenzo Camuccini, *Drawing*, Rome, private collection.**

National Gallery. He says that "this little panel picture in perfect condition was made by Raphael in his second manner for Maddalena Degli Oddi, nun in Perugia...".[30] Before continuing the analysis of Barberi's text, the reader should keep in mind that whoever was the patron of the original picture, whether it came from Perugia or not, whether it was carried to France as the re-

---

[30]From Penny (1992, p. 79, n. 31) who regards this notice with skepticism.

sult of a sale, and other related information about 'Maddalena degli Oddi', are the facts which pertain to the Ur or original picture. Under no circumstances can any of the speculation be connected specifically with the *Northumberland* painting. Consequently, the National Gallery's case is not really affected, even if Barberi's assertions turned out to be confirmed.

As for the story of the picture's origins and early history, on the surface Barberi's report is not implausible. Vincenzo after all had worked in Perugia and could have known the local lore about the Oddi, whose family history he illustrated. But I suspect that much of the provenance was an invention *ex novo*. Barberi, like his contemporaries, knew Vasari's *Lives of the Artists* almost by memory. The biographer mentions Maddalena degli Oddi as Raphael's patron but he calls her "Madonna" (that is, madam) not "*monaca*" (nun), as Barberi mistakenly does, presumably to embellish his story. In this case, the second manner reference is again a problem because *The Coronation of the Virgin*, which she commissioned, along with its predella, falls in the first manner and not the second, as recognized by Vasari and nearly all observers.[31]

---

[31] A possible explanation for Barberi's scenario is that Raphael went back to Madonna Maddalena for this picture later on, when he was painting in the second manner. But that is unlikely because the degli Oddi, who were in conflict with the ruling Baglione, were expelled from the city in the very years during which the *Pinks* was presumed to have been painted for Maddalena. Of course even in these circumstances not every member of a family would have been expelled, and one cannot be sure Maddelena was absent from Perugia at the time. But all of this discussion belongs to the land of speculation, not history. The "official" explanation of the gallery reiterated by D. Cooper ("New documents for Raphael and his patrons in Perugia," *The Burlington Magazine*, no. 1220, vol. cxlvi, 2005, p. 742) uses an *ex nihilo* argument, that her name does not turn up in the documents in the early 16th century because she joined a religious order, following Barberi's ingenious reference to her as a nun. Since she was not mentioned in Urbino at that time, perhaps she was a nun there. It would seem that the Gallery researchers were in luck not to find anything.

Barberi's account appears to have been based on an embellishment of Vasari, rather than on original documents. Today it is widely held that Vasari was actually wrong about the patronage of the *Coronation*: it was not commissioned by Maddalena degli Oddi, but by Alessandra degli Oddi, known as Leandra, and if anyone then ordered another picture from Raphael it would have been she. Barberi's account of the painting includes one element whose reliability even Penny questions outright.[32] According to Barberi, Raphael was supposed to have written a letter in which he says he is finishing a work for Maddalena, the little painting that was purchased by the National Gallery.[33]

Needless to say, the letter is a modern fiction, created to substantiate the invented provenance and a mistaken patron. If

---

They would do better to go after Leandra, I suspect, and they might yet. Cooper's identification of the patron as Maddalena, already laid out in D. Cooper, "Raphael's Altarpiece in S. Francesco al Prato, Perugia: Patronage, Setting and Function," *The Burlington Magazine*, vol. 143, Sept. 2001, pp. 554-561, has been corrected by V. Borgnini, "La Pala Oddi di Raffaello," *Kermes*, No. 58, April-June 2005, pp. 50 and *passim*. Alessandra Baglioni was married to Simone degli Oddi in 1460.

In all fairness all this argumentation might be academic fun, but is extremely removed of the issues surrounding the authenticity of the *Northumberland* painting.

[32] Penny, 1992, p. 79.

[33] In 1829, Francesco Longhena (in his already cited translation and amplification of Quatremère de Quincy's monograph on Raphael) speaks of a letter by Raphael which has failed to turn up, to the effect that Raphael, writing to a friend, said that "he [Raphael] had to finish a painting for donna Maddalena degli Oddi, who was a powerful woman who could bring him work." Nobody seems ever to have actually seen the letter which has no date attached to it. On the question, see J. Shearman, *Sources, op. cit.*, II, pp. 1452-53, Cat. F 3, that is, under the rubric of "False Documents." It appears to me that Barberi could have used the reference in Longhena's translation for his story.

Penny uses what is useful to his argument. He says part of the Barberi data "may well reflect precise documentation supplied", but he realizes that the claim that Maddalena degli Oddi Monaca in Perugia was the patron must be regarded with skepticism.

there were doubts before, at this point the overall reliability of Barberi collapses. Nor is it superfluous to remind the reader that the Camuccini brothers were known falsifiers not only of art objects, but also of letters from famous persons, and their collection or at least part of it, still exists.

Once set forth, Barberi's story became canonical in the Camuccini circle. In a subsequent reference to the picture found in a Roman inventory of 30 of May 1855 we find the following: "Raphaël Sanzio - La Vierge et l'enfant Jésus; peint pour Madeleine delli Oddi Baglioni, et connu sous el nom de la Vierge des Garofani." The persona of Maddalena may have been conflated with either Leandra or Atalanta Baglioni, another Raphael patron as already proposed.

At this point, one might wish to speculate about the provenance. The best explanation is that it was invented sometime after the death of Pietro in 1833 and probably following the death of Vincenzo in 1844. Was it his son's idea or was it Barberi's?

J.D. Passavant's extremely negative evaluation of what appears to be the *Northumberland* version, of about the same time was published in the 1860 French edition which seems to be identical with the 1839 German one:

"[Madone à l'Œillet] Dans la collection du cavaliere V. Camuccini, à Rome. La Vierge est assise à gauche et tournée vers la droite. L'exécution de cette copie est délicate, mais la couleur froide. C'est certainement un ouvrage de l'école du maître. Des retouches à l'huile, faites dans cette peinture, lui ont donné un aspect très-désagréable, y laissant des taches."[34]

---

[34] *Raphael d'Urbino e su pere Giovanni Santi*, 1860, II, pp. 62-63. Presumably he saw it a few years earlier before it left Italy for London, unless of course we are dealing with a third version owned by the Camuccini, an eventuality not totally out of the question. If this is the *Northumberland*, it must have been restored to correct the retouches.

The author gives a list of other copies and engravings, mentioning the Farrugia print as 1829. Notable is the fact that he favored the *Count Spada* version in Lucca which he knew however only by description and he reports

Passavant saw the picture in Rome in 1835, as established on the basis of his notebooks.[35] He seems on the mark, considering the "delicacy" of the copy and the cold color. The renowned Raphael specialist regarded it as a work of the school of Raphael, not Raphael himself. Some years later the French expert Eugène Müntz said that the *Pinks* was only known by old copies.[36]

Insights about the original or at least a near contemporary copy of the *Madonna of the Pinks* can be supplied.[37] A copy of the composition is known to have been among the possessions of Cardinal Silvestro Aldobrandini (1612) under the year 1606, made by a painter active in Urbino, a certain Archita Ricci.[38] From this, the earliest reference to Raphael and the composition of the *Pinks*, the original or a replica seems to have been in Urbino around the turn of the 17th century and it was already considered worthy of copying. Here again, this item, certainly of interest in building the history of the composition, has nothing

---

that on the back of the panel was written "Per la N. Donna SS ricevuto 80 scudi". This amount is consistent with the 100 scudi that the Camuccini copy had been estimated at in 1833. As for the original *Madonna of the Pinks*, Passavant said that it had not yet been found: "jusqu'à ce jour nous n'avons pu ne découvrir l'original."

[35]cf. C. Plazzotta, in *Raphael: from Urbino to Rome*, op. cit., p. 192, note 6.

[36]Cf. W. Armstrong, trans., *Raphael, His Life, Works and Times*, London, 1882, p. 200.

[37]I would like to thank Jan Sammer for the reference.

[38]The inventory is preserved in the Archivio Doria Pamphilii in Rome, Fondo Aldobrandini, busta 30, ff.1-15. Published by Laura Testa, "Novità su Carlo Saraceni: la committenza Aldobrandini e la prima attività romana," *Dialoghi di Storia dell'Arte*, 7, dic., 1998, p. 136, item 17: f.15-16 "Un quadretto ovè dipinta una Mad.a con il Bambino Giesù che sta seden. sopra ad un coscino bianco e vol pigliare un ramo de garoffoli che tiene la Mad.a nelle mani, viene da Raffaello, copiata d'Archita Ricci da Urbino, con cornige tutte dorate."

See also Francesca Cappelletti, "Una nota di beni e qualche aggiunta alla storia della collezione Aldobrandini," *Storia dell'Arte*, 93/94, May-Dec. 1998, pp. 341-347.

to do specifically with the *Northumberland* example, which is totally without a provenance prior to the 19th century, as I have demonstrated more than once in these pages.

In the final step toward an evaluation of the provenance of the *Northumberland* picture, the explanation provided by the proud new owners can be confronted. They challenge my claims that the provenance does not go back beyond the 19th century. Their report to the Trustees in recommending the purchase seems to me to be a scholarly presentation filtered through the museum's public relations machinery. The approach was to lay out some of the objections that had appeared in the press, and respond to them. To the objection that the provenance was non-existent before the 19th century, they respond:

"*This statement is not strictly true,*"

One is tempted to ask the Gallery experts to explain what "strictly true statements" are, or strictly false ones, for that matter.

We must conclude that the National Gallery, with the approval of the Trustees and a governmental commission, purchased a picture purportedly painted in the first decade of the 16th century, but whose verifiable provenance only goes back to shortly before 1833. They do not appear to be worried, however,

"*although even if it were [true], there are many, many paintings whose provenance cannot be traced beyond the Napoleonic upheavals of the late eighteenth/early nineteenth centuries. This would not be surprising or suspicious in any way.*"

They half concede that there may not have been an early provenance, but that does not make much difference. The argument is turned on its head: it is almost as if the absence of any early provenance was really good luck because after all "many, many" [*sic*] other pictures do not have them either. Of course, many, many pictures without adequate provenance turn out to be false. Excellent pictures with no better histories than the *Northumberland* picture do occur, but since the price of the painting was the highest paid by the National Gallery and public money was used, one might have expected a better understanding of what they were buying.

The report continues,

"*Although the picture's earlier provenance cannot as yet definitively be proved, the entry for it in an authoritative manuscript inventory of the Camuccini collection offers clues that are not at all incompatible with independent evidence.*"

The admission contained in this sentence is serious enough, and is at variance with the first line of this section. In terms either of clever communication skills or wishful thinking, by adding "as yet" the text makes the reader think that they are on to something which will be presented at any time. Apparently, the Gallery's experts got busy doing the work of checking, something which presumably should have been done before the picture was purchased. Their goal was to find in the Perugian archives evidence that this Maddalena degli Oddi was indeed a nun and could have been Raphael's patron in the first decade of the 16th century.

They did not uncover that much-hoped-for fragment of historical data in the Perugian archives, but that turns out magically to be in their favor. They are again able to call upon the negative as evidence, by asserting with a double negative that not finding any reference to Maddalena is "not incompatible" with the condition of documentation for nuns in Perugia in the early 16th century, or gypsies or prostitutes. For them, the absence of documentation about the woman proves that Barberi was right.

The insistence that Barberi's manuscript inventory is "authoritative" is unsustainable. There is no independent evidence that Vincenzo purchased the picture at all, and it was not his in 1833, but rather his brother's. Still, the Gallery report persists:

"This rather specific record, which may reflect documentation supplied by the painting's previous owner, states that the

Madonna of the Pinks was made for Maddalena degli Oddi, a nun in Perugia, from whose heirs a Frenchman acquired it in [sic] 1636, taking it to France. The very precise date given for the picture's migration to France is borne out by several French engravings made after it in the second half of the 17th century."

As Barberi's account moves increasingly into the twilight zone, so does the National Gallery's stance. While the Trustees and the adherents of the picture's authenticity might continue to hope that archival evidence will in the future support their case, those who deal with such material from the 15th and 16th centuries know all too well that you can never predict what you will or will not find. For the moment, the implications of non-finds on the Perugian horizon are a smoke screen for missing evidence. The Barberi manuscript was an excellent sales catalogue of the collection, so successful that the National Gallery can still with a straight face give heavy weight to its contents after 150 years. Like the Barberi catalogue, the National Gallery's report contains serious scholarly and moral lapses in an effort to defend the purchase. As for their provenance, their case lies limp at ground zero.

Chapter 5

Connoisseurship Gone Astray

Connoisseurship shows no decline in the face of a flourishing art market with a constant flow of new objects of every kind and culture requiring identification. Consequently, the need for a revival and revitalization of the activity continues to be as pressing as it is illusive. Almost every week in the international press, a headline article announces a new find, usually involving the biggest names in art, with Leonardo and Michelangelo in the forefront. A small wooden Crucifix owned by a dealer in Turin, which came to public attention recently, can serve to illustrate the process (Plates 13 and 14).

5.1 A wooden Crucifix.

The "discovery"—they are inevitably discoveries—was accompanied by a shiny, hardcover book in the guise of an exhibition catalogue with the title: *Proposta per Michelangelo. Un Croci-*

fisso in legno di tiglio.[1] The elaborate presentation of the object was similar to that employed for the gesso "*modello*" of the *David* nearly two decades ago by Frederick Hartt and may be regarded by now as standard procedure. A couple of decades before that, the *Little St. John*, a handsome marble figure in a New York private collection, was offered in the public arena as a lost early effort by Michelangelo.[2]

In the case of the new Crucifix, its advocates—not a lone optimistic scholar as is often the case—constitute a veritable "who's who" of art history in Tuscany. This aspect, which might be thought of as the sociology of the situation, is parallel to the connections represented by the proponents of the *Northumberland Madonna*. The group is headed by Antonio Paolucci, the powerful Soprintendente per il Polo Museale Fiorentino and a former Minister of Fine Arts in Rome. Other members of the team include the late Umberto Baldini, a Florentine art operative for over half a century on various levels, but with a special dedication to restoration as a former Director of the Istituto Centrale di Restauro (Rome), Giancarlo Gentilini, the well-regarded Professor of Art History and expert on 15th century Tuscan sculpture who edited the book/catalogue, Luciano Bellosi, Professor of Art History at the University of Siena (whose name comes up more than once in this book), mainly an expert on early Italian painting but with a side interest in sculpture, and Massimo Ferretti, Professor of Art History at the prestigious Scuola Normale di Pisa.

While the spokespersons do not have the international profile of the twenty-five *magnifici* assembled by the National Gallery,

---

[1] Giancarlo Gentilini, ed., *Una proposta per Michelangelo giovane. Un crocifisso in legno di tiglio*, Turin, 2004.

[2] A few years ago, I suggested, as did Carlo Pedretti independently, that it was a work by Pierino da Vinci, who was something of a late Michelangelo imitator. Cf. Carlo Pedretti, "Il nipote scultore" in M. Cianchi, ed., *Pierino da Vinci: atti della giornata di studio, Vinci, Biblioteca leonardiana, 26 maggio 1990*, Florence 1999, pp. 13-15, and J. Beck, *infra*.

5.1. A wooden Crucifix.

their presence is noteworthy and their explanations are specific and readily available.

The operation follows the modern approach in which support is sought in science and technology, a *sine qua non* these days for any attribution (or a restoration, for that matter). Thus we find injected into a purely connoisseurship issue contributions dealing with something called the "tomografia computerizzata" of the wood (which is linden, not cherry), and an anatomy lesson by two medical doctors *apropos* of the Crucifix. Not to be ignored among the *illustri* is Aurelio Amendola, the highly-esteemed art photographer, noted for his books on Luca della Robbia, Donatello and Michelangelo's sculpture. All together they would appear to constitute a winning team if there ever was one. But the question in the optic of the present study is different: does the connoisseurship behind the attribution awarding the object to Michelangelo hold up?

The Crucifix was placed on public view along with two related ones in May 2004 at the gem of a Museum, il Museo Horne in Florence. The exposition of the work accompanied by an obligatory public relations campaign hit big in the Italian media, although the echo in the international press was muted. Still one of the leading auction houses may get into the act sooner or later, bringing their masterful instruments into play. After all, when one considers that the National Gallery paid the equivalent of 65 million dollars for the *Northumberland Madonna of the Pinks*, which was after all "only" a Raphael, aspirations for a Michelangelo might be limitless.

Two full pages in Italy's most prestigious art monthly, *Il Giornale dell'Arte* which, lo and behold, is published by the very the same publishers who prepared the book/catalogue, Umberto Allemandi & C., were allotted to the story.[3] The headline is

---

[3] *Il Giornale dell'arte*, n. 232, May 2004, p. 18. As an aside, the example is proof of the power of the artistic-political lobby. Paolucci, a regular contributor to *Sole 24 ore*, wrote an article repeating his affirmations from

irresistible: "'Se non è Michelangelo è Dio!'" ["If it isn't Michelangelo it is God!"], allegedly quoting the late Federico Zeri, when he is said to have seen the sculpture. Zeri's words may not be entirely without irony especially knowing his habits and one could interpret the phrase as a rejection of the attribution to Michelangelo, since it is Dio, after all, who is represented.[4]

More to the point for a study devoted to connoisseurship is the determination of how the team achieved the attribution. Barbara Antonetto's article in *Il Giornale dell'Arte* supplies insights. The object, we learn, was purchased from a Florentine home about twenty years ago, the only tidbit offered for establishing the history of the Crucifix. The provenance, a fundamental building block for attributions as has been established in this study, is hardly overwhelming by anyone's standards: Florence, 1984.

According to the same article, Gentilini, Bellosi and Massimo Ferretti, all professors at Italian universities, studied the work "without rushing." They turned over again and again in their hands the 41 cm high object, incidentally only slightly taller than the *Northumberland* painting in its frame, suggesting, as if by free association, a series of possible authors. Through a process of elimination, we are told, they arrived at Michelangelo.[5] Hardly the 'lightning strikes' approach that generated the recent attribution of the *Fifth Avenue Cupid* (Fig. 2.1) and plaster model of the *David*, both ascribed to Michelangelo.

---

the book, and another influential art historian, Arturo Carlo Quintavalle, a frequent contributor to il *Il Corriere della Sera*, wrote a longish sycophantic article ending with a jingoistic appeal that the object should never be allowed to leave the country (like critic James Fenton's patriotic appeal about the *Northumberland Madonna*), suggesting that the government intervene, presumably by buying the work for the city of Florence.

[4]To use hearsay in the form of a remembered conversation is hardly convincing evidence in support of an attribution.

[5]Of course, they left out the ubiquitous "Giovanni Nessuno, Il Giovane" the most likely candidate, in my view.

5.1. A wooden Crucifix.

The recognition that the object was by Michelangelo evidently sank in only gradually. In point of fact, early on in the process Professor Bellosi actually had a low regard for the carving.[6] Over time, he experienced the Crucifix's power by stroking it, at which point the recognition penetrated into his brain that it was a "superb masterpiece." Perhaps he took Berenson's tactile values principle to heart, for nothing less than the marble *David* leapt to his mind. I wonder if he had stroked *il gigante* when the guards were not looking.[7]

Professor Bellosi reveals a favored methodology which he shares with a majority of his colleagues: comparisons (*confronti*). The 'evidence' he offered is exceptionally telling for any commentary on connoisseurship because the three works he singled out for comparison are all attributions themselves. In other words, he builds his attribution of the Crucifix on other attributions, constructing the edifice on an insecure foundation. The examples, none of which are documented as by Michelangelo and according to many, including myself, none of which are by him, constitute Bellosi's core list: the *Santo Spirito Crucifix* (Florence, Santo Spirito, the *Fifth Avenue Cupid* (New York) (Fig. 5.1), and the Angels in the *Manchester Madonna*, a painting in London's National Gallery. This system should be regarded as intolerable for the creation of a convincing new attribution and simultaneously it provides a clear example of the dangers of free-swinging attributions in the first place. Once out there in the public domain as accepted works, as is case of the trio used here, they give birth to new attributions, thereby creating a never-ending chain of ever more remote associations. This eventuality

---

[6]I cannot resist reminding the reader that among connoisseurs, their first and immediately reaction to an object is the preferred one: evidently Bellosi was right at the start too.

[7]This gives me an opportunity to go on record as stating that I believe that the cleaning was blatantly unnecessary and that the results diminished the appearance of the work without bringing improvements in its care.

already is coming to pass with the consensus acceptance of the *Northumberland* picture, which can and already has been used to produce further attributions to Raphael based upon it.

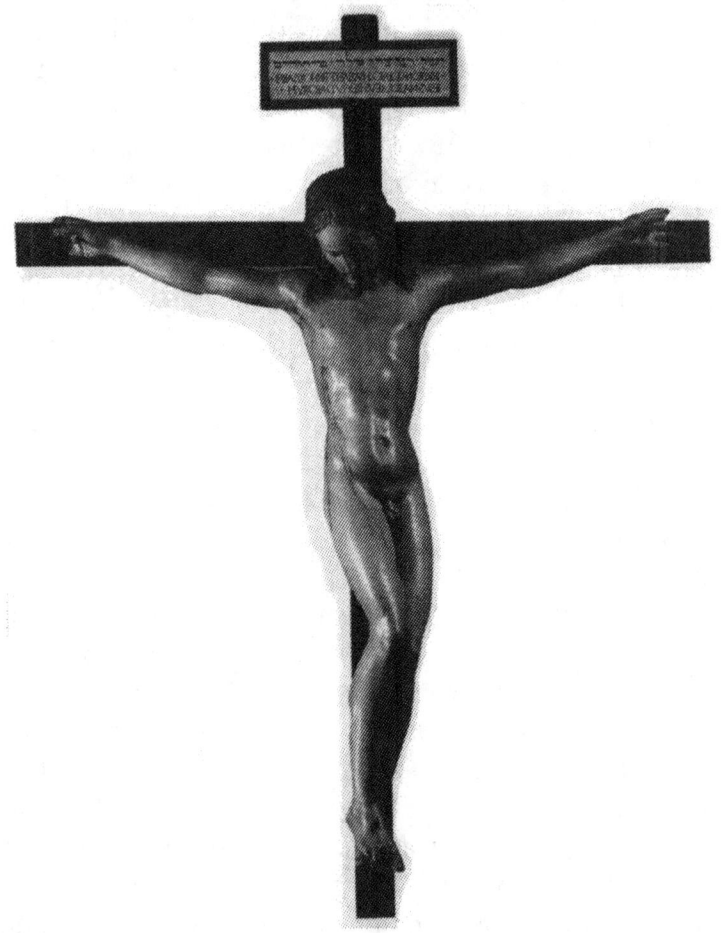

Figure 5.1: **Michelangelo, attributed to (here rejected).** ***Crucifix*, Florence, Santo Spirito.**

By and large all the contributors to the catalogue may be described as dipping their connoisseurship spoons into a steaming

5.1. A wooden Crucifix. 127

bowl of artistic "*minestrone*." Objects used for comparisons are taken from various genres, varying subjects, different sizes, diverse scales, questionable attributions, and from diverse periods in Michelangelo's development. Paintings, drawings, sculptures, sometimes hundreds of times larger, are used to create pseudo-analogies in which even vague parallels seems to be enough to give a dubious "confronto" credibility.

Of the three, to my eyes, the only remotely plausible comparison is with the *Santo Spirito Crucifix*, although suggested similarities pertain more to the fact that the two images represent the same subject and thus by definition share formal elements. Under any circumstances, I believe that the *Santo Spirito Crucifix* is not by Michelangelo, but by a Mannerist carver active in Florence around 1520 (Fig. 5.1).[8] The modeling of the *Santo Spirito Crucifix* is so smoothed out, the skin so tight on the matrix, the musculature so downplayed that the comparison fails to persuade anyway, leaving aside the issue of convincingly dating the objects.

Bellosi's emotional comparison of the new wooden Crucifix with the marble *David* is, in my opinion, far-fetched, due to the discrepancies in size, material, color and presumed date (1495 vs. 1504). The scholar used two different photographs of *David*'s torso to make his point, one dependent upon subjective, interpretative lighting and the other a more conventional "documentary" one. Whatever similarities he might seek to squeeze out from the idea, they are more closely related by the style of the photographs than the style of the sculpture represented in them.

Parenthetically, this neglected condition surrounding photographs used in the comparison process should not to be passed over without a comment. After all, each photographer like each copyist has his own style which cannot be eradicated from his

---

[8] J. Beck, "Benedetto da Maiano e Michelangiolo giovane," in *Giuliano e la bottega dei da Maiano, Atti del Convegno Internazionale di Studi*, Florence, 1994, pp. 176-181.

photographs. That style, furthermore, can change over the years, adding imponderables to judgments based upon his photographs. While this situation should be considered when depending upon reproductions of paintings, it is especially pressing when applied to in-the-round sculpture, which involves the translation of a three-dimensional object into a two-dimensional image.

The diversities between the *David* and the Crucifix are so pronounced in every respect, including an active *contrapposto* for the *Gigante* not present in the Crucifix, as to make Bellosi's point border on the ridiculous. He also offers a comparison between the Crucifix and the body of dead Christ from Michelangelo's *Pietà* in the Museo dell'Opera del Duomo (Florence), executed nearly a half century later, according to the presumptive date of the new object. The only convincing connection one can muster is that they are both nude male bodies of the same subject. The comparison offered in Ferretti's paper is equally tenuous. He illustrates the back of the marble *David* matched with the back of the wooden Cruficix, with its impossibly lumpy and inorganic shoulder blades and truncated, un-Michelangelesque cheeks of the derrieres.

In such cases the object put forward as a "glorious" discovery habitually undergoes a restoration to bring it to "perfection," and the Crucifix is no exception. According to Baldini, the cleaning and fix-ups took place in 1991, when significant adjustments to the surface were undertaken. Coincidentally or by intention, the *Northumberland Madonna* and the *Fifth Avenue Cupid* were likewise both given modern cleanings, the latter in preparation for an announced public exhibition at the Metropolitan Museum which was first heroically announced then appropriately aborted, although it made its pitiful appearance in an exhibition at Florence's Palazzo Vecchio.

I wonder how the Crucifix appeared before this recent cleaning, which now offers an off-putting pseudo-patina. The so-called *Croce di Savonarola da Montelupo* attributed to the sculptor

5.1. A wooden Crucifix.

Baccio di Montelupo, whose career overlapped that of Michelangelo, is, in my view, a higher quality object and, *pace* to the medical doctors Massimo Gulisano and Pietro Antonio Bernabei, whose anatomy and proportions are visually more satisfying than the one attributed to Michelangelo.

The report by the good doctors on the knowledge of anatomy demonstrated by the author of the Crucifix, according to *Il Giornale dell'Arte*, was determining for the attribution to Michelangelo, as science seems to come to the aid of common sense. They claimed that no other artist *from those years* (my italics) had the kind of practice and familiarity with cadavers and could have been able to achieve such a true anatomy ("ad avvicinarsi tanto al vero anatomico").

The support for the attribution from two medical professionals requires a comment. A fundamental part of the *modus operandi* of the doctors was accepting the date of ca. 1495 for the Crucifix, as their starting point. Although basic to their conclusions, no evidence for that date exists at all, so that their statement about the revealed control of the anatomy "at that time" is gratuitous. The only reasonable fact in this series of assumptions is that Michelangelo, according to old sources, had an opportunity to study dead bodies at Santo Spirito and that he made a gift of a Crucifix as a sign of gratitude. This seems to have taken place following his return from Bologna which is known to have been in late 1495 and hence the date of the *Santo Spirito Crucifix* is achieved by indirection, but the date of the newly-identified Crucifix is pure conjecture created out of thin air.

What the doctors fail to do is as remarkable as what they have done. They do not compare the use of anatomy of the *Santo Spirito Crucifix* with the new Crucifix (Cf. Plate 13, Figs. 2.1 and 5.1).

At the heart of what I regard as the weakness of their argument is the impossible assumption regarding Michelangelo's view of nature, one that runs entirely against what we see in his art, whether sculpture, painting or drawing. He surely studied the human body, dead and alive, but he never imitated it. That is to say, Michelangelo was not a hyper-realist, which is what one extracts from the doctors' reasoning. Rather, he used anatomy to understand how the body functions, always rendering the nude figure within the compass of his own artistic style. He sought a personally calibrated ideal type, one the ancient Romans knew well, which was not a clone of a cadaver, even a handsome one, but an interpretation. That the artist who made the Crucifix was familiar with human anatomy may be true, although I am doubtful that such an assertion can be made without further evidence. Besides, what guarantee is there that the carver did not have a drawing or another wooden cross which had these characteristics, which he merely copied? If he were a skillful artisan working in the back streets of Florence sometime on either side of 1550, which is when I would tentatively date the sculpture, that scenario is likely.

The doctors write: "...siamo in grado di affermare con certezza che l'autore conosceva alla perfezione l'anatomia umana per diretta e prolungata esperienza settoria e che aveva sua grandissima capacità di rappresentarla con precisione."[9] ("We are in a position to affirm with certainty that the author knew perfectly human anatomy by direct and prolonged experience in the area and that he had excellent ability to represent human anatomy with precision.") The proponents of the attribution fail to realize that their new discovery could itself be a work from a period later than they assume, at a historic moment when greater emphasis on the study of human anatomy is apparent.

Besides the anatomy, another level of "scientific" support for the attribution was claimed, techno-scientific examination and tomographic X-rays ("indagini tecnico-scientifiche e all'esame tomografico a raggio X") which, still according to the article, were

---

[9]Gentilini, *op. cit.*, p. 75.

conducted for the purpose of achieving a dating and to reveal the technique of the execution. The results could be related to similar tests taken on the *Santo Spirito Crucifix*.

Science these days is an essential ingredient for any new attribution, as we have already seen for the *Northumberland Madonna*, whether offering persuasive information or not. To repeat a point made earlier, the appearance of science seems to be enough, and when accompanied by complex computer illustrations or diagrams, all the better. That they do not tell a great deal is another matter, but the failure to test the pigment on the surface or the age of the wood is a puzzling omission. These tests could not totally resolve the question, but they would have gone a long way in giving greater authority to the entire operation. The bottom line is that this attribution does not rest on science, but is based purely on the visual judgment of those involved, using presumed relationships with other works, many not by Michelangelo. All the rest is irrelevant paraphernalia: there is no support whatsoever of Michelangelo's authorship beyond the elemental connoisseurship judgment, which I suggest is faulty. The operation surrounding the Crucifix, like that surrounding the *Northumberland Madonna*, threatens history and the dignity of art. The inventiveness and creativity of a Michelangelo or a Raphael is seriously diminished when credited with the authorship of such mediocre objects. One can be sure that other similar little Crucifixes will pop up in the years to come, with claims of Michelangelo's authorship. To protect the reputation of Michelangelo it is imperative that the cycle is broken before, as it were, the "*minestrone*" becomes "*ribollita*".

5.2 The Piccolomini '*modello*'.

The conditions surrounding the attribution of drawings to Raphael are analogous to those of his paintings. Let us take as an example the well-known *The Journey of Aeneas Silvius Piccolomini to Basle*, a drawing or really a *modello* of considerable fame (Plate 15). Modern criticism is unanimous in considering that it was created for expansion into a cartoon. In turn, the cartoon was thought to have been used by Bernardino Pinturicchio in his cycle treating the "Life of Enea Silvio Piccolomini" (Plate 16) in what is called the Piccolomini Library, an appendage to the Cathedral of Siena. Without trying to reconstruct the relation of invention to the final step, the painted fresco, changes have taken place between the phases, this *modello* probably already representing a second stage. A first stage was almost certainly developed in the form of one or more quick sketches and studies, while the cartoon constitutes the third stage. Finally, there is the fresco itself.

The drawing located in Florence's Gabinetto dei Disegni (Uffizi, 520E) is number 56 in Joannides' influential catalogue of Raphael's drawings. Quite recently it was the subject of an article by T. Henry,[10] and was discussed in the exhibition catalogue for *Raphael from Urbino to Rome* at London's National Gallery.[11]

The *modello*, all but universally regarded as by Raphael, appears to confirm Vasari's account of how the young genius from Urbino, then under twenty, came to design the prestigious frescoes for his much older colleague in Siena. Vasari, who was ostensibly an ardent admirer of Michelangelo but actually a hearty closet devotee of Raphael, reports: "... Pope Pius II had given the commission for painting the library of the Duomo at Siena to Pinturicchio; and he, being a friend of Raphael, and knowing him

---

[10]"Raphael and Siena," *Apollo*, October 2004, pp. 51-56, with earlier bibliography.

[11]H. Chapman, T. Henry and C. Plazzotta, *Raphael from Urbino to Rome*, op. cit., pp. 23-25. See also *La Libreria Piccolomini nel Duomo di Siena*, Salvatore Settis, ed., Modena, 1998; Alessandro Angelini, "Pinturicchio e i suoi: dalla Roma dei Borgia alla Siena dei Piccolomini e dei Petrucci," in *Pio II e le arti. La riscoperta dell'antico da Federighi a Michelangelo*, Siena, 2005, pp. 526-529.

5.2. The Piccolomini 'modello'.

to be an excellent draughtsman, brought him to Siena, where Raphael made for him some of the drawings and cartoons for that work. The reason that he did not continue at it was that some painters in Siena kept extolling with vast praise the cartoon that Leonardo da Vinci had made in the Sala del Palazzo of a very beautiful group of horsemen..." ["...era stato allogato da Pio Secondo pontefice la libreria del Duomo di Siena dal Pinturicchio, il quale, essendo amico di Raffaello e conoscendolo ottimo disegnatore, lo condusse a Siena dove Raffaello gli fece alcuni dei disegni e cartoni di quell'opera; e la cagione che egli non continuò fu che, essendo in Siena da alcuni pittori con grandissime lodi celebrato il cartone che Leonardo da Vinci aveva fatto nelle sale del palazzo in Fiorenza d'un gruppo di cavalli bellissimo..."].[12]

In other words, the young Raphael acquired fame in Perugia and Città di Castello, and when Pius II (actually Pius III) commissioned Pinturicchio to execute the frescoes for the Piccolomini Library, that painter sent for his much younger friend Raphael and once in Siena he produced certain drawings and cartoons for the cycle. However, Raphael, still according to Vasari, left Siena to study the battle cartoon that Leonardo was making in Florence. In his life of Pinturicchio, Vasari's account differs slightly. "... He [Pinturicchio] was summoned to Siena by Cardinal Francesco Piccolomini to paint the library made by Pope Pius II in the Duomo of that city. It is true, indeed, that the sketches and cartoons for all the scenes that he painted there were by the hand of Raffaello of Urbino, then a youth, who had been his companion and fellow-disciple under the same Pietro [Perugino]... One of these cartoons is still to be seen at the present day in Siena, and some of the sketches, by the hand of Raffaello, are in our book." ["...fu da Francesco Piccolomini cardinale chiamato a Siena a dipignere la libreria stata fatta da Pio II nel Duomo di quella città. Ma è ben vero che gli schizzi et i cartoni

---

[12]Giorgio Vasari, '*Vite*...', Gaetano Milanesi, ed., Firenze 1885, IV, p. 319.

di tutte le storie che egli vi fece, furono di mano di Raffaello da Urbino allora giovinetto, il quale era stato uno compagno e condiscepolo appresso al detto Pietro... e di questi cartoni se ne vide ancora oggi uno a Siena e alcuni schizzi ne sono di man di Raffaello nel nostro libro."][13]

The consensus among modern art historians is virtually absolute with regard to Raphael's authorship of the Uffizi drawing, together with studies and sketches connected with it. On the other hand, should we not be on guard for Gombrich's "plausible rhetoric," in which a *Sybil* by Michelangelo was proved to be by Raphael, not only with regard to contemporary critics, but also earlier commentators including Giorgio Vasari? In the first place, Pinturicchio could not have been "uno compagno e condiscepolo" of Raphael at Perugino's shop. After all, when Raphael was a pupil in the late 1490s or early 1500s, Pinturicchio had long since established a stellar career in Umbria and in Rome.

While it is not theoretically impossible that an older, well-established and famous master could call upon the services of a young and talented but unproven artist to design a major cycle, the chances are slight bordering on the negligible. By that time, Pinturicchio was regarded as second only to Perugino among the best painters in Italy by the influential patron, Agostino Chigi.[14] Making Vasari's case even more improbable, the contract for the frescoes specifically requires that Pinturicchio execute the designs. Of course, those who have dealt with artists' contracts of the Renaissance are fully aware that contracts were broken all the time. Yet one can speculate to the effect that it would have been precisely the role of invention that the master would have retained for himself, out of ego if for no other reason. He might

---

[13] *Ibid.*, III, pp. 494-497 and also the notes by Milanesi, pp. 515-528.

[14] Naturally with historical hindsight, of which Vasari had more than his share, one might like to see the brilliance of the genius unveiled, at the expense of a painter who was never popular among critics of art anyway, and certainly not with Vasari.

5.2. The Piccolomini 'modello'.

have less compunction to pass on the more mechanical tasks, like the transferring of the *modello* to a cartoon, or the cartoon to the wall, to young assistants, even highly qualified ones.

In terms of the chronology, Raphael had not yet produced a work that would indicate a genuine challenge to Pinturicchio's compositional skills in 1503. Of course the story is appealing: like Giotto and Cimabue, the young genius not only overtakes his master, Perugino, but his master's major competitor, Pinturicchio, from another generation. Vasari tells of a similar incident with the young Michelangelo, who is said to have made a copy of a portrait by his teacher Ghirlandaio so cleverly that the master took it as his own work. In fact Vasari's *Vite* are full of brilliant pupils outdoing their doltish masters.

If Vasari's motivation was to hammer home a favorite theme as well as to stress Raphael's powers, a further impulse can be suggested. Vasari may have been propelled to elaborate his theory in order to enhance his personal holdings of drawings, like all dedicated collectors. It appears from the account of the Piccolomini cycle that Vasari himself owned some of what he regarded as preliminary drawings. He seems to have enhanced the pre-eminence of the objects he owned.

The story of Raphael interrupting his activity with Pinturicchio to go to Florence to observe Leonardo preparing to paint the *Battle of Anghiari* for the Palazzo della Signoria (1505), does not fit in terms of a sensible chronology. In fact, nothing quite fits in to support the belief that Raphael was the designer of the Piccolomini Library frescoes.

The evidence is not determining about the date of the Piccolomini commission and work on it, especially any role for Raphael.[15] Joannides' commentary in his catalogue of Raphael drawings, which is followed by Dr. Henry, exposes the inflexibility of modern art-historical thinking as well as providing an

---

[15]Cf. J. Beck, "A New Date for Pinturicchio's Piccolomini Library," *Paragone*, 419-423, 1985, p.140-143.

indication of how Vasari's assertion, which was largely gossip, became gospel. The two experts, along with most others, call the Uffizi drawing a "*modello*" by Raphael, no doubts expressed, with the date given as c. 1502-03 or 1503. Joannides predictably spins off on the basic assumption by claiming that "Raphael's" *modello* is far superior to the finished fresco, which reveals a "conceptual inferiority."

Why the drawing is not by Pinturicchio himself, which would make the most sense, and as it surely would have been regarded without Vasari's intervention, is a possibility never even entertained by modern scholars.[16]

To use the drawing as a document and give it great authority, as Professor Shearman has done, is a serious error in terms of method. Actually, the Harvard scholar treats the *modello* as a fixed point in Raphael's chronology without any shadow of doubt and adds to the confusion by also presenting the other surviving "*modello*", *The Meeting of Frederick III and Eleanor of Portugal* (Morgan Library). This badly damaged drawing is, according to Joannides, also datable to ca. 1503 and he gives it prestige by proposing that the composition anticipated the *Marriage of the Virgin*, which is dated 1504 (Plate 10). Of course, this unlikely reconstruction has no basis whatsoever in the confirmable facts.

As can be predicted, the attributions of both these *modelli* as certain, unchallengeable Raphaels have given birth to a slew of attributions of other lesser drawings to the artist.[17] As a product of an undocumented, and in this case chronologically unlikely, attribution to Raphael, scholars have opened a Pandora's box stuffed with "related" drawings, ultimately constructing an imprecise and incorrect profile of the artist. Such spinoffs would be avoided by operating according to more rigorous standards,

---

[16] Another possibility can be raised, although I do not think it has great strength, namely that the drawing was made from the finished fresco, or from the cartoon.

[17] For examples see Joannides, numbers 57v to 61r.

5.2. The Piccolomini 'modello'.

I am sure, but it would also reduce the number of drawings optimistically called by Raphael in circulation. Simply speaking, the two drawings attributed to Raphael and regarded as from about 1503 cannot be used as documents nor regarded as works by Raphael, certainly not documented ones.[18]

---

[18]Regrettably, the most recent monograph on Pinturicchio continues to regard them as such, the power of the consensus being too strong to resist. See P. Scarpellini and Maria Rita Silvestrelli, *Pinturicchio*, Milan, 2004. I must add that the book, an indispensable study of the material, is full of new documents, new insights, and new observations.

Chapter 6

A Case Study: The *Metropolitan Duccio*

The triumph surrounding the purchase of the *Northumberland Madonna* by the London National Gallery was shared in intensity and elation across the Atlantic by the Metropolitan Museum of Art with their own acquisition of a *Madonna* regarded as by the great Sienese master, Duccio di Buoninsegna. The events have a number of factors in common. To begin with, both museums paid record prices in the history of their respective institutions for these pictures despite their diminutive sizes. Additionally, the two sales have in common some of the same individuals, while the vehicle of acquisition was in each case a world-class auction house. The Metropolitan's painting was known as the *Stroganoff* or the *Stoclet Madonna*, but henceforth will be referred to as the *Metropolitan Duccio* (Fig. 6.1, Plate 6).

The *Metropolitan Duccio* (27 x 21 cm.) is close in size to the *Northumberland Madonna* including its frame, although the painted surface, 23.8 x 16.5 cm, is substantially smaller, so that by the square centimetre it is even more expensive. The painting was regarded as by Duccio di Buoninsegna ever since the first of two public appearances just a hundred years ago, at which time

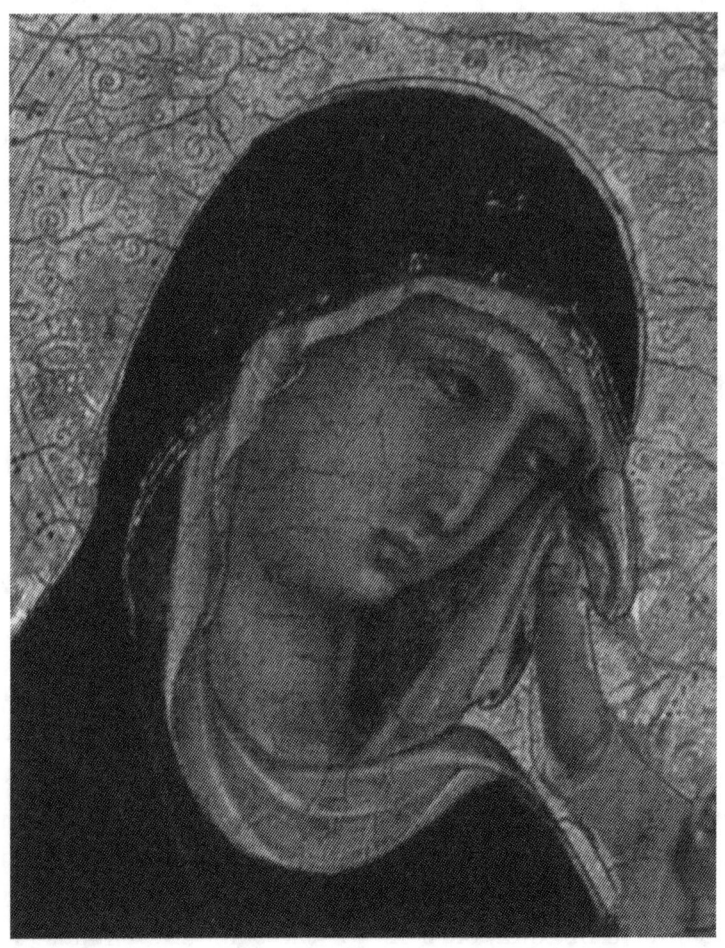

Figure 6.1: **Assigned to Duccio di Buonisegna (here rejected)**, *The Metropolitan Duccio* (detail), New York, Metropolitan Museum.

its first recorded home was a private collection in Rome.

The picture was unveiled at the historic 1904 exhibition of Sienese art in the Palazzo Pubblico as a late entry.[1] The fact

---

[1] *Mostra dell' Arte Antica Senese*, Siena, 1904, p. 38, no. 37. Coinciden-

remains that the *Metropolitan Duccio* has never been widely viewed "in the flesh," a circumstance which differs radically from that which surrounded the *Northumberland* picture. The two presumptive creators, apparently separated by 200 years, represent vastly diverse mentalities, epochs, period styles and personal languages. Duccio's visual idiom is tightly calibrated within a sophisticated Late Medieval visual tradition, Raphael's by a fully evolved Renaissance one.

The details surrounding the purchases of the pictures reveal analogies including exceptionally if not to say ridiculously high prices. It may not be relevant for the connoisseur to consider price or monetary value, but in both cases, since public money was involved and because the institutions are themselves public, at least an awareness of the expenditures seems to be in order. Nor can the involvement of the dominant auction houses be ignored. Christie's acted as an intermediary for the *Metropolitan Duccio* while Sotheby's had a central role in the sale of the *Northumberland Madonna*.

Additionally, both objects have abbreviated histories, and in fact the traceable provenance of the *Metropolitan Duccio* is significantly shorter than that of the London picture. Heirs of the Stoclet family of Brussels seem to have been the sellers, although an intermediary owner cannot be ruled out. The full story surrounding the sale remains to be told, including the exact amount of money paid.[2]

An article by Marco Grassi is a convenient starting point for a discussion of the *Metropolitan Duccio*, since it appears to

---

tally, to celebrate the 100th anniversary of the influential exhibition, another presentation also in the Palazzo Pubblico was held, with the title: "Il segreto della civiltà. La mostra dell'Arte Antica Senese del 1904 cento anni dopo" (Siena, Palazzo Pubblico, 18 Decembre 2005—5 Marzo 2006), where the old catalogue was displayed open to the page revealing the *Metropolitan Duccio*. This information was supplied to me by Piergiacomo Petrioli.

[2]Paul Jeromack, *The Art Newspaper*, 2004.

have a more or less official flavor.[3] A well-respected restorer, researcher, art lecturer and sometimes dealer based in New York City, Mr. Grassi is an international art market insider. He refers to the picture as the "miraculous newcomer" to the Metropolitan's collection which "has firmly maintained its place in the slim catalogue of Duccio... since it first surfaced in a Roman collection at the turn of the last century." Grassi continues by correctly reminding the reader that it was "inaccessible" for the past half-century, and "not one of the four scholars who have published full-dress monographic studies on Duccio since 1951 had ever seen the painting." From the point of view of proper connoisseurship, the fact alone that the object under scrutiny was not actually seen first-hand by experts for two generations constitutes a challenge to the seriousness of the enterprise and should have been a warning to potential buyers. At least in this respect, the circumstances are quite contrary to those surrounding the *Northumberland Madonna*, which was on public view at the National Gallery for over a decade prior to the consummation of the sale.

For the Duccio, then, the experts had to base their universally favorable (with one exception, and one by omission) evaluation of the attribution on an old black-and-white photograph of the work, which was furthermore in an uncertain state of conservation.[4] A respected and prolific expert of early Italian painting,

---

[3] Marco Grassi, "The Metropolitan Duccio," *The New Criterion*, Vol. 23/No. 6, February 2005.

[4] The Medievalist Florens Deuchler, who wrote a monograph on the artist (*Duccio*, Milan, 1984), questioned the attribution of the *Madonna and Child*, which he described as from "the orbit of Duccio." Cf. Calvin Tomkins, "The Missing Madonna: the Story Behind the Met's Most Expensive Acquisition," *The New Yorker*, 11 July 2005. Met Curator Christiansen describes the Swiss art historian's scholarship as "eccentric." Andrea Weber's recent monograph on Duccio (Cologne, 1997) left the picture out altogether, which is certainly not a sign of enthusiastic support for the work's status as an original.

University of Siena Professor Luciano Bellosi, whose name has occurred elsewhere in these pages, is an enthusiastic exponent of the painting's status as a genuine Duccio. He expressed his point of view in the impeccably produced catalogue of the acclaimed Duccio exhibition held in Siena in 2003-04.[5] That he himself had not seen the panel at the time he had written the entry is indicative if not actually shocking from the point of view of traditional connoisseurship.[6]

The unavailability of the work for hands-on study, from the point of view of a systematic methodology, provides a precarious foundation on which to base an attribution. To make the circumstances even more questionable, the Metropolitan Museum never tested the picture in their or any other independent laboratory *prior* to the purchase, but apparently only the year *after* (June-July 2005). Perhaps similar restrictions set forth by the Duke of Northumberland for the sale of his *Madonna* were also imposed by the unnamed owner of the *Metropolitan Duccio*.[7]

As it turns out, the favorable reception of the picture reverts back to opinions based upon the public presentation in 1904. After a century of virtually total obscurity, a viewing was en-

---

[5] *Duccio: alle origini della pittura senese, catalogo della mostra Siena, 2003*, Alessandro Bagnoli, Roberto Bartalini, Luciano Bellosi, eds., Milan, 2003.

[6] *Op. cit.*, p. 200, where Bellosi readily admits that "nessuno ha più visto con i propri occhi da molto tempo..." evidently including himself. What is even more revealing is that there was never a color illustration or transparency available to the Duccio experts until 2003. I can only assume that everybody used the old photos including the one reproduced in the catalogue of the 1904 exhibition.

[7] Without an independent, disinterested witness present, an element of doubt about the validity of the tests in the event the results prove negative has to be considered. The stakes are considerable, and heads could roll if the Metropolitan or the National Gallery reported that their new, expensive purchases are not what they were touted to be on physical grounds alone. One can only imagine the reaction of the members of the Boards of Trustees of the respective institutions.

thusiastically anticipated in late 2003 as part of the blockbuster Duccio exhibition, but that eventuality evaporated at the last minute. Apparently, at the time of the show the picture was in London being offered for private treaty sale through Christie's. Art gossip had it that the Louvre was interested in purchasing the little picture but had been out-maneuvered by the Metropolitan, which won the laurel by paying the 45-50 million dollar ticket. The well-informed and richly documented article by Calvin Tomkins in *The New Yorker* mentions that range.[8] Apparently the deep-pocketed Getty Museum had been approached as a potential buyer but passed on the picture as being too expensive.[9]

Like most of the writers on the subject, Grassi has high praise for the painting which he believes predates the completion of the *Maestà* (1308-1311) by a decade (Fig. 6.2). By placing it around 1300, he can contend that "one must realize that every aspect of this composition represents a departure from pre-existing convention." The early date requires that the painting be regarded as revolutionary. Incidentally, a pre-*Maestà* date presents problems for reconstructing Duccio's entire hypothetical development, although it does coincide with the consensus of the experts and the official position of the Metropolitan Museum. The precocious dating gives the object enormous art historical preeminence, especially with respect to the depiction of a shelf on brackets shown in perspective at the bottom. Christiansen goes so far as to assert (as quoted in Tomkins), "This is the first illusionistic parapet in European art."

For Grassi and implicitly for the Museum, Duccio would have set out the main lines of the *Maestà* years in advance: "one can

---

[8] Tomkins, 2005.

[9] This information was reported by *The Art Newspaper*'s Paul Jeromack (*op. cit.*). Perhaps the Getty saw themselves as over-committed for, after all, they had already agreed to purchase the *Northumberland Madonna*, but were outflanked by the National Gallery.

A Case Study: The Metropolitan Duccio   145

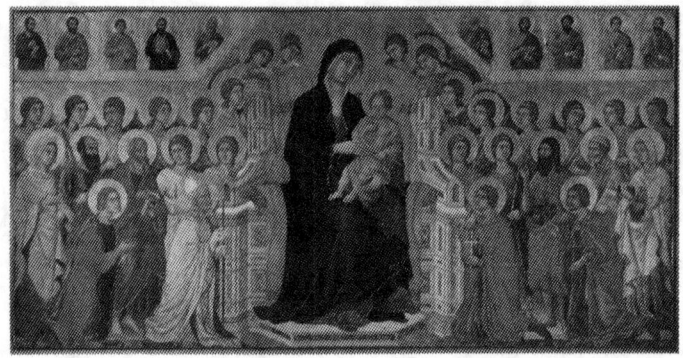

Figure 6.2: **Duccio, *Maestà*, Siena, Museo dell'Opera del Duomo.**

confidently state that Duccio had already achieved the high point of his stylistic development in the panel we can now admire at the Metropolitan." Such strong words lay a weighty burden on the tiny picture, one which, as will be demonstrated, it fails to support.

The preeminence of the picture on any level is difficult to maintain on the basis of the visual evidence. And, whatever the claims, the fact remains that the *Metropolitan Duccio* is a pure attribution to the Sienese master, which no documents or other historical evidence from the artist's lifetime confirm. What is more, there is no information about the painting's existence until 1901, six hundred years after the presumptive date of its creation.

The fact remains that the dating to ca. 1300 is extremely arbitrary, based upon comparisons with other undated and attributed works. The core object for Duccio's chronology has to be the *Maestà* with its chorus of images on the main fields (i.e. back and front) and in the predella scenes. That Duccio somehow modeled his brilliant and super-refined *Maestà* or even honed his style on this modest little picture is a stretch in common sense, whatever the experts singly or *en masse* might be prepared to assert.

Speaking in his guise as a restorer, Grassi's claim that the "image has survived in a remarkably fine state" should have considerable weight, although it is contradicted by earlier writers, a matter which I will address shortly. Grassi states that the Met's long-time Chief Curator Everett Fahy, along with Keith Christiansen, the Jayne Wrightsman, Curator of European Paintings, and Laurence Kanter, Curator of the Lehman Collection, constituted the team which promoted the purchase. Only Christiansen and the Director flew to London for the purpose of inspecting the picture firsthand, however. They were accompanied by Dorothy Mahon, the museum's head of painting conservation. The three "...spent a long time looking at it," Mr. Christiansen told *New York Times* interviewer Carol Vogel: "It's not only an incredibly beautiful picture; it's also unbelievably moving." He added that "it's a picture created for patient viewing...and as you look at it, the image grows in your imagination. Here Duccio has explored intimacy in a new way." *The New York Times*, who had an editorial praising the purchase described the work in an article by its chief art critic as "a sweet and melancholy masterpiece buoyed by grace." (Dec. 20, 2004)

The attentive reader might recognize an echo of an internalizing process on the part of the Metropolitan trio as they held the object in their hands (per Tomkins), similar to that described for the wooden cross discussed in Chapter 5 as well as Frederick Hartt's account of the gesso *'modello'* of Michelangelo's *David*.

I believe that it is fair to observe that none of the four Metropolitan museum staff members said to have been involved in the purchase are specifically experts of *Duecento* and *Trecento* painting, although Kanter has an impressive curriculum with regard to the study of Sienese art of the following century. But once Director Philippe de Montebello was convinced of the picture's validity, the Trustees were brought around to approving the record-breaking purchase, far and away the most expensive in the institution's history, out-distancing Jasper Johns' *White Flag* purchased in 1998 which cost less than half that amount.[10]

Mr. de Montebello's evaluation of the work can be summed up by his description of it as a "marvelous painting, small in size but immense in achievement and influence." He makes reference to what he regards as the picture's place in the history of art, evidently a motivating factor for the acquisition:

"Filling a gap in our Renaissance collection that even the Metropolitan had scant hopes of ever closing, the addition of the Duccio will enable visitors for the first time to follow the entire trajectory of European painting from its beginnings to the present. Moreover, the Duccio *Madonna and Child* is a work of sublime beauty. This was a unique opportunity not only to add a masterpiece to the Museum's holdings but to give its collections a new dimension."[11]

Besides being "marvellous" and "sublime" the explanation for the painting's acquisition lies with the high-minded educative aspirations of the museum. In this respect, the concept which rests on the history of art is worth rehearsing. The Metropolitan Museum's website explains that, together with Giotto, Duccio is considered "one of the two principal founders of Western European painting." While Giotto's place is assured by fact, Dante, tradition and scholarship, the claim for Duccio's commanding position is fragile, if not straight-out incorrect. Jan van Eyck certainly would be a better candidate, to name only one non-Italian.

While Italy's impact on the evolution of Western painting was weighty, other national traditions should not be ruled out.

---

[10] On the basis of square inches it must now seem like a particular bargain C. Vogel, "The Met Makes Its Biggest Purchase Ever," *New York Times*, 10 Nov. 2004. Cf. The website of the Metropolitan Museum of Art as well as a press release, dated 10 November 2004.

[11] Vogel, *op. cit.*

And if one were to seek another Italian many others come to mind ahead of Duccio, starting with Masaccio.

Duccio's place is in point of fact more provincial (Southern Tuscany) than pan-Italian, much less pan-European. He is definitely the founder of the Sienese School, which had an unusually tenacious life, with powerful, highly original contributions by Ambrogio Lorenzetti and Simone Martini, Duccio's influential pupils. Broadly speaking, their language continued to flourish well into the next century, although with much less impressive results in comparison with other Italian schools, including those of Florence, Venice, Padua and Ferrara.

My characterization is that despite the appearance of a really ranking if idiosyncratic personality, Sassetta, Sienese painting became something of a dead end following the transfer of Simone Martini to France toward the middle of the 14th century. A century later, masters of more than local reputation such as Vecchietta and Francesco di Giorgio finally managed to overcome the imprint of the Ducciesque tradition once and for all. One must conclude, consequently, that the Metropolitan considered it necessary to overstate Duccio's historical role to justify their expensive purchase to the Trustees, their donors and the general public, but it may have a harder time swaying the art historical community in the coming decades.

As the Museum correctly claimed, few if any Duccios were available for purchase. After all, Duccio's masterpiece, the *Maestà*, is housed in the Museo dell'Opera del Duomo in Siena and other works by him are in churches and museums, mainly in Italy. A few minor but magnificent portions of the *Maestà* were sold off in the 18th century, of which one, the *Temptation of Christ*, found its way to the Frick Collection on Fifth Avenue, eight city blocks from the Met, as one of that superb collection's crown jewels. The Frick picture is certainly contemporary with the rest of the *Maestà*, and few doubt its autograph status as Duccio's. To make their new acquisition more distinctive, however, the Met found it necessary to belittle such "fragments"—that is the word they used—while their Madonna is a "complete and independent work." Even this self-serving claim does not appear to be true: at least some scholars have expressed the opinion that it was once part of a triptych, in which case it would be a 'fragment' too.[12]

I believe that the connoisseur these days must be aware of the socio-anthropological realities of modern culture. Institutional explanations about almost anything connected with their operations are motivated by media considerations, as is the case with the National Gallery and the *Northumberland*. Consequently, the public as well as the specialist must be wary of claims about works of art from even distinguished museums. Fund raising considerations lie behind actions and positions offered to the public. The connoisseur should recognize the risk that history itself is manipulated for the sake of *"bella figura,"* to please sponsors, trustees, governmental agencies and the general museum visitors.

For the new owner of the Duccio-like Madonna, Mary Logan's exhibition review of 1904 in the *Gazette des beaux-arts* is a lynchpin for their attribution. Mr. Christiansen termed it an "eloquent appraisal" and he characterized Logan as an "influential connoisseur of Italian Renaissance art." She is quoted in an English translation of the original French by the Met as, "Perhaps the most perfect work [in the exhibition] is the little Madonna of Duccio belonging to Count Gregory Stroganoff... which, small though it is, offers so much majesty, dignity, and profound sentiment. Taken alone, it is worth all the other paintings exhib-

---

[12]Vittorio Lusini, *In onore di Duccio di Buoninsegna e della sua scuola*, Siena, 1903, p. 140, cat. # 5, where he described it as a "tavola rettangolare CON CORNICE RIFATTA [my caps]; già parte di un trittico a sportelli [*sic*]. Richard Offner's opinion is reported in *Duccio: alle origini della pittura senese, op. cit.*, p. 200. The wings, if there ever were any, have not been identified.

ited under the name of Duccio."[13] Mary Logan was the wife of Bernard Berenson, whose home, Villa I Tatti, is now Harvard's sumptuous Renaissance study center in the hills above Florence. Unlike the opinions of her husband, Mary Logan's are not especially treasured in the annals of art history. However, Berenson appears also to have held a high opinion of the picture, although the representative of Duveen, a firm with whom he worked for decades, is quoted in a letter of 1936 as describing it as "very small and ineffective." Besides, Duveen's agent goes on to lament that the painting's condition was unsatisfactory "and there was

---

[13] M. Logan, "L'Exposition de l'ancien art siennoise," *Gazette des beaux-arts*, xxxii, 3e période, Sept. 1904, p. 210. The entire passage related without interpolations to the Duccio reads: "L'oeuvre la plus parfaite peut-être est la petite Madone de Duccio appartenant au comte Greogri Stroganoff (salle XXVII, no. 37) qui, toute petite qu'elle soit, offre tant de majesté, de dignité et de profondeur de sentiment. Elle vaut, à elle seule, tous le autres tableaux exposés sous le nom de Duccio. Ils sont, pour la plupart, de travaux d'atelier qui ressemblent à Duccio par la facture et le dessin, mais sans avoir le sentiment subtil de la forme et de la ligne qui lui est propre." And can be translated as follows: [Translation by the author] "The most perfect work may be the little *Madonna* by Duccio belonging to Count Gregori Stroganoff (salle XXVII, no 37) which, besides being as little as it is, offers so much majesty, dignity and profound sentiment. It is worth, all by itself, all the other panels exhibited under the name of Duccio. They are for the most part works of the workshop which resemble Duccio for its structure and in term of design, but without having the subtle sentiment of the form and of line which is precisely his." The Met's placement of the insert in brackets "[in the exhibition]" is disingenuous and misleading, because it gives a certain priority to the picture over all pictures in the entire exhibition which was not her intention. In fact, it was not even illustrated in her article. The phrase should not have been inserted at all, but if one were to insist it would better have been placed in the second sentence as "all the other paintings '[in the exhibition]' exhibited under the name of Duccio," whatever miserable pictures they were. In other words for Logan it was perhaps the best of a mediocre lot of Duccios, which were all from his workshop. Hence among the Met's few eye-witnesses Logan's praise of the picture is relative and hardly merits a triumphal purchase.

no colour left in the picture."[14] Can such a damningly negative judgment over the quality and the condition be easily dismissed as simply self-serving, especially when the goal was business? Nor is the Museum's assumption that the painting's "unknown owner must have appreciated the privileged access to the sacred figures that Duccio's innovations gave him" be taken as anything other than pure fantasy.

In seeking to construct a provenance for the *Metropolitan Duccio*, all that can be said with confidence is that it was acquired by Count Gregory [Grigorii] Stroganoff, of *beef alla Stroganoff* fame, for his collection in Rome, shortly after 1900. How the picture was obtained is open to disagreement. According to Stroganoff's own testimony, he found it in an antique shop somewhere in Tuscany and apparently made the attribution to Duccio himself, while Met Curator Keith Christiansen thinks it is more convincing that the Count acquired the painting from a Roman dealer.[15] The picture and the entire Stroganoff collection was sold off, beginning in 1910 after the Count's death, with the final dispersal occurring in 1925, according to Grassi. Paul Jeromack's information differs slightly, as he has it purchased by

---

[14] As reported by Tomkins, *op. cit.* Given the negative evaluation of the picture's condition, one has to assume that considerable restorative work was undertaken after 1936.

[15] According to Tomkins the author Antonio Muñoz in the catalogue of the Stroganoff collection (Part II), claimed that "the Count found his Duccio in an antique shop 'in Tuscany,' had it restored [*pace* Christiansen], and personally identified it as a work by Duccio." Why Christiansen dismissed the report from a source intimate with the Count (i.e. Muñoz) needs a better explanation than the one he offers, namely that it does not seem to have been heavily restored, a condition which, if true, would for him speak against an antique dealer's possession. Besides, in my opinion, the painting does show ample restorations, although the Met Curator insists: "It is in excellent condition" and alternatively, "It's in a very pure state." The *New York Times* (Dec. 20, 2004) goes further referring to it as "a miracle of preservation." Of course, it would not be such a miracle if it were 125 years old, not 700.

Adolphe Stoclet of Brussels in 1923 from the Stroganoff heirs in Rome, while Grassi says that the picture was purchased by the Stoclets from a Florentine dealer soon after World War I and not directly from the Russian owners. The evidence such as there is indicates the transfer occurred in early 1923, arranged through the Sangiorgi auction house in Rome to the Stoclets, according to correspondence in the Duveen files as cited by Tomkins.[16]

Since provenance can be helpful for the creation of a convincing attribution, a few more lines about the *Metropolitan Duccio* in this regard are in order.

The work was one of many acquired shortly after 1900 by Count Stroganoff as he was filling his newly finished Roman palace with an array of art objects from diverse periods, media and categories. In other words, he had constructed a substantial collection *ex novo*, comprised of big name artists and apparently impressive artefacts. Obviously the Russian aristocrat must have had the help of one or more dealers and scholars who were able to locate appropriate works for him. As was the case with an overwhelming majority of objects which the collector acquired along with the *Metropolitan Duccio*, they were unpublished (*"inediti"*). In other words, the objects were unknown or at least had not appeared in scholarly monographs, journals, catalogues, or been presented in exhibitions, and consequently had not been subjected to evaluation within the discipline. Along with the others, the *Metropolitan Duccio* was, in effect, a new object to the field, with no previous history.

As an aside, the Stroganoff collection was filled with mediocre works, including possible forgeries and fakes, as well as a handful of more convincing objects. Among the latter was at least one other picture which ended up in the Met, the very fine *Griggs Crucifixion* sometimes attributed to Giovanni Toscani (and quite recently to Fra Angelico), and a tabernacle in the Hermitage related to Fra Angelico.

---

[16]Tomkins, *op. cit.*

As an example of a large number of problematic works, I am illustrating a medieval sculpture known as the *Veronese Madonna*, and although there are experts who would vouch for it, Dossena or another forger of his ilk seems to me its likely author[17] (Fig. 6.3).

As already mentioned, the *Metropolitan Duccio* was presented to the art public in 1904 in the memorable exhibition, *Arte Antica Senese*. Besides the praise from Mary Logan, it was singled out in a review by F. Mason Perkins which appeared in *The Burlington Magazine*, and was reprinted in Italian.[18] A decade later, the local scholar Vittorio Lusini wrote that it was part of a triptych and its frame had been remade.[19] This account also runs contrary to the view put forth by Dr. Christiansen, who says that "it remains in its original frame, singed along the bottom edge by devotional candles."[20] Christiansen is also quoted as saying "Photographs of the work from the 19th century reveal two burns on the bottom edge of the frame, no doubt from candles lighted over many years in which the 'Madonna' was used as a devotional object, probably in someone's bedroom." To my knowledge, no photographs of it from the 19th century are known. The indentations, which are still visible on the object's frame today, could very well have been man-made, fashioned to give the appearance of age and wear. Neither of the two unequal indentations is in the middle of the picture where one would expect to find them, if burned by a candle, or at least aligned below each of the sacred figures. And of course, if Lusini was

---

[17]About the sculptor and forger Alceo Dossena (1878-1937), see Lidia Azzolini, *Alceo Dossena: l'arte di un grande "falsario"*, Cremona, 2004; *Falsi d'autore: Icilio Federico Joni e la cultura del falso tra Otto e Novecento*, exh. Cat. Gianni Mazzoni, ed., Siena, 2004; Walter Lusetti, *Alceo Dossena scultore*, Roma, 1955.

[18]F. Mason Perkins, "The Sienese Exhibition of Ancient Art," *The Burlington Magazine*, 1904, pp. 581-584.

[19]Cf. V. Lusini, *op. cit.* See note 12, above.

[20]Vogel, 2004,*op. cit.*

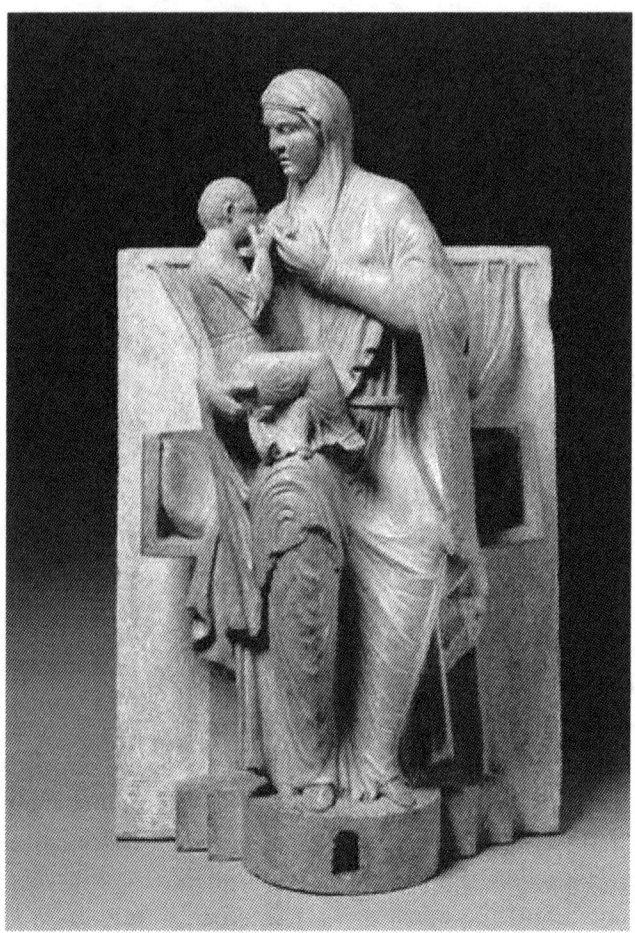

Figure 6.3: *Madonna del Veronese*, **unknown collection (formerly Rome, Stroganoff Collection).**

correct about the frame having been remade, why the burns anyway? Instead of supporting the authenticity of the picture, could they be understood as a serious challenge? Unquestionably the authenticity of the frame leaves unanswered questions.

Including a discussion of the *Metropolitan Duccio* in a book entitled the *Crisis of Connoisseurship* permits the introduction of an issue or aspect of the connoisseur's task which has yet to be faced squarely: that of quality, in distinction to the identification of authorship. A painting may be an original Duccio, Raphael, Giovanni Nessuno or Amico di Sandro and still be uninspired or downright poor in terms of quality.

Defining the quality of a work of art is inevitably a daunting task which lies to the east of a never-never land of taste and a viewer's concept of beauty, however one might wish to define that impossible concept. Yet most "art people" know exactly what is meant. That is, one can have great Raphaels, good ones, and uninspired ones, a condition presumably true for all artists, including Duccio. An example of this wide range is found in Picasso's vast *oeuvre*, where all levels of quality and invention, whatever standards one might seek to apply, appear to be represented. Of course, a raft of copies and outright forgeries are around too, but this is not the issue at hand.

Added to the fundamental task of isolating authorship, then, should not the connoisseur also call attention to those works which he regards as inferior or "minor"? It seems to me that such a function is not only appropriate but obligatory. All Picassos are not created equal, nor are all Raphaels, nor all Duccios. Formulating distinctions is a service to the public as well as to specialists. Of course, there will always be disagreements, even radical ones, among experts, *de gustibus non est disputandum*, but such is the nature of the beast. I believe that notwithstanding skirmishes, substantial agreement can be expected when it comes to absolute quality, once vested interests, communication operatives, and outside pressures are swept aside.

What can be said beyond the indications already raised about the excellence of the *Metropolitan Duccio*? As we have seen, in public statements Met officials were ecstatic about the quality of the little picture, as was the sycophantic press, led by the *The New York Times*.

Before pursuing the point, we must concede that quality and authenticity are not entirely separable. After all, the connoisseur cannot avoid the issue of attribution whether the object is good or bad. Hence in one schema of classification the *Metropolitan Duccio* could be:[21]

1. *An original work by the hand of Duccio;*

2. *A picture emanating from Duccio's workshop, that is, executed by his "school" with some intervention of the master;*

3. *A work from a shop (bottega) in Siena contemporary with Duccio which imitates his style;*

4. *A copy of a lost work by Duccio from an undisclosed period;*

5. *A work from the early trecento pertaining to one of the previous possibilities, which survived in very poor condition and which was "revitalized" at different times;*[22]

6. *An imitation or reconstruction, in simple terms, a straight-out fake, based upon indications found in works by or presumed to be by Duccio, not long before its purchase by Stroganoff (ca. 1901).*

---

[21] I do not insist upon the primacy or infallibility of this plan but rather offer it as an effort to organically begin the development of such a schema, with the goal of eventually achieving one that can be applied widely.

[22] Since the back was cleaned of everything except bits of gesso residue presumably in the cracks, it is possible that an old wreck of an image there had been removed. Had there been any clues about what was there originally, they would have been effectively removed. In this hypothetical and speculative reconstruction of events, eventually the back was covered with a wooden grid, supposedly to keep the wood stable. One suggestion is that the old back was used to make an entirely new (fake) picture, which would be the *Metropolitan Duccio* as it appears today. Naturally it had to have been prepared with some sort of ground before the painting and gilding was applied.

The technical evidence and the historical data which relate to all these possibilities were not available to the Museum at the time they purchased the painting. In the summer of 2005, long after the sale had been consummated and after the picture had been put on public display, the picture was brought to the Met's lab for evaluation and possible treatment, but apparently nothing dramatic has been found, and as far as I can gather, noteworthy treatment was not deemed necessary.

The limited provenance already referred to is a troubling consideration shared with the vast majority of works from the Stroganoff Collection which was, after all, formed *ex novo*. Besides, the fact that few if any experts have examined the work firsthand in the past half century or more does little to establish an atmosphere upon which to build confidence in its authenticity. Furthermore, differences of opinion regarding its state of preservation and the originality of the frame as well as its form as conceived—either as part of a triptych or as an independent unit all to itself—must leave the disinterested connoisseur uneasy. Having examined it on the wall of the museum, I am prepared to make observations about its quality.[23]

As a preamble, one must recognize the existence of a special love affair for what in the past was referred to as the Italian Primitives, a phenomenon which goes back at least to the early 19th century. Sienese art in particular captured the affection of Anglo-American and German collectors. In this context, Duccio, the Sienese *caposcuola*, has always had an enormous appeal which rests upon the brilliance of the *Maestà* and its justified fame. Art experts have favorite domains, and for many Italianists including Berenson (who purchased for his own collection at I Tatti more than one fake), Millard Meiss and John Pope-

---

[23] As is my custom, I often go to picture galleries and museums accompanied by artist friends, and in this case I wish to thank Michael Daley who shared with me his insights upon first seeing the newly acquired picture at the Met.

Hennessy, one was *trecento* Siena. As a result, over time, even the most minor, inept, and often nameless Sienese practitioners of 14th- and 15th-century have found a place in the hierarchy constructed in the handbooks, monographs and exhibition catalogues.

Unquestionably Sienese painting deserves a distinctive cubicle within the labyrinth of Western art history, based upon the distinctive contributions of Duccio, Ambrogio Lorenzetti and Simone Martini. At the same time, their followers and imitators have been consistently overvalued. Lesser Madonna and Child paintings with gold backgrounds which were produced by the hundreds if not thousands represent an antiquarian's dream, but they are not especially rewarding as artistic artifacts. In simple terms, no fairness principle is operative in the history of art or art criticism. Not every artist, whether good, bad, or indifferent, automatically gets a turn at bat or a moment of glory.

I suggest that the enthusiasm for the little painting reflects a reservoir of affection for Sienese art and for Duccio, combined with nostalgia for the college classroom where his *Maestà* is inevitably shown in every Introduction to Western Art course. The presenter can be counted upon to recount how the entire city of Siena was out cheering in the streets when the giant double-sided altarpiece was carried to the high altar of the Cathedral in 1311.

Hence if only by transference, the name of Duccio alone could inspire admiration for the little picture now at the Met, a situation which has nothing to do with whether it is genuine or not, or of high quality or not. To the extent it embodies elements of Duccio's language and reflects, even obliquely, Duccio's remarkable artistic statement, the painting functions as a Duccio in a society which sees as much with its ears as with its eyes.

Even a fake or objects of minimal value can engender genuine passion and stir in the memory authentic images which have the power to uplift. After all, one experiences authentic emotions when contemplating a slide, reproduction or a copy, so why not with fakes? An echo, shadow, or hint of the uniqueness of the original can come across, bringing with it rewards. If the picture is *not* by Duccio *nor* his immediate circle, *nor* of his time period, which I believe to be the case, something of Duccio's aura still surrounds it.[24] The Metropolitan's Director and various curators surely were moved; but, of course, that does not change the status of the object nor transform a fake into something genuine.

We often find that with extended contemplation, as described specifically in the case of the *Metropolitan Duccio* and the *Michelangelo Cross*, the viewer's involvement increases geometrically. The power assumed to be found in the art work increases which, in turn, affects the judgment of the quality of the object. Just as a viewer can contemplate for hours objects of high quality so can he contemplate ones of little artistic consequence, like the *Northumberland Madonna*, those notorious fake Vermeers, an absurd Magdalene attributed to Leonardo, fake Modigliani sculptures, the "*modello*" of Michelangelo's *David*, or an oversize Etruscan Warrior and come away with a compelling experience.

I do not doubt for a moment that upon confronting the object, the Met experts were deeply taken with it, unquestionably in large measure because of its reputation as a Duccio. And the longer they looked the more enthusiastic they became in a self-generating cycle. In my opinion, this proves absolutely nothing about the authenticity of the object. Actually most connoisseurs rely upon their immediate, gut reaction to an art object, after only a few moments, nearly a blink of the eye, to provide indications about authenticity and quality.

Let us now turn to the *Metropolitan Duccio* for a hard look, both in terms of quality and in terms of what is presented. In my view, the most damaging if not shattering element for an identification of Duccio as its author is precisely the revolutionary feature which ironically has been much vaunted by the Museum and by the painting's proponents. The parapet or shelf is lo-

---

[24]Bellosi, *loc. cit.*

cated not merely below but on a plane *in front of* the image of Mary and the Child. With brackets rendered in an elementary perspective, the parapet's pictorial function has been compared to its usage by Giovanni Bellini nearly two hundred years later (Fig. 6.4).[25] Professor Bellosi writes that the parapet is highly innovative, almost "futuristic", because it constitutes a precedent for many European paintings of the 15th century. ("Il davanzale in basso, formato da un piano aggregante che viene sorretto da una fila di mensole... è in se stesso un'invenzione novissima e quasi futuribile, perché costituisce precedente per tanti dipinti del Quattrocento europeo.")[26] I find the language somewhat obscure in English, and possibly in Italian too, so I have reproduced the original text.

We are asked to believe that the little picture represents a formidable leap into the future of Western painting by establishing a plane in front of Mary and the Child, characteristic of Renaissance (not Medieval) pictures. The feature has to be considered a unicum for the period of around 1300, and as such is regarded as constituting an unparalleled innovation, which for the proponents of Duccio's authorship somehow guarantees their case. Instead, the parapet and the concept which gave rise to it must be taken as a devastating challenge to Duccio's authorship altogether and to the presumptive dating to the early 1300s.

Max J. Friedländer, one of the most insightful writers on connoisseurship in the previous century, has provided a warning which his modern colleagues at the Metropolitan and elsewhere appear to have overlooked. "Experienced and ingenious forgers," he reminds us, "aim at extracting from several archetypes an apparently new whole. In putting together heterogeneous parts they give themselves away. They will imitate, say, the 15th century manner of painting, but will choose a motif or movement

---

[25] The perspective is also somewhat puzzling because it is not central, which would be expected.

[26] Bellosi, *loc. cit.*

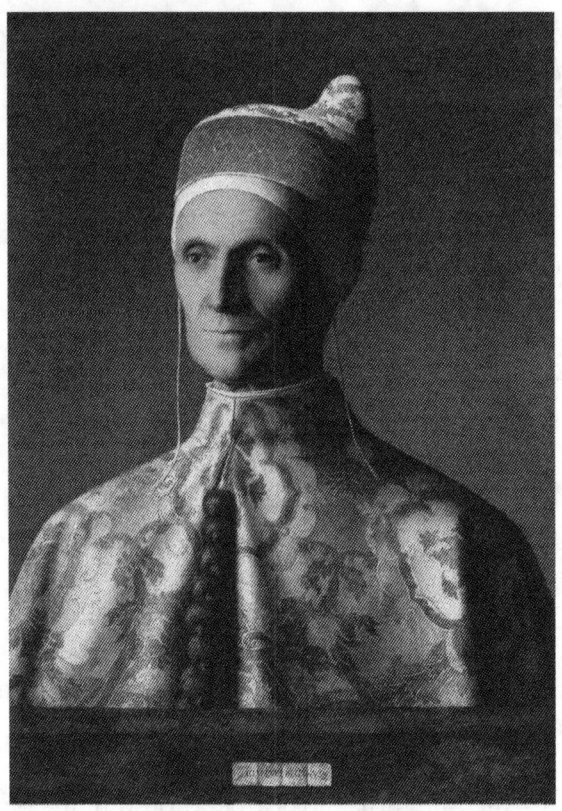

Figure 6.4: **Giovanni Bellini,** *Portrait of the Doge Leonardo Loredan,* **London, National Gallery.**

characteristic of the 16th century; or they will place a head-gear of the 16th century on the cranium with a coiffure of the 15th century. *Confusion of styles and disharmony are typical of a forgery...*" (italics added).[27]

---

[27]M. J. Friedländer, "On Art and Connoisseurship" (1942), reprinted in R. D. Spencer, ed., *The Expert versus the Object: Judging Fakes and False Attributions in the Visual Arts*, Oxford and New York, 2004, pp. 39-40. Needless to say, these remarks can be effectively applied to the *Northum-*

The issues surrounding the *Metropolitan Duccio* and the *Northumberland Raphael* are reflected in a longtime dispute over the authenticity of another even smaller picture, *St. Jerome in his Study*, located in the Detroit Institute of Arts. In the face of a consensus which regards the picture as by Jan van Eyck, challenges to its authenticity have been put forward, in particular by R. H. Marijnissen and L. Kockaert.[28] Among the shared factors with the *Metropolitan Duccio* is the lack of a longtime history of the object (ironically it is said to have come from Italy), the absence of evidence of transfer, and as with the *Northumberland*, claimed *pentimenti*, and, again like the London painting, the appearance of lapis lazuli and lead-tin yellow. (p.38) Marijnissen regards the Detroit picture as probably a fake of the "pasticcio-type." His general observation can be fittingly applied to the *Metropolitan Duccio*.

No other Sienese paintings of the Madonna revealing the innovative parapet functioning as a plane from Duccio's time and even a century later have been found. Certainly none exist among Duccio's confirmed works. Consequently, we are asked to believe the impossible: Duccio at a fairly young age made a breakthrough which he himself totally ignored in his other works. True enough, the motif of a foreshortened shelf on brackets is found in early wall painting, especially in the circle of Giotto in Assisi and objects dependent upon that tradition as Bellosi has indicated, but in addition to being vastly different in scale, the element does not operate as a form *in front of* an image but instead serves as a kind of base for the figuration, and therefore can hardly be regarded as the same thing.[29]

---

berland *Madonna* as well.

[28]"The Detroit Saint Jerome. The story of an interdisciplinary approach," in *Mededelingen van der KoninklijkeAcademie voor Weternschappen, Letteren en Schone Kunsten van Belgie*, 1996, n. 1, offprint.

[29]The shelf on brackets becomes a typical motif for relief sculptors, especially Andrea Pisano on the first bronze doors of the Florentine Baptistery, but spatially the figures stand on, rather than behind, it.

One must apply the test of common sense, advocated right along in these pages, and seek an explanation for this revolutionary element in the *Metropolitan Duccio*. Can a major invention be forgotten by the very artist who is said to have formulated it, and can it be ignored by his greatest pupils and neglected for more than 100 years? An answer is, obviously, no. Clear-headed logic therefore brings us to an explanation. Whoever produced the *Metropolitan Duccio* must have been aware of of the depiction of space and planes in Renaissance painting. He must have worked up this aspect of his picture from hindsight rather than foresight. Thus the innovation represented by the parapet offers a *post quem* for the little painting of after ca. 1450 in Italy, and probably a generation earlier in the Netherlands, in either case a century after the lifetime of Duccio di Buoninsegna (Figs. 1.2, 1.3, 6.4).

Another puzzling aspect of the picture is the treatment of the Virgin's garment. The typical highlighting of linear gold patterns derived from Byzantine painting for Mary's clothes, quite common for pictures even after 1300 in Siena, are absent in the *Metropolitan Duccio* (Plate 6). But more revealing is the treatment of the gold-accented borders of Mary's garment which proves to be yet another unsettling element which speaks against the attribution to Duccio. These borders or edges are confused, inelegant and hesitant, forming dreary swings which are uncharacteristic of Duccio's confirmed works, like the *Madonna of the Franciscans* in Siena's Pinacoteca (Fig. 6.5). In other words, Duccio's impeccable control of design is totally absent in the Metropolitan's painting.[30]

The Child's raised arm which appears like that of an amputee, constitutes another disconcerting element. While nobody should expect Duccio to draw with the anatomical precision of

---

[30] One must also wonder about the status of the London National Gallery's *Duccio Triptych* in a "perfect state of preservation" which reveals similar features, and which the Gallery dates 1300-1305.

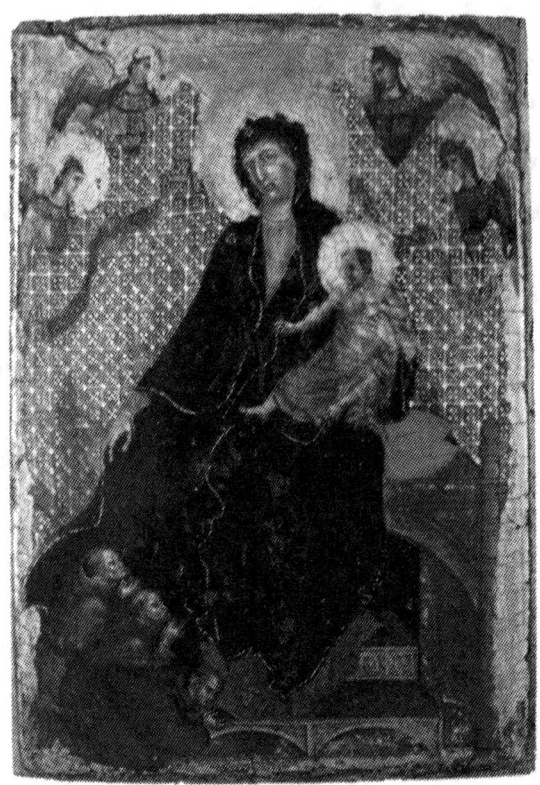

Figure 6.5: **Duccio di Buoninsegna**, *The Franciscan Madonna*, **Siena Pinacoteca**.

a Leonardo da Vinci, one might expect the limbs and hands in the little painting to be consistent with Duccio's treatment in securely documented works, which is not the case.

The report in the *New Yorker*, citing the Met's head conservator of paintings, to the effect that the Madonna's blue dress was painted very skillfully with azurite and lead white caught my attention.[31] I was surprised to learn that for a precious painting

---

[31]Tomkins (2005) was told by conservator Dorothy Mahon that "the mod-

instead of using the rarer and more expensive blue, lapis lazuli, otherwise known as natural ultramarine, the artist applied the cheaper azurite. My point may appear to be nitpicking but it presents yet one more question mark surrounding the authenticity of the painting.

Issues already raised about the frame also serve to undermine the attribution of the painting to the early *trecento*. As things now stand, we cannot be sure whether it is the original or was remade as at least one specialist proposed and in which case, when and why. The suffering the frame has experienced could be the product of natural aging and wear and tear, although against this possibility is the fact that the picture surface seems to have suffered less. The frame's signs of age could have been created intentionally, for the purpose of making the little altarpiece appear old, a trick frequently used by forgers.[32] Federico Zeri reminds us that Siena and Florence at the beginning of the 20th century were a true "factory of forgers" who frequently used old pictures which were poorly preserved and of low quality for making their forgeries, in such a manner that a fake can have old portions.[33] Another element which is incongruous with the early 14th century dating is the way in which light appears to fall on the top of the parapet or bracket.

Bearing in mind the serious challenges to Duccio's authorship

---

elling of the folds in the Virgin's deep-blue mantle was largely intact. Duccio had used a high-quality blue made from azurite". Mahon said, "The buildup was so skillfully done with different colors of azurite and then lead white in the final one."

[32]Since fakers regularly use old materials including old wood for their panels and for their frames, the age might turn out to be old. If it is from the wrong century, however, the credibility of the Duccio attribution would be further endangered.

[33]F. Zeri, *Dietro l'imagine. Conversazioni sull'arte di leggere l'arte*, Milan, 1990, Capitolo/conversazione 4. The reader might also keep in mind that Stroganoff obtained the picture in Tuscany. See also Gianni Mazzoni, "Falsi Ducceschi", in *La Diana*, I, 95, pp.65-77 and *Falsi d'Autore. Icilio Federico Joni e la cultura del falso fra Ottocento e Novecento'*, op. cit.

raised already, we might finally return to the question of quality, an issue which is part of the connoisseur's province. How does the *Metropolitan Duccio* hold up under analysis? Some weaknesses of the picture have already been alluded to, such as the treatment of the hands, the design formed by the edges of Mary's dress, and the awkward perspective revealed in the parapet. Two elements concentrated in the lower right corner of the little picture raise further doubts over the quality. The sleeve of the Virgin's dress does not operate properly, and appears cut off arbitrarily, creating an unpleasant silhouette. Furthermore, the gold leaf background applied in that area creates a confused distinction between background and foreground. The other sleeve seems to reveal incongruous gilding at the wrist. The feeble gold decoration found in the halos is yet another dismal element in the *Metropolitan Madonna*.

The high praises for the picture's emotional content and humanity emanating from the museum on Fifth Avenue and 82nd Street as well as modern journalists who have written about the purchase do not apply to this picture at all. As far as the presentation of the subject, obviously a crucial matter in establishing the quality of the little painting, I confess that I find it deficient. The action of the Child who fumbles with Mary's veil appears to be based on the *Madonna* from Crevole in the Museo dell'Opera del Duomo, itself a work not without attributional problems, but misunderstood. The conception of the Child's gourd-like head is hardly rewarding and is quite at odds with the same element in the confirmed and documented paintings by Duccio.

While the rapport between the two sacred figures, to the extent that it captures the aura of Duccio's humanity from his genuine works, is appealing, it is hardly of that level. Here I am thinking of course of the *Maestà*, but also works that date from earlier in his chronology, like the *Rucellai Madonna* and the tiny *Madonna of the Francescani* (Fig. 6.5). In other words, the bottom line of my discussion is that whoever was the author of the

Metropolitan Duccio—Duccio, a pupil, a follower, or my choice a faker—the picture cannot be regarded as a work of distinction in the larger compass of masterpieces nor within the narrower view of its genre.[34]

6.1 Addendum.

A controversy erupted in London and New York over the authenticity of the Metropolitan Museum's "Duccio" with echoes elsewhere, after this book was written.[35]. The Met continued to emphasize their basic contention and really the only solid plank in their position, that "virtually" all the experts have supported the attribution. In expressing their contention, however, they disregarded the judgement of several scholars including Florens Deuchler, who Christiansen dismissed as "eccentric." Deuchler, a respected Medievalist whose curriculum vitae includes having been a curator at the Met did not accept the Duccio attribution in his monograph on Duccio published in 1984.[36]

As for other rejections of Duccio's authorship, Frances Vieta, a writer who came up with the same conclusion I did over the authenticity of the Met picture, generously brought to my attention a number of fascinating observations, including a reference to the first known citation to the "quadruccio," (1901) one missed by Met scholars. It has to be regarded as a rejection because it was regarded as not by Duccio at all but the work of

---

[34] Ideally, if this work is a fake, suggesting a date for its manufacture is also a task for the connoisseur. Here one might wish to bring into the discussion the amazing 19th and early 20th century tradition which had unfolded in Italy, especially in Rome, Florence, and Siena. The skill was exemplified by an eye-opening exhibition in Siena recently (see, for example, *ArtNews*, June 2005). As a guess, however, I am inclined to date it to the late 19th century.

[35] See *The Times* of London, July 6th, 8th and 12th, 2006 and *The New York Times*, July 7th and 8th, 2006

[36] Florens Deuchler, *Duccio*, Milan, Electa, 1984.

Sano di Pietro, a minor 15th century Sienese painter.[37] Three years later, the head of the Uffizi Gallery Corrado Ricci (1904) placed the picture among works not by Duccio but among those "in the manner of Duccio" (Duccesca).[38] Significantly the only early advocates of the picture were amateurs: Mary Logan whose evaluation is not altogether emphatic and F. Mason Perkins a trained musician and a protégé of Berenson.

To further cloud the waters, it turns out that Count Stroganoff owned at least six other small Sienese paintings of similar size, besides the Met 'Duccio" and the so-called Simone Martini which was in the exhibition in Siena in 1904 alongside the *Madonna*.

The Simone was willed to the Hermitage by Stroganoff heirs and is widely regarded as a fake, not detected by either Logan or Perkins. In the same year, 1904, Stroganoff lent the six items to an exhibition called "Pictures of the School of Siena" organized by R. Langston Douglas for The Burlington Fine Arts Club in London.[39]

As for the wood panel upon which the *Metropolitan Duccio* is painted, Mr. Christiansen generously informed me that a cradle on the back was removed by the Met and that they found that the back had been cleaned off of any signs of its history at an uncertain time, leaving only a few bits of gesso. Once again we must regard with suspicion a situation similar to that surrounding London's *Madonna of the Pinks* with its obscured back. The cradle, in the case of such a tiny panel was evidently put on for

---

[37] See Giorgio Bernardini's survey of the Stroganoff collection, in *Rassegna d'arte*, 1901, p. 119.

[38] *Il Palazzo Pubblico di Siena e la Mostra d'Antica Arte Senese*, Bergamo, Istituto Italiano d'Arte Grafiche, 1904, p. 68.

[39] *The Sienese School of Art*, The Burlington Fine Arts Club Exhibition, London, 1904, pp. 43-44 and 49-50; "Scenes from th Life of Christ" (respectively: "The Descent from the Cross", "The Pentecost", "The Ascension", "Pietà", "The Resurrection", "The Descent into Hell"), attributed to an Unknown Artist.

6.1. Addendum.

cosmetic effect as well as to hide the back from scrutiny. As for the so-called candle burns on the bottom of the frame, to my knowledge this is another unique situation, which also should be regarded with considerable skepticism.

In *The New York Times* article of 7 July 2006, prominence was conceded to the opinion of Professor Luciano Bellosi, who enthusiastically supported the attribution without reservation. It was a well orchestrated inclusion whose purpose it was to give authority to the Met's purchase and to cripple my assertions. Undetected by the *Times*, Bellosi has never seen the painting, a fact he confirmed to the journalist Lee Rosenbaum, a day or two after the publication of the *Times* article in response to her question:

"No, unfortunately I didn't see it with my own eyes; only by photographs... I know it is a very important question. It is always necessary to see the works of art in reality to be sure what they are... Art historians like Keith Christiansen and Everett Fahy [of the Met] are very capable to judge the works of art with their eyes. I know their capacity. I trust in them for that".

His admission confirms my basic point: *none* of the experts whose opinions were much vaunted by the Met actually saw the picture. This condition is totally inappropriate from the point of view of proper connoisseurship, as Bellosi concedes. His statement also confirms one of the subtexts of this book, that there is an interconnection of loyalties within the Art Establishment, where transparency is unheard of. I offered this spectacular admission to *The New York Times* but apparently it did not fit into their plan to protect to Metropolitan Museum at all costs and was never used; nor was an op-ed piece I innocently prepared for them. I also notified the Chairman of the Met's Board who is also a Harvard *magnifico* of this matter, but never received an answer. So much for freedom of exchange, transparency and academic honesty. An Italian word describes the situation: *Ver-*

gogna [Shame]. The New York Times, Vergogna, Harvard University.

Bellosi is also the proponent of the relationship between the Met Duccio with a much cut down and heavily restored *Madonna and Angels* in Museo Civico of Montepulciano (Fig. 6.6).

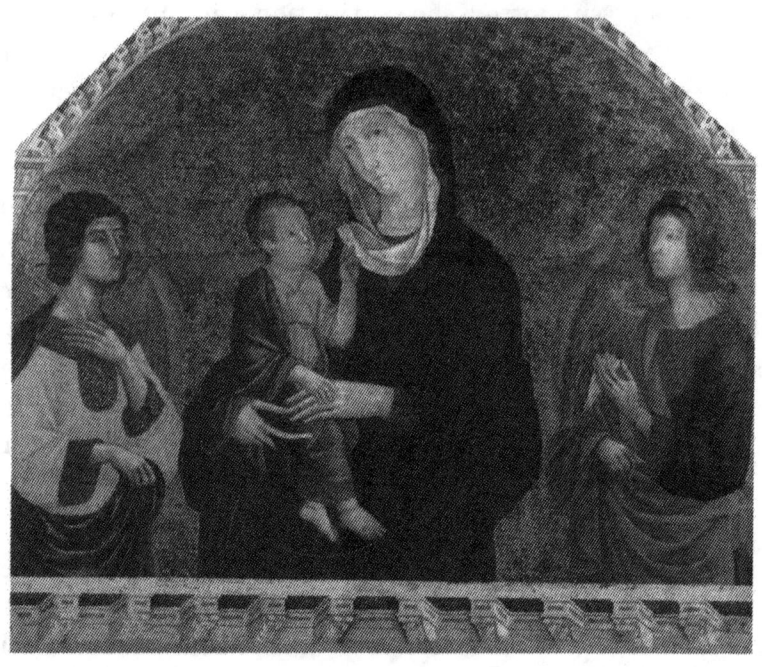

Figure 6.6: **Anonymous Sienese painter,** *Madonna and Child with Angels*, **Montepulciano, Museo Civico.**

The Met says that the parapet or perspective shelf in their painting influenced that picture. Actually the heavily restored and cut-down object is irrelevant to the discussion because of the immense differences in size, scale, format, function and the Assisi tradition to which it belongs. All parapets do not function in the same way nor do they belong to the same typological origins. The concept of the parapet, the type and the perspective is fundamentally different between the two works. The *Montepulciano Madonna and Angels* has three standing figures within a truncated Gothic arch, while the Met's tiny picture is a rectangular mini-tableau with a single group, a conception congenial to 15th century Flemish and Italian Renaissance portraits, where the parapet operates spatially as a plane in front of the figure.[40]

The bottom line is that the Met asks us to believe the impossible: a nameless artist has appropriated what would have been a revolutionary element created by Duccio, but the Master himself never used it. Nor did any of his great pupils, Pietro Lorenzetti, Ambrogio Lorenzetti or Simone Martini. Such a sequence of events is unknown in the history of art.

Somewhat surprising as well in the recent outburst of exchanges has been the overall silence on the part of art experts world-wide, unlike the conditions surrounding the National Gallery's *Northumberland Madonna*. There has been no outcry among specialists supporting the Metropolitan Museum's picture.

The New York Times insists that I never inquired about the technical issues connected with the painting and that I had held off expressing my doubts about its authenticity to the Met. The evidence is, however, quite to the contrary as confirmed by an exchange of e-mails with Mr. Christiansen, which unfolded in July 2005. Following an answer to my letter asking about technical information when he mentioned the cleaning of the back and the cradle, I wrote on Tuesday, July 19, 2005:

"Dear Keith: ......I would be dishonest if I did not men-

---

[40]See Laura Martini, *Memorie d'arte antica: restauri a Montepulciano*, Montepulciano, Le Balze, 2003. On the transformation of the icon into a portrait in the early Renaissance see the brilliant article by Hans Belting "The Invisible Icon and the Icon of the Invisible: Antonello and New Paradigms in Renaissance Painting," in Catterson, L. and M. Zucker, eds., *Watching Art: Writings in Honor of James Beck*, Todi: Ediart, 2006, pp. 73-83.

tion to you that I personally have some problems with the painting..."

The claims circulated within the Metropolitan Museum and in the press that samples of pigments verified that the picture was 700 years old are totally unsupported by accompanying technical evidence or citations of recognized experts. The fact remains that pigments *per se* cannot be dated; only their presence can give clues as to the history of their usage. What the Met did not mention is that a test to determine the age of the wood, which can claim a fifteen-twenty year margin of error, has yet to be undertaken.

The art historian John White, an author cited by the painting's proponents appropriately observed, "The prime cause of the uncertainty surrounding the *Stoclet Madonna* is the presence of the marble parapet..."[41] The uneasiness surrounding the function of the parapet in the painting leads to an observation offered by R. H. Marijnissen and L. Kockaert[42]: "Any baffling work of art becomes automatically suspect. Clumsy fakes do not succeed because they are bad. The very essence of a nice forgery is its misleading character."

---

[41] John White, *Duccio. Tuscan Art and the Medieval Workshop*, London, 1979, p. 62.

[42] R. H. Marijnissen and L. Kockaert, *The Detroit Saint Jerome. The story of an interdisciplinary approach,* in "Mededelingen der Koninklijke Akademie van Wetenschappen, Letteren en Schone Kunsten van België", 1996, n. 1, offprint, p. 32.

Coda

Is speaking of Connoisseurship and with it official Art History as in a state of crisis an exaggeration? I think not. The very legitimacy and integrity of the field as an academic discipline practiced in the universities and especially in its role of training students to confront and evaluate works of art has gone seriously awry and the effects are widespread. A solid consensus within the art establishment has awarded the authorship of the National Gallery's so-called Raphael *Madonna of the Pinks* also known as the *Northumberland Madonna* as well as the Metropolitan Museum's so-called *Duccio Madonna* also known as the *Stroganoff Madonna* to those famous masters. In the case of the Metropolitan Museum's example the opinion of the experts was achieved without ever having seen the picture first-hand, an intolerable condition in terms of the unwritten rules of proper connoisseurship. Not even up-to-date photographs were available, and none at all in color. As far as is known, no in-depth technical test results were presented in support of the object's authenticity before the purchase since: nothing of the kind has been circulated.

In the case of the *Northumberland Madonna* testing before the purchase (2004) was severely hamstrung by the seller, yet no one in authority at the Gallery nor from a UK governmental commission which approved the acquisition raised any objections to the restrictions. Evidently the possibility of passing on the purchase was never a serious option, whatever the limitations of the evidence might have been. The most convincing element in the eyes of the proponents of the picture's originality turns out to be a "pseudo-underdrawing," really a composite image generated by computer, hardly reliable data for the rigorous connoisseurship in evaluating authorship, because the drawing cannot be actually seen directly and effectively does not actually exist *per se*.

Mind you, these examples of recent connoisseurship gone a-muck are not penny ante matters. Nor do they involve an argument over whether a given picture is by the young Titian or by Giorgione or even by the School of Titian or the School of Giorgione. Such are relatively harmless academic disputes, where one's university reputation may be tarnished or belittled but no irreparable injury to the artistic heritage results. On the other hand, when the debate is whether the diamond is genuine or paste, other issues come into play, including honesty, ethics, and the squandering of public and private resources. Economic and sociopolitical factors cannot be brushed aside when examining multimillion-dollar purchases such as those of the *Northumberland Madonna* and the *Metropolitan Duccio*. After all, in both public money is involved, directly in the case of the London picture, and indirectly with the New York one, since the Metropolitan benefits from tax exemptions as well as substantial support from the City of New York. Enormous sums were spent on pictures of minimal artistic luster, and even the general museum-going public despite the hoopla has shown extremely little interest in these paintings.

Imagine how those dollars and pounds sterling might have been used to purchase objects that garner fewer headlines but would genuinely fill holes in the collections; instead the present purchases add next to nothing to their holdings, even were they what they are supposed to be. The National Gallery already has its share of quality Raphael paintings, so it hardly benefits from the addition of an ambiguous one, actually called a "dud" by the London art critic, Brian Sewell. The Metropolitan's overall collection of Italian Late Medieval and Renaissance paintings is mediocre to begin with, so the 50 million dollars spent on a single, questionable work is an even greater disappointment. Instead, the money might have been used to purchase a number of quality drawings to expand the museum's already impressive holdings. Alternatively the museums might have spent the money buying works by living artists. Consider how many lives and careers could have benefited from an injection of 100 plus million dollars emanating from New York and London?

In distinction to most humanistic disciplines, Art History and with it connoisseurship are surrounded by a sea of money accompanied by waves of power, influence, and prestige. The museum network, the universities, wealthy foundations, and the international auction houses are part of an equation in which billions of dollars a year change hands, yielding monstrous profits. We humans being what we are, and money and power having their own mechanisms, the field cannot be expected to sort out deficiencies all on its own any more than can the medical profession. Society is quite unwilling to leave health policy and medical treatment exclusively to the pharmaceutical manufacturers, health insurers, hospital boards, or the doctors for that matter, without oversight, supervision, regulations, and legal constraints originating from the body politic. Our artistic heritage which is essential in sustaining our much threatened civilization deserves nothing less. Here, as in medicine, the common good should take precedence over other considerations.

Will the specific objections, suggestions, and challenges raised in this book have an impact upon the institutions involved, upon the Art Establishment, or upon the wider public? Will the larger world of culture and, in particular, the universities on the one hand and the media on the other accept a share of responsibility for the decline of connoisseurship and take up the matter with resolve and courage? Or will they continue to leave the decisions to the self-appointed, self-selected experts protected by powerful Boards of Trustees? My expectation is that the Establishment will do everything in its mighty power to totally ignore the issues. The vested interests—the trustees and donors, the professors and the auction houses—will seek protection by engaging media consultants and will call upon political connections, as they have in the past. They will sweep the sweep-able under the carpet as they shout jingoistic slogans and self-righteous rhetoric.

Once an object has found its way into an imposing collection it is virtually immune to serious challenges over authenticity. The likelihood is strong that such will be the fate of the *Metropolitan Duccio* and the *Northumberland Raphael*. The vested interests will keep a lid on the situation and frustrate transparent debate. The interlocking connections and interlocking directorates which I have signaled in the text are very much to the point with respect to the Metropolitan Museum's *Duccio*. The Chairman of the Met's board is one of the five members of the billion-dollar Harvard Corporation, that is, the governing body of that great and powerful institution. He is also on the boards of a number of international business giants. With its Board the Met is essentially untouchable and one can even imagine that they could make a Duccio a Matisse, if they really try. As further evidence of the interaction between Harvard and 1000 Fifth Avenue, the Museum's long-term Director is a Harvard graduate and in June 2006 was awarded an honorary doctorate from the University. *The New York Times* is a key ingredient in the mix. Arthur Ochs Sulzberger, longtime chairman of the Met and of *The New York Times*, holds a degree from Harvard's Business School and is emeritus Chairman of both New York based institutions.

After all, who gains from denouncing the dismal fakes, besides Duccio and Raphael and with them all art, whose dignity and integrity have been belittled and besmirched by ignorance, greed and cruel disinterest?

Bibliography

Angelini, Alessandro. "Pinturicchio e i suoi: dalla Rome dei Borgia alla Siena dei Piccolomini e dei Petrucci," in *Pio II e le arti. La riscoperta dell'antico da Federighi a Michelangelo*, Siena, 2005; pp. 526-529.

Azzolini, Lidia. *Alceo Dossena: l'arte di un grande "falsario,"* Cremona, 2004.

Bagnoli, Alessandro; Roberto Bartalini; Luciano Bellosi; Michel Laclotte. *Duccio. Siena fra tradizione bizantina e mondo gotico*, Milano, 2003.

Bagnoli, Alessandro, Roberto Bartalini and Luciano Bellosi, eds. *Duccio: alle origini della pittura senese*, catalogue of the exhibition, Milano, 2003.

Barberi, Tito. *Catalogo ragionato della Galleria Camuccini in Rome descritto da Tito Barberi, XIX secolo*, (unpublished manuscript).

Barberi, Tito. *Della collezione dei quadri e di altri oggetti d'arte posseduti da Monsignor Federico de Falloux*, Rome, 1869.

Beck, James. "Connoisseurship: A Lost or a Found Art? The Example of a Michelangelo Attribution: 'The Fifth Avenue Cupid,'" in *Artibus et Historiae*, 37, 1998; pp. 9-42.

Beck, James with Michael Daley. *Arte Violata*, Firenze, 2003.

Beck, James. "A New Date for Pinturicchio's Piccolomini Library," in *Paragone*, n. 419-423, 1985; pp. 140-143.

Beck, James. "Benedetto da Maiano e Michelangelo giovane," in *Giuliano e la bottega dei da Maiano. Papers of the International Meeting in Fiesole, June 13 - 15, 1991*, edited by Daniela Lamierini, Marcello Lotti, Roberto Lunardi, Firenze, 1994; pp. 176-181.

Beck, James. "Raphael's Madonna of the Pinks: a connoisseurship challenge," in *Source. Notes in the History of Art*, n. 2, 2005; pp. 50-59.

Beck, James. "Restoration II: Debunking the 'have you seen it?' myth," *Source. Notes in the History of Art*, n. 2, 2000: pp. 2-5.

Belting, Hans. "The Invisible Icon and the Icon of the Invisible: Antonello and the New Paradigms in Renaissance Painting," in L. Catterson and M. Zucker eds., *Watching Art: Writings in Honour of James Beck*, Todi, 2006; pp. 73-83.

Benedetti, Sergio. *Caravaggio e la collezione Mattei*, ed. Claudio Strinati, catalogue of the exhibition Rome 1995, Milano, 1995; pp. 124-126.

Berenson, Bernard. "Amico di Sandro," in *Gazette des Beaux-Arts*, 1899, 1, XLI, pp. 459-471; 2, XLI, pp. 21-36, reprinted in Bernard Berenson, *Study and Criticism of Italian Art*,London, 1901; pp. 46-69.

Bernardini, Giorgio. "Alcuni dipinti della collezione del conte Stroganoff in Roma," in *Rassegna d'arte*, 1901; pp. 116-120.

Borgnini, Valentina. "Alcune novità sull'Incoronazione della Vergine: la 'Pala Oddi' di Raffaello," in *Kermes*, 58, April-June 2005; pp. 49-58.

Cappelletti, Francesca. "Una nota di beni e qualche aggiunta alla storia della collezione Aldobrandini," in *Storia dell'Arte*, 93/94, May-December 1998; pp. 341-347.

Catterson, Lynn and Mark Zucker eds. *Watching Art: Writings in Honor of James Beck*, Todi, 2006.

Cappelletti, Francesca. "La Galleria Camuccini nel racconto di un prezioso manoscritto," in *Strenna dei Romanisti*, 35, 1974; p. 133.

Chapman, H. T. Henry and C. Plazzota. *Raphael from Urbino to Rome*, Catalogue of the exhibition, London, 2004.

Cianchi, Marco. *Pierino da Vinci: atti della giornata di studio, Vinci, Biblioteca Leonardiana, 26 maggio 1990*, Florence, 1999; pp. 13-15.

Constantin, Abraham. "Idées Italiennes sur Quelques Tableaux Célèbres," Stendhal, *Oeuvres*, Paris, vol. 35, 1927-1938; p. 133.

Cooper, Donal. "New Documents for Raphael and his Patrons in Perugia," in *The Burlington Magazine*, 146, 2004; p. 742.

Cooper, Donal. "Raphael's Altarpiece in S. Francesco al Prato, Perugia: Patronage, Setting and Function," in *The Burlington Magazine*, 143, 2001; pp. 554-561.

Corbo, A. M. "Il restauro delle pitture a Roma dal 1814 al 1823," in *Commentari*, XX, 1969; p. 236.

Coremans, P. B. *Van Meegeren's faked Vermeers and De Hooghs: a scientific examination*, Amsterdam, 1949.

Department for Culture, Media and Sport of the U.K. *Export of Works of Art 2002-2003*, Case 18.

Deuchler, Florens. *Duccio*, Milano, 1984.

Dunkerton, J. and N. Penny. "The infra-red examination of Raphael's *Garvagh Madonna*," in *National Gallery Technical Bulletin*, 14, 1993.

Falconieri, Carlo. *Memoria intorno al rinvenimento delle ossa di Raffaello Sanzio con breve appendice sulla di lui vita*, Rome, 1833.

Ferino Padgen, Sylvia. *Disegni umbri del Rinascimento da Perugino a Raffaello*, catalogue of the exhibition, Firenze, 1982.

Finocchi Ghersi, Lorenzo. "Il moccolo che va avanti, fa lume per due: Pio IX, il Marchese Campana e la vendita della collezione Camuccini," in *Rivista dell'Istituto Nazionale d'Archeologia e Storia dell'Arte*, 57 (III serie, XXV), 2002; p. 371.

Frezzato, Fabio. *Il Libro dell'arte di Cennino Cennini*, Vicenza, 2003.

Friedlander, Max J. *On Art and Connoisseurship*, Boston, 1946.

Gentilini, Giancarlo, ed. *Una proposta per Michelangelo giovane. Un crocifisso in legno di tiglio, Firenze, Museo Horne*, catalogue of the exhibition, Torino, 2004.

Godley, John. *Master Art Forger: The Story of Han Van Meegeren*, New York Wilfred Funk, 1951.

Grassi, Marco. "The Metropolitan Duccio," in *The New Criterion*, XXIII, 6, February 2005.

Hartt, Frederick, "David by the hand of Michelangelo: the original model discovered," in *National Gallery of Art, Center for Advanced Study in the Visual Arts: research reports and record of activities*, 8, 1987-1988; p. 32.

Henry, Tom. "Raphael and Siena," in *Apollo*, CLX, 2004, 512; pp. 50-56.

Hiesinger, Ulrich. "The paintings of Vincenzo Camuccini, 1771-1844," in *The Art Bulletin*, 60, June 1978; p. 301.

Hirst, Michael. "The New York 'Michelangelo': a different view," in *The Art Newspaper*, VII, 61, 1996; p. 3.

Il Giornale dell'Arte, 232, may 2004; p. 18.

Il segreto della civiltà. La mostra dell'Antica Arte Senese del 1904 cento anni dopo, catalogue of the exhibition, Siena 2005.

Jeromack, Paul. *The Art Newspaper*, 2004.

Joannides, Paul. "Raphael: a sorority of Madonnas," in *The Burlington Magazine*, 2004, CXLVI; pp. 749-752.

Joannides, Paul. *The drawings of Raphael: with a complete catalogue*, Oxford, Phaidon, 1983.

Kemp, Martin, Leonardo, Oxford and New York, 2005.

Kuehn, Hermann. "Terminal Dates for Paintings Derived from Pigment Analysis," in *Application of Science in Examination of Works of Art*, Papers of the meeting, June 15-19, 1970, edited by W.J. Young, Boston, Museum of Fine Arts, 1973.

Leonard, George. "Raphael Saved," in *Jackdaw*, 39, June 2004.

Logan, Mary. "L'Exposition de l'ancien art siennois," in *Gazette des Beaux-Arts*, XLVI, 1904; p. 210.

Lusetti, Walter. *Alceo Dossena scultore*, Rome, 1955.

Lusini, Vittorio, *In onore di Duccio di Buoninsegna e della sua scuola*, Siena, 1913.

Mancinelli, F. "La Trasfigurazione e la Pala di Monteluce: considerazioni sulla loro tecnica esecutiva alla luce dei rcenti restauri," in *Princeton Raphael Symposium Science in the Service of Art History*, edited by J. Shearman and M. B. Hall, Princeton, 1990; pp. 149-50.

Marijnissen, R. H. and L Kockaert. "The Detroit Saint Jerome. The story of an interdisciplinary approach," in *Mededelingen van der Koninklijke Academie voor Weternschappen, Letteren en Schone Kunsten van Belgie*, 1996, n. 1; p. 32.

Martini, Laura. *Memorie d'arte antica: restauri a Montepulciano*, Montepulciano, 2003.

Matthaes, G. *Manuale illustrato del collezionista d'arte: saper distinguere tra autentico e falso*, vol. I, Milano, 1997.

Mazzoni, Gianni, ed. *Falsi d'autore: Icilio Federico Joni e la cultura del falso tra Otto e Novecento*, catalogue of the exhibition, Siena, 2004.

Mazzoni, Gianni. "Falsi ducceschi," in *La Diana*, I, 1995, pp. 65-77.

Meyer zur Capellen, Jürg. *Raphael, a Critical Catalogue of His Paintings*, I, *The Beginnings in Umbria and Florence, ca. 1500-1508*, Landshut, 2001.

Morandi, Giovanni. *La beffa di Modigliani. Tra falsari veri e falsi*, Firenze, 2004.

Mostra dell'Antica Arte Senese, catalogue of the exhibition, Siena, 1904; Bergamo 1904, 308, n. 37 (1960).

Müntz, Eugene. *Raphael, His Life, Works and Times*, translated into English by W. Armstrong, London, 1882.

Müntz, Eugene. *Raphaël, sa vie, son oeuvre et son temps*, Paris, Hachette, 1881.

Oberhuber, Konrad. *Raphael. The Paintings*, New York, 1999.

Parronchi, Alessandro. *Opere giovanili di Michelangelo*, Firenze, 1968, pp. 131-148.

Parronchi, Alessandro. *Proposte per Leonardo scultore*, Milano, 2005.

Passavant, Johann David. *Rafael von Urbino und sein Vater Giovanni Santi*, Leipzig, 1839.

Passavant, Johann David. *Raphael d'Urbin et son père Giovanni Santi*, Paris, 1860.

Penny, Nicholas. "Raphael's *Madonna dei garofani* Rediscovered," in *The Burlington Magazine*, 134, 1992; pp. 67-81.

Penny, Nicholas and Roger Jones. *Raphael*, New Haven, 1983.

Perkins, F. Mason. "The Sienese Exhibition of Ancient Art," in *The Burlington Magazine*, XVIII, September 1904; pp. 581-584.

Pezzini, Grazia Bernini, ed. *Raphael invenit: stampe da Raffaello nelle collezioni dell'Istituto Nazionale per la Grafica*, catalogue of the exhibition, Rome 1985.

Pollak, Ludwig and Antonio Muñoz. *Pièces de choix de la collection du Comte Grégoire Stroganoff à Rome*, Roma, 1911.

Quatremère de Quincy, Antoine Chrisostome. *Histoire de la vie et des ouvrages de Raphaël*, Paris, 1824.

Quatremère de Quincy, Antoine Chrisostome. *Istoria della Vita e delle Opere di Raffaello Sanzio da Urbino*, trans. by Francesco Longhena, Milano, 1829.

Ricci, Corrado. *Il Palazzo Pubblico di Siena e la Mostra d'Antica Arte Senese*, Bergamo, 1904.

Scarpellini, Pietro and Maria Rita Silvestrelli. *Pinturicchio*, Milano, 2004.

Seracini, M. "Il Disegno Sottostante nella Pittura di Raffaello, Esempi dei periodi Fiorentino e Romano," in *Raffaello e l'idea della bellezza*, catalogue of the exhibition edited by A. Vezzosi, Perugia, 2001.

Settis, Salvatore. *La Libreria Piccolomini nel Duomo di Siena*, Modena, 1998.

Shearman, John. "Raphael at the Court of Urbino," in *The Burlington Magazine*, 112, 1970; pp. 72-78.

Shearman, John. *Raphael in Modern Sources, 1483-1602*, New Haven and London, 2003.

Spencer, R. D. *The Expert versus the Object. Judging Fakes and False Attributions in the Visual Arts*, Oxford and New York, 2004.

Spezzaferro, Luigi. *Caravaggio e l'Europa. Il movimento caravaggesco internazionale da Caravaggio a Mattia Preti*, catalogue of the exhibition, Milano 2005.

Stendhal, *Promenades dan Rome* (1828), ed. by V. Del Litto, Grenoble, 1993.

Strelke, C. B. and C. Frosinini. *The panel paintings of Masolino and Masaccio: The Role of Technique*, Milano, 2002.

Sutton, P. C. "Rembrandt and a Brief History of Connoisseurship," in R. D. Spencer, *The Expert versus the Object. Judging Fakes and False Attributions in the Visual Arts*, Oxford and New York, 2004.

Testa, Laura. "Novità su Carlo Saraceni: la committenza Aldobrandini e la prima attività Romana," in *Dialoghi di Storia dell'Arte*, 1998; pp.130-137.

The Sienese School of Art, The Burlington Fine Arts Club Exhibition, London, 1904.

Tomkins, Calvin. "The Missing Madonna: the Story Behind the Met's Most Expensive Acquisition," in *The New Yorker*, 11 July 2005.

Van Asperen de Boer, J. R. J. "Current Techniques in the Scientific Examination of Paintings," in *Princeton Raphael Symposium Science in the Service of Art History*, edited by J. Shearman and M. B. Hall, New Jersey, 1990.

Vasari, Giorgio. *Vite de' più eccellenti pittori, scultori, architettori moderni da Cimabue insino a' giorni nostri*, Firenze 1550, edited by Luciano Bellosi and Aldo Rossi, Torino, 1991.

Vasari, Giorgio. *Vite de' più eccellenti pittori, scultori, architettori moderni da Cimabue insino a' giorni nostri*, Firenze 1568, edited by Gaetano Milanesi, Firenze, 1885.

Verdone, Luca. *Vincenzo Camuccini pittore neoclassico*, Roma, 2005.

Visconti, P. E. *Vita di Camuccini pittore*, Roma, 1845.

Vogel, Carol. "The Met Makes Its Biggest Purchase Ever," in *The New York Times*, 10 November 2004.

Waagen, Gustav Friedrich. *Kunstwerke und Kunstler in Baiern, Scwaben, Basel, dem Alsass und dem Rheinpfalz*, Leipzig, 1845.

Weber, Andrea. *Duccio*, Cologne, 1997.

White, John. *Duccio. Tuscan Art and the Medieval Workshop*, London, 1979.

Zeri, Federico. *Dietro l'immagine. Conversazioni sull'arte di leggere l'arte*, Milano, 1990.

Index

Aldobrandini, family, 116
Aldobrandini, Silvestro, 116
Allemandi, Umberto, 123
Amendola, Aurelio, 123
Amico di Sandro, 27, 155
Andrea Pisano, 162
Andreis, Bruno, 80
Angelico fra, Guido di Pietro called, 24, 30, 152
Angelini, Alessandro, 132
Antonello da Messina, 24, 32, 34, 171
Antonetto, Barbara, 124
Armstrong, W., 116
Assonitis, Alessio, 11, 12
Assunto, Rosario, 101
Azzolini, Lidia, 153

Baccio di Montelupo, 129
Baglione, family, 113
Baglioni, Alessandra, see: Oddi, Alessandra degli
Baglioni, Atalanta, 115
Bagnoli, Alessandro, 24, 143
Baldini, Umberto, 122, 128
Barberi, Tito, 106-115, 118-119
Barker, Sheila, 11

Bartalini, Roberto, 24, 143
Bartolomeo fra, Baccio della Porta called, 57
Beck, James, 12, 40, 49, 122, 127, 135, 171
Bellini, Giovanni, 26, 160, 161
Bellosi, Luciano, 24, 26, 28, 122, 124-125, 127-128, 143, 159-160, 162, 169, 170
Belting, Hans, 171
Benedetti, Sergio, 31
Berenson, Bernard, 27-28, 74, 125, 150, 157, 168
Bernabei, Pietro Antonio, 129
Bernardini, Giorgio, 168
Bibb, Barbara, 11
Blumenthal, Gabriel, 11
Boccaccio, Giovanni, 12
Borgia, family, 132
Borgnini, Valentina, 114
Botticelli, Alessandro Filipepi called, 30
Boulanger, Jean, 64, 69
Bristol, lord, 109
Brown, Beverly, 45
Brown, David Alan, 45, 47-48
Budd, Denise, 11

Buonarroti, Michelangelo, 18, 23, 26, 40, 43-45, 48-49, 121-132, 134-135, 146, 159
Burri, Alberto, 32
Butler, Kim, 46

Campana, marchese, 103
Camuccini, collection, 50-51, 55, 98, 101-106, 108, 110, 112, 115, 118
Camuccini, Pietro, 12, 72-73, 84, 93-95, 98, 102-106, 108, 110, 115
Camuccini, Giovanni Battista, 73, 106
Camuccini, Vincenzo, 12, 14, 65, 72-73, 80, 84, 93-95, 98, 101-103, 105-110, 112-113, 115, 118
Camuccini, Vincenzo, Baron of Rome and Cantalupo, 11, 104
Cappelletti, Francesca, 116
Caravaggio, Michelangelo Merisi called, 31, 95
Carracci, Annibale, 105
Castiglione, Baldassarre, 72
Catterson, Lynn, 171
Cavalcaselle, Giovanni Battista, 28, 60
Cecchi, Alessandro, 46
Ceccopieri Maruffi, F., 106, 107
Cennini, Cennino, 93
Cézanne, Paul, 32

Chapman Brown, Hugo, 46-47, 49, 74, 108, 132
Chigi, Agostino, 134
Christie's, auction house, 46, 52, 141, 144
Christensen, 91
Christiansen, Keith, 48, 142, 144, 146, 149, 151, 153, 167-169, 171
Cianchi, Marco, 122
Cimabue, Cenni di Pepo called, 24-26, 135
Clifford, Timothy, 48
Constantin, Abraham, 104
Contini Bonacossi, collection, 110
Cooper, Donal, 46-47, 108, 113, 114
Corbo, A. M., 95
Coremans, P. B., 44
Corot, Camille, 35
Couvay, Jean, 63, 67, 69
Crowe, John Archer, 60

Da Maiano, Benedetto, 127
Da Maiano, Giuliano, 127
Daley, Michael, 11, 52, 157
Dangles Deeds, Lisa, 11
De Hooghs, 44
De Kooning, Willem, 32
De Montebello, Philippe, 146, 147
Del Litto, V., 101
Della Robbia, Luca, 123
Dente, Marco, 56
Desiderio da Settignano, 57

Deuchler, Florens, 142, 167
Duveen, Joseph, 150, 152
Donatello, Donato di Niccolò called, 123
Doria Pamphilii, family, 116
Dossena, Alceo, 153
Duccio di Buoninsegna, 13-14, 17-20, 24, 26, 31, 48, 82, 139-160, 162-168, 170-174, 176
Dunkerton, J., 91

Ekserdjian, David, 46-47
Elam, Caroline, 46-47
Eleanor of Portugal, 136

Fahy, Everett, 48, 146, 169
Falconieri, Carlo, 106
Falomir, Miguel, 46
Farrugia, Giovanni, 84-85, 97-99, 101-103, 115
Federighi, Antonio, 132
Fenton, James, 124
Ferino-Pagden, Silvia, 46-47
Ferretti, Massimo, 122, 124, 128
Fidolini, Marco, 11
Finocchi Ghersi, Lorenzo, 103, 104
Francesconi, Chiara, 12
Francesconi, Enrico, 12
Frederick III, 136
Frezzato, Fabio, 93
Frick, colletion, 148
Friederich, Caspar David, 35
Friedländer, Max J., 160-161

Frosini, C., 29

Garofalo, Benvenuto, 107
Gentilini, Giancarlo, 122, 124, 130
Ghirlandaio, Domenico Bigordi called, 26, 135
Ghirlandaio, Ridolfo, 96
Giorgione, 35, 174
Giotto, 24-26, 135, 147, 162
Giulio Romano, Pippi Giulio called, 74
Godley, John, 44
Gombrich, Ernst, 134
Gonzaga, Eleonora, 47
Grassi, Marco, 141-142, 144, 146, 151-152
Gratziu, Corrado, 11
Gulisano, Massimo, 129

Hall, M.B., 72, 87
Hartt, Frederick, 122, 146
Henry, Tom, 46-49, 74, 108, 132, 135
Hiesinger, Ulrich, 109
Hiller von Gaertringen, Rudolf, 48
Hirst, Michael, 46

Jacopo della Quercia, 28
Jaquotot, madame, 100
Jaquotot, M. Victoire, 15, 99-101
Jeromack, Paul, 141, 144, 151
Joannides, Paul, 55, 132, 135-136

Jones, Roger, 47
John, Jasper, 147
Joni, Icilio Federico, 153, 165

Kanter, Laurence, 146
Keihm, Young-June, 11
Kemp, Martin, 80
Kilbracken, lord, 44
Klein, Franz, 32
Kockaert, L., 162, 172

Laclotte, Michel, 24
Langston Douglas, Robert, 168
Leonard, George, 86
Leonardo da Vinci, 23, 26, 35, 39, 54, 57, 60, 76, 80, 89, 95-96, 121, 133, 135, 159, 164
Lichtenstein, Roy, 32
Logan, Mary, 149-150, 153, 168
Longhena, Francesco, 52, 101-103, 107, 114
Longhi, Giuseppe, 98
Longhi, Roberto, 28, 31
Lorenzetti, Pietro, 171
Lorenzetti, Ambrogio, 148, 158, 171
Lorrain, Claude, 35
Lusetti, Walter, 153
Lusini, Vittorio, 149, 153

Mahon, Dortohy, 146, 164-165
Mancinelli, Fabrizio, 71
Marijnissen, R. H., 162, 172
Martini, Francesco di Giorgio, 148

Martini, Laura, 171
Martini, Simone, 148, 158, 168, 171
Masaccio, 29, 148
Masolino da Panicale, 29
Mason Perkins, Frederick, 153, 168
Matisse, Henri, 32, 176
Matthaes, G., 92
Mazzoni, Gianni, 153, 165
Meiss, Millard, 157
Meyer zur Capellen, J., 110
Michelangelo, *see*: Buonarroti Michelangelo
Milanesi, Gaetano, 133-134
Modigliani, Amedeo, 52, 159
Morelli, Giovanni, 28
Moscato, Alessandra, 11
Muñoz, Antonio, 151
Müntz, Eugène, 116

Nagel, Alexander, 46-47
Nanni di Banco, 28
Natali, Antonio, 46
Nesselrath, Arnold, 46-47, 49
Northumberland, Duchess of, 51
Northumberland, Duke of, 30, 50-51, 84, 98, 106, 143

Oberhuber, Konrad, 74
Oddi, Alessandra degli, 114
Oddi, family, 107, 113
Oddi, Leandra degli, *see*: Oddi, Alessandra degli

Oddi, Maddalena degli, 112-115, 118, 119
Oddi, Simone degli, 114
Offner, Richard, 149

Paolo Uccello, Paolo di Dono called, 31
Paolucci, Antonio, 122-123
Parronchi, Alessandro, 40, 57
Pasinati, Giovanni Antonio, 104
Passavant, Johann David, 28, 65, 115-116
Pedretti, Carlo, 122
Penny, Nicholas, 43, 46-47, 49, 55, 57-58, 66-70, 75, 80, 82, 84-85, 89, 91, 97, 99-101, 105, 108-109, 112, 114
Perugino, Pietro, 26-27, 48, 53, 72, 133-135
Petrioli, Piergiacomo, 11, 141
Petrucci, family, 132
Pfister, Kerri, 11
Phillips, auction house, 102, 103
Picasso, Pablo Ruiz, 32, 155
Piccolomini, Francesco, 133
Piccolomini, Enea Silvio, 132-133
Piccolomini, family, 132-133, 135
Piels, Manya, 11
Pierino da Vinci, 122
Piero della Francesca, 24, 26
Pinturicchio, Bernardino di Betto called, 132-137

Pius III, pope, see: Piccolomini Francesco
Pius II, pope, see: Piccolomini, Enea Silvio
Plazzotta, Carol, 46, 49, 74, 108, 116, 132
Pollock, Jackson, 32
Pon, Lisa, 46
Pope-Hennessy, John, 29, 158
Preti, Mattia, 31
Puddu, Paolo, 11, 73

Quatermère De Quincy, Antoine, 101, 103, 107, 114
Quintavalle, Arturo Carlo, 124

Raphael, 11, 13-14, 17-20, 23, 26, 30, 39, 43-44, 46-61, 66-83, 86, 88-91, 93-97, 100-116, 118, 123, 126, 131-137, 141, 155, 162, 173-174, 176
Rembrandt, Harmenszoon Van Rijn, 17, 23, 33, 87, 91
Ricci, Archita, 116
Ricci, Corrado, 168
Rosenbaum, Lee, 169
Rossi, Aldo, 28
Roy, Ashok, 72
Rubens, Peter Paul, 23
Rubin, Patricia, 46-47
Russell, Francis, 46

Sammer, Jan, 11, 12, 58, 95, 97, 99, 102, 116

Sangiorgi, auction, 152
Santi, Giovanni, 65, 115
Saraceni, Carlo, 116
Sassetta, 148
Sassoferrato, Giovan Battista Salvi called, 51, 107
Saumarez Smith, Charles, 46, 75
Scarpellini, Pietro, 11, 137
Schama, Simon, 87
Scrase, David, 48
Seracini, Maurizio, 57, 91
Settis, Salvatore, 132
Sewell, Brian, 175
Shearman, John, 46-47, 55, 72, 75, 87, 114, 136
Silvestrelli, Maria Rita, 137
Sloser, Carolina, 11
Spada, count, 105, 115
Spencer, Ronald D., 87, 92, 161
Stendhal (Henri Beyle), 101, 104
Stock, Robert, 11
Stoclet, Adolphe, 15, 152
Stoclet, family, 141
Strehlke, Carl Brandon, 29
Strinati, Claudio, 31
Stroganoff, Gregorii, 14-15, 31, 139, 149-152, 154, 156-157, 165, 168, 173
Sulzberger, Arthur Ochs, 176
Sutton, Peter C., 91

Talvacchia, Bette, 46-47
Titian, 26, 35, 174

Tomkins, Calvin, 142, 144, 146, 151-152, 164
Torrigiani, Pietro, 56
Toscani, Giovanni, 152
Turner, William Mallory, 35

Van Asperen de Boer, J. R. J., 87
Van Eyck, Jan, 32-33, 147, 162
Van Meegeren, Han, 44, 52
Vasari, Giorgio, 27-28, 43, 113-114, 132-136
Vecchietta, Lorenzo di Pietro called, 148
Vermeer, Jan, 44, 52, 159
Verrocchio, Andrea del, 26, 60
Vezzosi, Alessandro, 11, 91
Vieta, Frances, 11, 167
Visconti, 110
Vogel, Carol, 146-147, 153

Waagen, Gustav Friedrich, 50-51
Warhol, Andy, 32
Weber, Andrea, 142
Weil-Garris Brandt, Kathleen, 40
Weston-Lewis, Aiden, 46-47
Whistler, Catherine, 46-47
White, John, 172
Wocher, 51
Wrightsman, Jayne, 146

Zeri, Federico, 29, 124, 165
Zucker, M., 171

Anthropology of Contemporary Culture Series
directed by James H. Beck

Luisa Accati, *Beauty and the Monster. Discursive and Figurative Representations of the Parental Couple from Giotto to Tiepolo*

Teresa Hoefert de Turègano, *African Cinema and Europe: close-up on Burkina Faso*

James H. Beck, *L'Arte Violata. Una valutazione sulla cultura del restauro*

Ester Fintz Menascé, *Una Musica canta nell'Anima*

Pavan-Garzonio, *L'Italia nella Casa di Puškin*

Other EPAP publications

Luisa Accati, *Madri Pervasive e Figli Dominanti*

Eleonora M. Beck, *Giotto's Harmony. Music and Art in Padua at the Crossroads of the Renaissance*

Virgil Hawkins, *The Silence of the UN Security Council. Conflict and Peace enforcement in the 1990s*

Riccardo Gori-Montanelli, *Il Federalismo e la Corte Suprema degli Stati Uniti*

Violeta Beširević, *Euthanasia: Legal Principles and Policy Choices*

European Press Academic Publishing (EPAP)
http://www.e-p-a-p.com
http://www.europeanpress.it
orders@e-p-a-p.com

www.ingramcontent.com/pod-product-compliance
Lightning Source LLC
Chambersburg PA
CBHW071158240526
45470CB00017B/295